"I can best summarize my feelings about this book by saying it is the best one I have read on the topic . . . (Potter's) "up-front" comments about the ethics of behavior modification are some of the more open and honest statements I have seen in print by an author . . . topics are explained at the appropriate level . . . chapters are really very good . . . I would have to give this book very high marks for technical merit. It is thoroughly researched, well-documented with detail, and highly readable."

> Paul M. Muchinsky
> Director, Industrial Relations Center
> Iowa State University
> PERSONNEL PSYCHOLOGY

"This book is about managing: yourself as well as others. As one who has a tendency to confuse management with either manipulating or "bossing," I found it reassuring as well as stimulating. The method Potter uses has an ethical spine running through it which keeps it from being manipulative, and a respect for the individual which eliminates bossiness. If you need to develop or hone management skills, the techniques explained here can increase your effectiveness. If you work alone, or do a minimun of supervising and managing, you will discover new and satisfying ways of working."

> Camille Pronger
> Palo Alto
> TALENT SOURCE: A PUBLICATION OF THE
> RESOURCE CENTER FOR WOMEN

". . . instead of turning to more exotic modern management concepts such as strategic planning or matrix structures to improve their effectiveness, the modern manager may be better off following Potter's behavioral guidelines for managing personnel selection, authority, meetings and conflicts."

> Fred Luthans
> Professor of Management
> University of Nebraska
> CONTEMPORARY PSYCHOLOGY

"A book of outstanding merit for business people."

> Paperback edition: CHANGING PERFORMANCE ON THE JOB
> SOUNDVIEW EXECUTIVE BOOK SUMMARIES

"I was able to immediately apply Potter's tools for interviewing, managing conflict and giving directives that work. I recommend Potter's book above all others for entrepreneurs who want to manage more professionally — starting right now!"

Carter L. Schelling
President, McArdle-Desco Corp.
Chairman, The 3655 Group for Entrepreneurs
New Castle

"If you are interested in developing your employees' full potential read this book. In *Turning Around,* Dr. Potter has translated the latest scientific research into practical management techniques that, when used, will result in optimal job performance."

Mike Modena
Training Officer
U.S. Dept. of Energy
San Francisco Operations Office

"Dr. Potter is an exciting author and speaker who shows us how to make the words we use when giving a directive more effective in getting what we want done."

Marty Maskall
Data Processing Management Association
Sacramento

"...Dr. Potter has contributed substantially to the literature with fresh insight, specifically in the area of motivating by kindness and compassion."

Larry Chasen
Library Manager
General Electric Company
Space Systems Division
SPECIAL LIBRARIES

Turning Around

Keys to Motivation and Productivity

Dr. Beverly Potter

Ronin Publishing, Inc.
P.O. Box 1035
Berkeley, Ca 94701

To my father,
Campbell McLeod Potter
who initiated me into the Way of the ronin

Library of congress Cataloging in Publication Data

Potter, Beverly A.
    Turning Around

        Includes index.
            1. Organizational behavior.   2. Management.
    I. Title.
    HD58.7.P67   658.3   79-54847
    AMACOM ISBN 0-8144-5533-6
    RONIN ISBN 0-914171-00-3
    RONIN ISBN 0-914171-16-X

RONIN Edition 1983 ISBN 0-914171-00-3 cloth, $19.95
RONIN Edition 1988 ISBN 0-914171-16-X paper, $9.95

Forward, Introduction and Appendix added to 1980 AMACOM
edition. Rights granted to Beverly A. Potter and RONIN
Reprinted with permission from AMACOM.

RONIN Publishing, Inc.
PO Box 1035, Berkeley, Ca 94701
415-540-6278

"Job Burnout: A Management Challenge,"

© 1981 Beverly A. Potter, was first published in
PIMA Magazine, December, 1981.

"The Potter Principle: There Is No Peter Principle," is
reprinted by permission from Boardroom Reports,
Management's Source of Useful Information,
330 West 42 Street, NY, NY 10036.

Foreword

Change can be difficult. Helping others to change is a delicate process as well as a difficult one. This process is an important aspect of the work of anyone charged with managing organizational performance or supervising others. Understanding behavioral change and knowing how to help bring it about can strongly influence how well managers and supervisors accomplish and enjoy their jobs. Implementing change effectively leads to progress; implementing it ineffectively, on the other hand, can cause regression.

Beverly Potter understands both the elements of personal change and the ethical questions inherent in helping others to change. Dr. Potter also understands how to explain what she knows in the context of the work place. In *Turning Around*, she applies psychological principles of learning and behavior to self-management, then, through steps that can be followed, she clarifies how the principles can be used in four crucial work place situations: employee selection, assignment of work, confronting conflict, and working with groups of people in meetings.

Dr. Potter's wide range of experience as a management consultant and producer of training programs is evident in the realism of the many examples she uses, often in the form of dialogues with explanatory notes. What results from her combination of principles, action steps, and examples is an immediately practical book for readers who seek models for action along with reasons the action works.

Turning Around is a book to be read in several ways. It is, first, a consistently interesting explanation of a compelling subject. It is also a reference work to be consulted when the situations it treats present themselves and require effective responses. It is finally a book to be returned to when a refresher course in the "how to" of productive human resource management and supervision is needed. In short, *Turning Around* is a book for the "active" section of your professional library.

Judy Moss
Coordinator
Staff Development
Stanford University
Summer, 1983

Also by Beverly Potter

The Way of the Ronin
Riding the Waves of Change At work

Beating Job Burnout
*How to Transform Work Pressure
into Productivity*

Preventing Job Burnout
A Workbook

Introduction
To The Ronin Edition

If America is to regain its leading edge, business must renew its ability to be innovative and foster the entrepreneural spirit. But over-reliance on the analytic has led to an abstract, soulless philosophy that has all but killed this spirit. As Camus said, "Without work, all life goes rotten, but when work is soulless, life stifles and dies."

The business of innovating, of developing successful new products, is not a step-by-step, carefully planned, rational process. Rather it is through experimentation and mistakes that we break through to new ways of doing things. If we are to be on the cutting edge and are to keep our employees highly motivated and productive we must organize and manage to encourage this nonlinear, nonrational process.

Innovation usually pivots around what Tom Peters and Robert Waterman (in their groundbreaking report, *In Search of Excellence,*[1]) call a product champion, the fanatic who inspires the extra effort and pushes the project through and around the bureaucratic maze. But today in American business there are too few of these Corporate Ronin. The Ronin workstyle has been considered to be at odds with the way most businesses manage. Too often Ronin are regarded as disruptive and challenging, even embarrassing. Consequently, they are not hired, and if hired, they are not promoted or rewarded. Instead, organizations kill the spirit of the champions they so desperately need.

The manager, more than any other individual in the organization, is saddled with satisfying the needs of the organization and the individual. Yet, the responsibility for achieving organizational goals through individuals often seems like an impossible *catch 22* because the relationship of the individual and the organization is inherently paradoxical. Organizations, which are created by, of and, presumably, to serve individuals, develop a consciousness of their own that is suspicious of, even antagonistic to individuals.

For example, organizations strive for certainty and predictability, yet individuals often act in unpredictable ways. Organizations prize clarity, but individuals who work within them are ambiguous. Organizations demand perfection even though individual workers are not perfect; they make errors. While organizations call for risk taking, they punish even small failures, thereby stamping out the seedbeds in which new ideas germinate. Organizations abhor dependence upon any individual. So much so that through specialization, the pyramid structure, and standardized job descriptions, they strive to mold individuals into standardized, replaceable parts in the organizational machine. Yet, individuals are unique and want to feel they are making an indispensible contribution. Likewise, organizations are structured along the military model to ensure that no one individual has too much power. The resulting powerlessness has led to a demoralized, burnt-out workforce. As I discussed in my book, *Beating Job Burnout*,[2] to be mentally healthy and productive we, as individuals, must feel we control our lives and our work.

Peters and Waterman report that there is one striking feature of excellent companies: The ability to manage ambiguity and paradox. While mainstream American business has swung toward the overly rational and toward satisfying the needs of the organization at the expense of individuals, excellent companies have found a middle path, bridging the paradox. They treat people, not money or machines, as *the* natural resource.

Many books, workshops, and seminar leaders admonish bewildered managers to promote participation, gain commitment, improve communication, foster innovation, and encourage entrepreneuralism. But few provide how-to steps for doing so. This is what *Turning Around* is all about: A practical hands-on approach. The first two chapters describe the basics of behavior modification which is an experimental model — pinpointing, trying something, observing the results and then trouble shooting. Subsequent chapters describe how to enlist employees in this process. The key is for the manager to function not as a drill sergeant barking orders or as the nice guy cajoling employees into working. Instead, an excellent manager is like the conductor of an orchestra. A conductor does not play the drums, then blow on the flute for a few bars. The conductor takes all of the sounds, the individual outputs, and brings them together with the right timing and in the right measure to produce the symphony. Similarly, excellent managers orchestrate employees' output.

For this new edition, two papers have been added to the appendix. "The Potter Principle," reprinted from *Boardroom Reports*, challenges the Peter Principle, which suggests that individuals have a topping out point, a maximum capability causing them to rise to one step beyond their level of competence where they then remain. Instead, I suggest that what is really happening is that the best technicians and professionals are being promoted into managerial positions without the essential training they need to succeed in the new role. As a consequence they must fly by the seat of their pants as they attempt to identify and teach themselves the needed skills while still performing at their former high level. Some master this challenge, many do not. Those who do are promoted repeatedly until they can no longer reinvent the wheel.

In the second appendix you will find a step-by-step process, TASC+, for integrating the four essentials for maintaining high motivation — goal setting, feedback, participation and acknowledgement —into the daily managing process. TASC+ (*T*ell how performance compares to the standard, *A*sk for information and suggestions, *S*et action objective, *C*heck progress, and *P*lus — acknowledge/reward good work) is a method of providing employees with direction without sabotaging their feelings of control over their work. "Tell" and "Set objective" work in concert to set goals and give feedback on movement toward them. "Ask" elicits participation. The "Check" step is an opportunity to oversee without overcontrolling. And "Plus" reminds the manager to give the vital acknowledgement for on-task performance that makes us feel like winners.

Utilizing TASC+ fulfills a number of organizational metagoals. For example, organizational structure provides for getting information from the top down. The problem is how to get the information up from the botton line where the action is. Asking is the key. Managers often forget that individual employees know more than anyone else about the problems of their jobs and possible solutions. TASC+ is a way of tapping that informational goldmine. Likewise, managers are continually advised to develop employees, to train and prepare them for advancement. But daily deadlines make it unlikely that any manager has time to sit down and teach employees. TASC+ provides a means of teaching while managing. The good teacher doesn't tell but asks: "What happened?" "What do you suggest?" "How would that work?" Such are the types of questions that stimulate thought and encourage innovation. Additionally, TASC+ is a positive way to handle failure. Errors are precious. We must not squelch these seeds of innovation. With TASC+ we can harness what is learned from mistakes. Finally, TASC+ helps create involvement and cooperation by enlisting employees into the problem-solving and decision making processes.

Asking, the secret of orchestrating employee output, is an artful skill that can be learned. Chapter 4, "Managing Personnel Selection," discusses the do's and don'ts of question asking. The same principles apply whether you aim to gather information from a candidate about suitability for a position, to brainstorm with an employee the next logical step in solving a problem (See Chapter 5, "Managing Authority: How To Give Directives"), to learn from warring employees the nature and scope of the dispute (See Chapter 7, "Managing Conflicts") or to promote discussion among members in staff meetings (See Chapter 6, "Managing Group Meetings").

During the next decade managers will face even greater challenges. The baby-boom generation, for example, will reach their peak performance years. But there are too few slots in the pyramid for this wave of highly trained humanity. How will managers motivate these ambitious workers raised on great expectations during the post-war growth era? Economic swings and technological advances further aggravate the problem.

Out of these oppressive and antiquated work conditions, this "corporate feudalism," is emerging a new breed of worker, the Corporate Ronin. I draw my metaphor from traditional Japan where a ronin was a samurai who had broken away from his feudal warlord to live by his wits as his own master. Some became scholars, other poets; some marketed themselves as freelance bodyguards; others opened schools of martial arts. Likewise, Corporate Ronin are not beholden to the mandated one-life-one-profession career strategy. Nor do they subscribe to climbing the corporate ladder and overspecialization which leads to lopsided development and vulnerability to change. They strive for self-actualization through work and, as generalists, they make lateral moves that bring challenge while increasing their repertoire of skills and broadening their sphere of influence. With the Ronin lie hope for a renaissance at work.

In *The Way of the Ronin: Riding the Waves of Change at Work*,[3] you will meet the Corporate Ronin. We need more Ronin in the workplace because they bring a mix of excellence and innovation to the corporation. But leading and managing Corporate Ronin is management's challenge. TASC+ and the other techniques in *Turning Around* are keys for doing so.

Beverly A. Potter
Berkeley, 1983

1. Thomas J. Peters and Robert H. Waterman, Jr., *In Search of Excellence*, Harper & Row, 1982.

2. Beverly A. Potter, *Beating Job Burnout: How to Transform Work Pressure into Productivity*, (Previously published by Harbor/Putnam, 1980, & Berkley/Ace, 1982), Ronin, 1985.

3. Beverly A. Potter, *The Way of the Ronin: Riding the Waves of Change at Work*, AMACOM, 1984, & Ronin, 1988.

Preface

Because this book is about behavior control—how to use scientific knowledge to manage people more effectively—the question of the right and wrong uses of control presents itself immediately.

Control. Just the printed word seems to have the power to make images of Big Brother come to mind. I personally dislike this picture with its implied punishment and loss of individuality.

The ethics of control is a basic issue that I was confronted with throughout my training in rehabilitation counseling and counseling psychology. Without fail, the first question my clinical supervisors put to me when reviewing my work with a client was: Who determined that this is an appropriate goal for this person? And often during this scrutiny I discovered I had assumed a godlike role by thinking I knew what was best for another person. The specific issues of concern to psychologists differ greatly from those facing business and its managers. And I am not so presumptuous as to assume that I know the right and wrong uses of control within the organization. At best I can only pose a few of the questions and hope that those in a position to control others in the workplace will seriously ponder these questions.

How those in a position to control others' behavior feel about this power is illuminating. Of the gamesman, a new breed of executive, Michael Maccoby said, "By controlling himself so successfully and maintaining control over the organization, he begins to enjoy control for its own sake." There is a danger here, and some of the leaders Maccoby interviewed share this concern. Wakefield, one of the brilliant gamesmen, said, "But getting power assumes you have responsibility for what you do with it. You have to have philosophical goals. Power has to nestle somewhere, and I'd like to see it nestle with honest, sincere people who have a philosophy I understand."*

Don't all of us believe ourselves to be honest, sincere people with the best of motives? I certainly do. And when I think this I must

*Michael Maccoby, *The Gamesman* (New York: Simon and Schuster, 1976).

remind myself that those managed (or controlled) are sovereign human beings with inalienable rights. At what point is their dignity violated?

Suppose as a manager you decide competitiveness will increase the performance of your sales team and you actively use behavior modification techniques to foster and reinforce competitive behavior. Is this ethical? Is it permissible to use knowledge to shape others in this way? Yes, you may say. But where should the line be drawn? Is encouraging people to become so involved in work that they neglect other important aspects of their lives and personal development good or evil? And what about the possibility of behavior modification's being used in the service of more dubious goals? Suppose that it is used to subtly enforce compliance and conformity? Wakefield's words testify that the danger of abuse has always existed, but the appearance in the organization of the science of behavior—a systematic and effective technology for behavior control—demands that questions of responsibility be confronted.

In pondering the implications of these questions, I was forced to consider alternative views of behavior control, and it made me conceive of an image that I find more hopeful than the Brave New World many people fear. I have called this new image the "Garden of Eden dilemma." Nearly everybody knows the story: Yielding to the serpent's temptation of godliness, Adam and Eve ate the forbidden fruit from the Tree of Knowledge and became aware—they learned the difference between good and evil. When God asked them how they had gotten this knowledge, each blamed the other for the transgression, and this denial resulted in God's casting them out of the Garden and into the world of consequences.

This image suggested to me that scientific knowledge, control, and responsibility are an inseparable trio. When the balance among the three is altered, work becomes toil—working to avoid some sort of punishment—and this is where Big Brother fits in. But the Eden dilemma holds out hope. Implied in the story is that had responsibility not been denied, there would have been a different outcome, possibly Adam and Eve's remaining in the Garden. That is, a balance among the three can create a nourishing environment that supports abundance or productivity.

Using this image, I reformulated one of the basic questions posed by the use of behavioral techniques in management (When should organizational goals be primary and when should they be secondary to human freedom and dignity?) and decided to look for the midpoint or balance between these seemingly contradictory priorities.

Two programs described in Chapter 8 highlight this issue. The program for reducing absenteeism in a South African factory is an example in which organizational goals were primary. Here an intervention was conceived and implemented without any apparent consideration of the unique individuals who were the targets of the change program. In contrast, the program that modified safety behavior in a wholesale bakery, in my opinion, balanced organizational goals and human dignity by directly involving the target employees in the change process.

As I stated before I think what many find particularly disturbing about the prospect of being controlled in the workplace is the threat to individuality—being one of a mass made to march along unnoticed and unconsidered. And I believe that the potential for this type of abuse—treating people as commodities—is real. Incentive programs applied thoughtlessly and uniformly are a movement in this direction. Over the long run most have failed, however, because they overlook individuality. Not everybody is motivated by the same incentive. A self-evident, yet often forgotten fact. One danger with such programs is that the individual who does not respond to the incentive may be deemed unmotivated when, in fact, the problem lay in the environment and not within the individual. But the way in which incentives can be used to shape people is secondary to the major question of outcome. In the service of what goals is it permissible to control people? And who shall decide? This is the dilemma I keep returning to.

Perhaps if managers could develop the behaviors that Maccoby calls "qualities of the heart"—including independence, a critical attitude to authority, compassion, and idealism—they would be better prepared to answer these questions. Answers must be more than abstract philosophical statements; they must be concrete statements made in daily decisions in managing those in subordinate positions. This is no easy challenge. The organizational environment extinguishes, and at times punishes, the qualities needed to answer these questions. It is difficult to develop qualities of the heart when you are in an environment that does not nourish their growth. The self-management techniques described in Chapter 3 can help, but they are insufficient to meet the challenge. The real challenge is for management as a profession to develop a philosophical and ethical position and for the professional manager to work within self-imposed limits derived from this basic position.

The destructiveness of a negative work environment can pervade every aspect of a person's life, whereas a positive work environment can provide the prompting and support needed to develop latent capabilities as well as a sense of self-worth and purpose. Many organizations expound the importance of employee development, yet what happens on a daily basis is often antithetical to this stated goal. I have written this book because I believe that one's work is the single most important factor in one's life. And I believe that the principles and techniques described herein can, if employed responsibly, simultaneously develop employees' capabilities and accomplish organizational goals.

I thank my friends. Each played a special role in shaping this book: Sharon Anthony Bower, Chris Coultas, L.D., Howard Gold, Helen Loceff, Vicki Katz-O'Brien, Charles T. Peers, Jr., Doug Pies, Silva M.C., Suzanne, Ann Modersohn Straight, and C.J. Singh Wallia.

I also thank the managers and supervisors who participated in my workshops.

Beverly A. Potter

Contents

1

Basic Principles

THE multitude of problems that plague managers suggests that the traditional theories and techniques of management have not been effective. A new technology of behavior promises to prove effective in managing behavior within the organization. Unlike other theories of management, behavior modification principles and procedures were first developed in systematic and carefully controlled laboratory research. Until recently, however, most controlled practical application has been restricted to behavior problems within the traditional domains of psychology, education, and corrections. Although the field of organizational behavior modification is in its embryonic stage, the results to date have been dramatic. Companies that have instituted behavior modification programs have been able to reduce absenteeism, improve customer services, and increase quality control.

It is important to understand the theory that underlies the management techniques. There are two basic factors in the behavior modification model of what causes behavior: learning and environment. Social-learning theory states that behavior is learned through interactions with the environment. This means that counterproductive behaviors are regarded as having been learned. Thus, a learning approach should be used in effecting behavior change. Applied to the job situation, this means that one would alter undesirable employee behavior by teaching employees to behave in desired ways. Because environment plays a critical role, one would view the behavior of a subordinate within the context of the work environment.

ABCs: Antecedents, Behaviors, Consequences

The ABCs is a conceptual way of thinking about behavior and its causes. *Antecedents* are cues that inform the individual which behaviors are appropriate in a given situation. For example, the ringing of a bell at 8:00 A.M. could be a cue that informs assemblers that work is about to begin. An antecedent that is always present when a person behaves in a certain way can actually evoke that very behavior, or at least set the occasion for it. For example, an advertisement for a delicious steak dinner may evoke desire for such a steak—even in the absence of physiological hunger; rock music may evoke dancing; the presence of an ashtray may evoke smoking; and so forth. Usually we are unaware of the cues that elicit our behavior unless our attention is specifically directed toward them.

Behavior is divided into two broad categories: *respondent* and *operant* behavior. This is an important distinction, because there is a difference in the underlying processes by which these behaviors are learned. Respondent (also called reflexive or involuntary) behaviors are not learned; they are present at birth, or develop as a result of physical maturing. A person ordinarily has no control over whether to engage in them. They include physical reflexes such as the constriction of the pupil when a bright light is directed into the eye, the jerking of the knee when a doctor taps it in a specific way, or the startled reaction to a loud and unexpected noise.

Although respondent behaviors themselves are not learned, a person can learn to perform the behavior in the presence of something (an *antecedent stimulus* or *cue*) that ordinarily would not elicit it. For example, to respond with some manifestation of fear to a loud noise is inborn, but through a process called *classical conditioning* a person can learn to respond fearfully in situations that are not physically dangerous. In short, although respondent behaviors themselves are unlearned, a person can learn to carry them out in a wide variety of situations.

Operant behaviors (also called instrumental or voluntary) are learned, and are not a result of physical functioning. Operant behaviors include such things as hitting a baseball, programming a computer, dancing, or typing. The process by which one learns operant behaviors is called *operant conditioning*. Most behaviors of concern to managers are operant behaviors.

Consequences are events that immediately follow a behavior. The kind of consequence (positive, negative, or neutral) exerts a powerful influence on whether a person will engage in that behavior again. People are more likely to repeat a behavior that is followed by a positive consequence and less likely to repeat a behavior that is followed by a negative consequence. For example, when the bell rings at 8:00 A.M., the assemblers will receive positive consequences if they begin work immediately and negative consequences if they continue to socialize.

Classical Conditioning

Although most managers will not directly employ the principles of classical conditioning, it is important for them to understand the process. First, it can help explain why punitive or disciplinary actions should be avoided or used with caution. Second, managers may find an understanding of classical conditioning useful in modifying their own behavior. This discussion is presented as an alternative explanation to theories that emphasize internal needs and unresolved conflicts as the basis of so-called neurotic behavior.

The basic principles of classical conditioning were first discovered in Pavlov's experiments with dogs. Figure 1 shows how this form of learning works. At step one Pavlov presented meat (the *unconditioned stimulus*) to a hungry dog, and the dog responded with the unconditioned response of salivation (called "unconditioned" because it is an unlearned, or reflexive, stimulus-response association). Next, through a process called *pairing,* Pavlov rang a bell at the same time that he presented the meat to the dog. Again, the dog responded by salivating. Pavlov repeated this step many times. Finally, he rang the bell but did not present the meat, and the dog salivated anyway (step three), because it had learned to salivate at the sound of a bell. The bell is the conditioned stimulus and the salivation is the conditioned response. The association is called "conditioned" because dogs don't normally salivate at the sound of a bell.

Classical conditioning is the process by which phobias or irrational fears as well as emotional reactions to certain situations (the manifestation of such respondent behaviors as increased heart rate, rapid breathing, and sweating palms) are learned. Suppose you were riding a horse and it threw you off: Being thrown through the air would be the unconditioned stimulus, and the fear you experienced would be the unconditioned response. As a result of this incident, you may very likely have learned to respond with fear to sitting on a horse—or even to the sight of a horse—because of its association with your having been thrown. Folk wisdom would tell you to get right back on the horse, because by doing so you can break the fearful association and thus unlearn or extinguish your fear of horses.

Consider the dog once again. In step four, Pavlov paired a light

Figure 1. Classical conditioning.

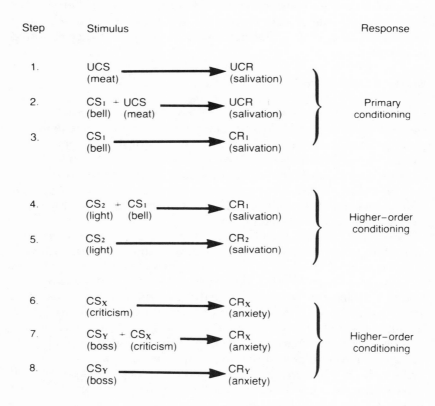

with the bell and found that once again the dog salivated. After repeating this procedure a number of times, the dog salivated at the sight of the light alone. This is called *higher-order conditioning,* because a conditioned stimulus was used in the pairing.

Most emotional reactions are learned through the process of higher-order conditioning. Suppose somebody has learned to respond anxiously to criticism. If this person is then criticized several times by the boss, that individual may learn to respond anxiously in the boss's presence, even when the boss is not being critical, because the boss has been paired with the *aversive* (unpleasant or painful) stimulus of criticism. Through higher-order conditioning, the boss will eventually become a conditioned stimulus that elicits anxiety. It is called "higher-order" because the stimulus used in the pairing or conditioning is itself conditioned, i.e., the employee's anxiety. Higher-order conditioning is one way in which some people learn to display strong emotional reactions to certain minority groups or nationalities—even though they have had little or no personal contact with these groups. Higher-order conditioning also refers to the way in which words can have different connotations to different people.

For conditioning to occur, a person need not be aware of the process, nor is the selection of the conditioned stimulus a conscious choice in most cases. (People who understand the laws of learning, however, can employ these laws to condition themselves in ways they choose. This will be discussed in Chapter 3.) Anything that is present in the situation when a person experiences an aversive stimulus might become paired with that stimulus, and thus condition the same emotional response. For example, in the case of the critical boss, the office in which the critical remarks were made might also come to elicit anxiety in the person who was the object of the boss's criticism.

People who experience a lot of vague anxiety might be conditioned to respond with anxiety to many stimuli of which they are unaware. The color green might elicit anxiety in someone who, as a child, was severely spanked on a green carpet; small rooms might elicit anxiety because the spanking occurred in a small room, so that when in the presence of green or in a small room, this individual might feel vaguely anxious and be unaware that small rooms and the color green are the conditioned stimuli that are eliciting this anxiety. Positive emotional responses to environmental stimuli are learned in the same manner. In most cases conditioning will be extinguished or lose its hold on the individual if the unconditioned stimulus is never again paired with the conditioned stimulus. For example, in the case of the hungry dog, if the meat is never again paired with the bell, the dog will eventually stop salivating at the sound of the bell.

However, when the conditioned response is anxiety or another strong emotion, the conditioning can become self-perpetuating because the sensation of anxiety is itself uncomfortable. Thus, when the conditioned response is anxiety, the feeling of anxiety is continually paired with the conditioned stimulus and is continually reconditioning the person. Thus, the person who was spanked on the green carpet might continue to respond with anxiety to the color green, even if such a punitive incident were never to occur again.

Conditioning is not a static process; it may generalize or become more discriminative. Conditioning "generalizes" when stimuli similar to the conditioned stimulus can elicit the conditioned response. The classic experiment that established this phenomenon was the case of an 11-month-old child, "Little Albert."[1] By repeatedly pairing a white rat with loud noise in front of Albert, experimenters were able to condition the child to cry (a fear response) at the sight of a white rat. The psychologists who performed the experiment discovered that after the conditioning Albert also cried at the sight of other white furry things, such as a white rabbit, a white dog, and a hairy Santa Claus mask. In this case, the conditioning "generalized" to several white furry objects.

Discrimination is essentially the opposite process. Discrimination occurs when the conditioned stimulus elicits the conditioned response only under certain conditions. Discriminative learning takes place when there is a third stimulus that is present each time the pairing occurs but that is not present when the pairing does not occur. For example, the anxious employee may learn to discriminate among the critical boss's expressions: The boss is critical only when he frowns; but when he doesn't frown, he does not criticize. In this case, the employee could learn to respond anxiously only when the boss frowns.

Operant Conditioning

B. F. Skinner discovered *operant conditioning,* the process by which most behaviors of concern to managers are learned. The principles of operant conditioning explain how operant (instrumental or voluntary) behaviors (such as hitting a baseball, typing, or dancing) are learned and how respondent behaviors evoked through classical conditioning are maintained. In operant conditioning the consequence (what happens immediately after the behavior) is crucial, because reinforcing consequences increase the likelihood that the behavior will recur, and punishing consequences reduce that likelihood. For example, a pretentious engineer might throw a tantrum in the presence of certain environmental cues such as a request to do his own typing. The probability of his throwing tantrums in the future will be determined by the consequences of that behavior. If the supervisor gives him special attention (*commiserates*) or finds someone else to do the typing (*reinforcement*), then the tantrums will probably recur more frequently. On the other hand, if the engineer is reprimanded or deprived of a privilege (*punishment*), his tantrums will probably recur less frequently.

Four types of consequences are illustrated in Table 1. A *reinforc-*

TABLE 1. Reinforcement and punishment: kinds of consequences.[2]

Something Positive	*Something Negative*
Positive Reinforcement	Positive Punishment
Negative Punishment	Negative Reinforcement

ment is a consequence that makes a behavior more likely; *positive reinforcement* occurs when something positive is presented or "turned on" after a behavior. For example, the supervisor who commiserates with the engineer is positively reinforcing the engineer's tantrum behavior (commiseration is positive attention). And if the supervisor were to find someone else to do the typing, the tantrum behavior would be *negatively reinforced* because something negative was removed or "turned off."

There are also two types of punishment. (Punishment is a consequence that makes a behavior less likely.) *Positive punishment* occurs when something negative or unpleasant is presented or turned on. By reprimanding the engineer, the supervisor would be positively punishing tantrum behavior. Being reprimanded is a negative event after the tantrum behavior. *Negative punishment* occurs when something positive is removed or withheld (turned off). Depriving the engineer of a privilege would be negative punishment of the tantrum behavior because something positive is withheld.

How Antecedent Cues Are Established

As stated earlier, antecedents are events or stimuli that signal that a certain behavior should be performed. Antecedent cues can be established in two ways. With respondent behaviors, the antecedent usually gains its power through classical conditioning or association. Recalling Pavlov's dogs, when an unconditioned stimulus such as meat is paired repeatedly with a neutral one such as a bell, the neutral stimulus will eventually elicit the salivation by itself. In other words, the bell has become the cue that elicits the salivation. If this conditioned salivation is then reinforced repeatedly, the association between the bell and salivation will become permanent and it will never again be necessary to pair the bell with the meat.

As another example, consider Little Albert again. Little Albert learned to cry at the sight of a white rat because he associated it with a loud and frightening noise. And this learning generalized to white rabbits, white dogs, and a hairy Santa Claus mask. Now suppose Little Albert sees a rat or a Santa Claus (the *antecedent cue* or *conditioned stimulus*) and begins to cry (the *learned* or *conditioned response*). When his mother hears him crying she gives him a lollipop. That is a positive consequence, since the lollipop is a positive reinforcer. If this sequence were repeated several times, Albert would probably learn that the sight of a white rat or a Santa Claus is a cue to cry and thereby receive a lollipop. Thus, the power of the white rat (antecedent) to evoke crying (behavior) would have been established through classical conditioning and maintained with lollipops (consequence) through operant conditioning. It would never again be necessary to pair the loud noise with the rat, because the crying behavior would be maintained by the reinforcement delivered by the mother.

In contrast with operant behaviors, the antecedent cues are established by repeated association with a particular behavior-consequence sequence. *When a behavior is consistently reinforced or punished in the presence of a stimulus, the stimulus becomes an antecedent that cues the person to the likely consequences of that behavior in that situation.* In other words, antecedents cue a person to the "if-then" (or contingent) relationship between a behavior and its probable consequence—that is, if I do this, then a particular event is likely to happen.

Antecedents can become so powerful that they evoke certain behavior. For example, because ashtrays are usually present when one smokes cigarettes, the sight of an ashtray alone can evoke smoking behavior. And each time the smoker enjoys smoking after seeing an ashtray, the association is established even more firmly. Expressed in terms of the ABCs, the ashtray is the antecedent cue, smoking is the behavior, and enjoyment is the reinforcing consequence. In short, behavior is influenced by what precedes it and by what follows it. The antecedents elicit or set the occasion for the behavior, and the consequences strengthen or weaken the behavior.

The establishment of antecedent cues is crucial in the development of *stimulus control*. This means that the likelihood of certain behaviors is increased in the presence of some antecedents and decreased in the presence of others. For example, consider Jeff, the office gossip. Suppose that whenever Jeff tells John a juicy story, John responds with interest, whereas whenever Jeff gossips to Susan, she responds with irritation. John's interest reinforces the gossiping, and Susan's irritation punishes the gossiping. Very quickly Jeff's behavior will come under stimulus control: John's presence becomes an antecedent that cues gossiping, and Susan's presence becomes an antecedent that discourages gossiping.

Stimulus control is established through discriminative learning in which the individual learns that a particular behavior pattern (such as wearing sexy clothes) will be reinforced in the presence of certain environmental cues (such as friends at a party), but punished in the presence of others (such as the supervisor at the office). It is through stimulus control or discriminative learning that an employee can learn such things as where and when to look busy, who can be trusted with privileged information, how to identify a defective product, or who will provide an answer to a difficult problem.

It is also possible for a particular response to *generalize* to more than a single environmental setting or cue. Generalization occurs when the same behavior is reinforced or punished in the presence of a variety of environmental cues. It may also occur when a behavior is reinforced in the presence of a cue similar to but different from the original one. This is the way in which many children learn to respect people who wear uniforms. A child might be praised for acting respectfully toward a police officer, and because a police officer's uniform is very similar to a fireman's uniform, the child might then act respectfully toward a fireman. After many such experiences, the child learns to act respectfully toward anyone wearing a uniform. Over time, acting respectfully might generalize from people in uniform to anyone in a position of authority.

The phenomenon of generalization is important in any training program. It would be a waste of time to train people to deliver a sales pitch if they could do so only in the presence of the trainer. The trainer is hoping that what the trainees learn will generalize from the classroom to the work setting.

Functional Analysis: Identifying the ABCs

An event is not labeled as an antecedent, behavior, or consequence because of something inherent in that event; rather, it is the *function* the event serves that is important. Consider the following sequence:

Boss criticizes Joan	→	Joan starts crying	→	Ted sympathizes with Joan	→	Joan stops crying	→	Ted buys Joan some coffee

Which event is the antecedent? Which is the behavior? And which is the consequence? The analysis depends on which behavioral event is the focal point and what functions the other events serve relative to that behavior.

Figure 2 shows a functional analysis of this series of events. As can be seen, an event can function as an antecedent, a behavior, or a consequence. For example, Ted's sympathy with Joan functions as a positive consequence and also as an antecedent to Joan's cessation of her crying. And of course Ted's sympathy is a behavior evoked by the antecedent cue of Joan's crying, and is negatively reinforced by the cessation of Joan's crying.

This is the essence of what is commonly called the "vicious cycle": Ted's sympathetic attention maintains Joan's crying behavior and Joan's cessation of her crying maintains Ted's sympathetic behavior. Experientially, however, Joan and Ted probably both feel the other is "making" them behave the way they do, and probably neither is aware of how they stimulate and maintain the other's behavior. This dynamic is particularly evident in conflicts in which both parties point to the other as the cause or instigator of the problem. Most people are unaware of how their actions and reactions control others, but are very aware of how others' actions and reactions control them.

On the basis of this functional analysis, one could predict that Joan

Figure 2. A functional analysis of a vicious cycle.

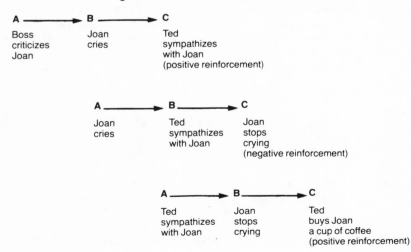

will cry more when criticized by the boss and Ted will sympathize more when Joan cries. A careful functional analysis is an essential step in modifying a behavior such as crying at work. The analysis reveals the factors that prompt and maintain each behavior in a cycle, and a manager could use this to determine the most appropriate point to intervene.

Chained Behavior

Thus far we have reviewed how a single behavioral event is learned, but most work performance is a series of numerous behavioral events. The principle of chained behavior explains how performance is prompted and maintained. (Figure 3 depicts graphically the dual consequence/antecedent relationship of the behavioral events involved in such a simple performance as making a sale.)

Almost all work performance is a chain of behavioral events. Functionally analyzing the ABCs that make up a performance chain is important in three ways. First, it is a guide for the training director who wants to teach a particular performance. By breaking the performance into its chain of behavioral events, the trainer can arrange learning experiences to teach each behavior in the chain. Second, analyzing the chain can assist managers in identifying the locus of the problem when performance is inadequate or incomplete. That is, a manager can observe the discrete behaviors of an employee who is unable to carry out a performance successfully, so that the manager will know where to intervene by having identified which behavioral event needs to be learned or modified. Finally, by examining chains, managers can identify behavioral events that are irrelevant or counterproductive to desired performance.

Avoidance and Escape Behavior

The principles of aversive antecedent cues and negative reinforcement explain how many nonproductive work behaviors are established and maintained. All too frequently a person engages in various work behaviors not to gain a positive consequence but to avoid or escape a negative one. To explain how avoidance and escape behavior is established, consider the case of Joe. Suppose that Joe has been criticized several times by his boss for loafing. And suppose that Joe has learned that when he does work his boss does not criticize. This is a situation in which the presence of the boss (an *aversive antecedent*) stimulates work behavior (*avoidance behavior*), which is negatively rein-

Figure 3. Chained behavior: making a sales call.

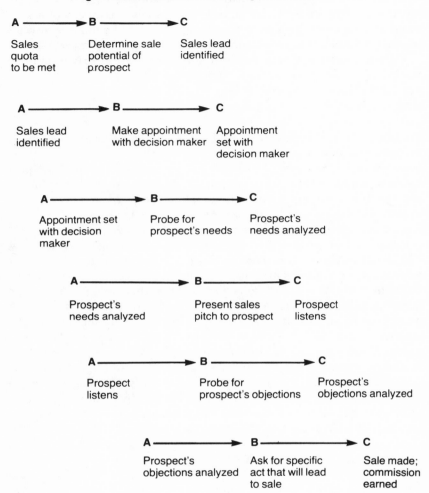

forced by the absence of criticism (the withholding of something un-pleasant). When the boss is not present, Joe is likely to loaf, because such behavior in the boss's absence does not bring the danger of criticism. In fact, loafing in the absence of the boss might be positively reinforced by the pleasure of socializing with others. Thus, Joe's loafing is now under stimulus control. When the boss is present, Joe avoids criticism by working but when the boss is absent, Joe loafs and enjoys the pleasure of socializing. The boss and the company have a

serious problem: Working to avoid criticism or other negative consequences is inefficient. The only way the boss can increase Joe's efficiency is to monitor Joe's work continually, with the implicit threat of
criticism if work is not performed.

Escape behavior is similar to avoidance behavior in that it is established and maintained through negative reinforcement. But whereas
avoidance implies that the person engages in a behavior *within* the
situation, escape behavior means that the person leaves the situation
entirely: Absenteeism, for example, is frequently an escape behavior.
Suppose that during the biweekly supervisory meeting, Ruth is frequently criticized. The day of the meeting could then become an
antecedent cue that signals probable negative consequences. If Ruth
is absent on the day of the meeting, she will escape the possibility of
criticism, so Ruth's absenteeism is negatively reinforced. Consequently, the frequency of Ruth's absence on the day of the meeting is
likely to increase.

Clearly, the threat of discipline and other punitive measures can
have far-reaching negative consequences for the company and the
manager as well as for the employees. Managers who use punitive
methods are inadvertently teaching employees to be unproductive
workers. Such employees become limited in their capacity to function
appropriately in a work setting and in their ability to gain positive
consequences (feelings of accomplishment, self-esteem, promotions,
pay increases, and so forth). The use of punitive control methods is
one cause of the disgruntled, uncommitted, and unproductive workforce that is found so often today.

It is often difficult to perform a functional analysis of avoidance
and escape behaviors. If the person is successful in avoiding or escaping the negative consequence, then that negative consequence will
never occur. One can only guess what is likely to happen if the person
does not engage in escape or avoidance behavior. In a functional
analysis, identifying the antecedents becomes very important: It is
often the only clue as to what is controlling the behavior.

Dangers of Punishment[3]

Most behavioral psychologists advise against the use of punitive
methods, and advocate positive methods of behavior control. Punishment usually results in only a short-term behavior change, and it is
often accompanied by undesirable and unpredictable side effects. As
was illustrated in the case of Joe and his critical boss, the supervisor
who uses punishment can become an antecedent that signals pending

punishment. Not only does this usually result in many avoidance and escape behaviors such as absenteeism, nonproductive work, and obsessive agreement with the supervisor; it makes it almost impossible for the supervisor to function as an administrator of positive reinforcement. That is, it becomes physically impossible for the supervisor to deliver a positive reinforcement to someone who is avoiding him or her. When the punitive boss attempts to be positive, it is likely to arouse the suspicions of subordinates and to discredit any potentially positive reinforcement delivered.

Because the dynamics of emotional responses are so complex and are not completely understood, it is difficult to predict the emotional response to a punitive experience. Thus, punitive experiences frequently elicit dysfunctional emotional responses such as angry outbursts, breaking of equipment, threats, and sabotage. Related to avoidance and escape behavior is the problem of a temporary suppression of the undesired behavior. The undesired behavior, such as Joe's loafing, is suppressed only as long as the punitive boss is present; but as soon as he leaves, the undesired behavior usually returns. Another problem is the probability of behavioral inflexibility. A behavior that is viewed as undesirable at one time may at another time be considered highly desirable. Yet as a result of past punishment, the behavior may be inhibited or permanently suppressed. For example, the suggestions of a management trainee may be suppressed by derogatory remarks from the supervisor, so that later on, when the supervisor actively solicits suggestions, the trainee may be unwilling or unable to generate any ideas.

A very serious problem with the use of punishment is that punishment begets punishment. The more people use punishment, the more likely they will be to use it again. Punishment is usually followed by the immediate cessation of an undesired behavior (*negative reinforcement*) and possibly by the appearance of a desired behavior (*positive reinforcement*). In short, the consequences of punishment tend to reinforce the punitive behavior of the supervisor who delivered the punishment. Once again we have a vicious cycle, one that results in an increase in the frequency of punishment.

Suppose a foreman's job is threatened by a drop in production (*antecedent*) and that in response to this drop, the foreman upbraids the subordinates and threatens that heads will roll if there isn't an immediate increase (*punishing behavior*). In response, subordinates work faster (*consequence*) and production increases. As would be expected, after several days the subordinates again slow down. The foreman will again most likely engage in punishing behavior because it has been both positively and negatively reinforced. The foreman's threats have been positively reinforced by the increase in production and negatively reinforced by the temporary removal of the threat to his or her own termination. The final problem with the use of punishment is that, although it suppresses undesirable behaviors, it does not teach *desired* behaviors. An awkward teenager's invitation for a date may be punished by rejection. The rejection will tend to suppress socially inept behavior, but it does not teach the teenager how to extend an invitation that will be accepted.

Extinction

Extinction is the process by which conditioning or learning is reversed. In general, conditioned or learned responses established through classical conditioning can be extinguished by continued presentation of the conditioned stimulus in the absence of the unconditioned stimulus. Thus, if the conditioned and unconditioned stimuli are never again paired, the conditioned stimulus will lose its power to elicit the conditioned response. For example, if the dog in Pavlov's experiment had heard the bell ring hundreds of times yet did not get any meat, the bell would have eventually lost its power to make the dog salivate.

There are two exceptions to this general rule. First, if the conditioned response is itself aversive, the conditioning will tend to remain intact. Responses such as anxiety and fear are inherently painful. Consequently, these uncomfortable sensations themselves become associated with the conditioned stimulus (such as the rat's causing Little Albert to cry) and tend to maintain the learned response (crying). The second exception is the case in which the conditioned response is followed by reinforcement. Each time Little Albert cries, his mother gives him a lollipop. The lollipop is a positive consequence that reinforces and maintains crying behavior. In this situation we would not expect the crying behavior in response to a white rat to extinguish even though the rat is never again paired with a loud noise. Avoidance and escape behaviors are difficult to extinguish because they are negatively reinforced. For example, a dog who has learned to jump out of a compartment in response to a flashing light and an electric shock will probably continue to do so when the light flashes even though the light is never again paired with the shock. Escape behavior is negatively reinforced by the very act of escaping.

In contrast, behaviors established through operant conditioning can be extinguished by withholding any consequence. For example,

when gossip behavior is ignored and is no longer followed by a reinforcing consequence such as attentive listening, it will probably stop.
In some cases the process of extinction is functionally similar to that
of negative punishment. Negative punishment is the withholding or
removal of something positive. When the gossip who is accustomed to
receiving attentive listening is ignored, that lack of attention can be
experienced as negative punishment. Thus, it is best to simultaneously reinforce a behavior that is *incompatible* with the behavior to
be extinguished. For instance, talking about work-related topics is
incompatible with gossiping, because one cannot do both at once. To
extinguish gossip behavior most efficiently, a manager should ignore
all gossip talk and listen attentively to work-related talk. This principle of reinforcing desired incompatible behavior rather than punishing undesired behavior can be applied to all areas of the work environment. (Examples of incompatible behaviors include standing–
sitting, tension- relaxation, loafing–working, laughing–crying, frowning–smiling, and assertiveness–passivity.)

Principles of Reinforcement

For a stimulus to function as a reinforcer, it must meet two conditions. First, it must be *contingent* on the performance of a specific
behavior—that is, the delivery of the reinforcement must be based on
an "if–then" relationship: *If* the behavior is carried out, *then* the specific consequence will follow. A behavior change strategy usually includes alteration of the contingency of if- then relationships. The
manager who wants to modify gossip talk must change the contingent
relationship from "if Jeff gossips, then I will listen" to "if Jeff gossips,
then I will look away and if Jeff talks about work-related topics, then I
will listen." In this example the manager has rearranged the
contingencies.

Second, to be effective the reinforcement must be desired by the
person carrying out the behavior. Whereas a lollipop might be an
effective reinforcer for Little Albert, it will not be an effective reinforcer for the pompous engineer. Although some consequences—such
as praise and other positive attention—are desired by most people, it
is a serious mistake to assume that one reinforcer will be desired by all
employees. What constitutes a desired consequence varies considerably from individual to individual. Thus, identifying and utilizing a
desired consequence is an essential step in developing a successful
behavior change strategy (see Chapter 2).

The power of a reinforcer to establish and maintain a behavior is determined by *when* and *how often* it is delivered. The timing of reinforcement refers to how long after the manifestation of the target behavior the reinforcement is delivered. The sooner the reinforcement is delivered, the more effective it will be. Common sense tells us that to say "thank you" for a favor immediately has more impact than to say "thank you" a month later. Obviously, in a work situation it is not always possible to deliver a reinforcement immediately after the performance of each desired behavior. As a general principle, *to establish or teach a behavior, the reinforcement should be delivered each time the behavior is carried out,* but once the behavior is learned it can be maintained most efficiently by a different schedule or frequency of reinforcement. There are five different schedules of reinforcement, and each one has a different effect on the target behavior.

Continuous Reinforcement

A schedule of continuous reinforcement is one in which a positive consequence follows each enactment of the target behavior. This results in a steady high rate of responding as long as the reinforcement continues to follow every response. This is a schedule appropriate for establishing or teaching new behaviors and increasing the frequency of existing behaviors. Continuous reinforcement has two drawbacks: First, the behavior weakens or undergoes extinction rapidly when the reinforcement is discontinued. For example, assistants who are accustomed to being thanked each time they get coffee for their supervisors are likely to stop getting coffee if they are not thanked a few times. The second drawback is that the reinforcer may lose its power to reinforce or its desirability. If a supervisor uses the word "terrific" in response to every suggestion a subordinate makes, "terrific" may lose its power to reinforce suggestion giving. *To maintain a behavior once it has been established, the schedule of reinforcement should be gradually changed from continuous to intermittent.*

Intermittent Reinforcement

When reinforcement follows some but not all manifestations of the behavior, it is said to be intermittent. There are two kinds of intermittent reinforcement: the *ratio schedule* and the *interval schedule.* Ratio schedules refer to reinforcements received after a number of responses, whereas reinforcement available only after a lapse of time is on an interval schedule.

Both ratio and interval schedules may be either fixed or variable. A *fixed schedule* is one in which a specific length of time or number of responses is required before the reinforcement is delivered. Piecework is an example of a fixed-ratio schedule; the workweek is an example of a fixed-interval schedule. With piecework the worker is paid for completing a specific number of items; with the workweek the worker is paid for spending a specific amount of time on the job. With both the fixed-interval and the fixed-ratio schedules, every response is not reinforced and the reinforcement is delivered intermittently and predictably.

Fixed schedules have one major drawback: The rate of responding usually drops immediately after the reinforcement is delivered. This is because the responses that occur immediately after the reinforcement are never reinforced. Therefore, in a fixed schedule we find that the frequency of responding is highest just before reinforcement and lowest just after reinforcement. The longer the fixed time or the larger the fixed number of responses required, the longer will be the pause after reinforcement before responding is resumed.

Although in theory, pay is supposed to reinforce work, it is actually contingent on the amount of time (number of days) one spends on the job. Thus, we would expect that the rate of absences among salaried workers would be highest at the beginning of a pay period (the day after receiving a paycheck) and lowest at the end of the pay period (the day the paychecks are issued). Likewise, those working on a task or piecework basis are likely to work harder when the task is near completion. This explains why many pieceworkers find it difficult to begin a new project. The pieceworker who must complete many items before being paid is likely to pause longer at the beginning than one who must complete fewer items before being paid. Similarly, we would expect more absences at the beginning of a monthly pay period than at the beginning of a weekly pay period.

A *variable* schedule is one in which the length of time or the number of responses required to obtain the reinforcement varies randomly. Because their actual delivery of reinforcement is unpredictable, variable schedules do not usually result in the problem of workers' pausing immediately after reinforcement. The reason for this is that, owing to the unpredictability of the variable schedule, the first response after receiving a reinforcement might also be reinforced, whereas there is always a fixed space between reinforcements with the fixed schedule—that is, in the fixed schedule the first response after reinforcement would never be reinforced. Consequently, that first response would be subject to extinction which results in a short pause.

If, for example, paychecks were issued on a variable-interval schedule, we would predict that the rate of absenteeism at the beginning of the pay period would drop, since the workers would not know on which day they would receive their pay. Likewise, slot machine players are likely to continue playing at a high rate because sometimes they will win twice in a row and sometimes they will win only after many turns (variable-ratio schedule). Making sales is another example of a variable-ratio schedule: The salesperson never knows how many calls will be required to secure a sale. (This could explain the perseverance of many salespeople.)

There is an exception to the general principle of continued high rates of response when using variable schedules. When the *average* interval or ratio required to secure reinforcement is very big, the person may pause after the reinforcement. That is, although sometimes the first response or first time segment is reinforced, the probability of this decreases as the interval or ratio increases. Hence, the person learns that another reinforcement will usually not be forthcoming for a long time or until many responses have been evidenced. A quality control inspector in a company that produces very few defective items is more likely to become lax immediately after finding a defective item than is an inspector who works for a company that produces many defective items. In general, when the average intervals or ratios are moderate, response will remain constant and high. Thus, behavior is most efficiently maintained by variable or random schedules of reinforcement.

Resistance to Extinction

A behavior is said to be resistant to extinction when it repeatedly occurs after reinforcement is discontinued. Behavior that has been maintained on an intermittent schedule will be more resistant to extinction than will behavior that has been maintained on a schedule of continuous reinforcement. Suppose that the call button for the elevator in your building is defective and you have discovered you must push it three times to call the elevator. You are likely to continue to use that button to call the elevator as long as it always comes after three pushes. However, if one day you push the button three times and it doesn't come, you may continue to push it three, six, or even nine times more. But if the elevator still does not come, you will probably give up and use the stairs. If for a few days in a row the elevator does not come after pushing the button three or six times, you are likely to stop approaching the elevator altogether and begin going directly to the stairs each day. On the other hand, the manager who is trying to stop the engineer's temper tantrums may occasionally give in to them, without realizing that giving in intermittently will make the tantrums extremely resistant to extinction. But if the manager has always given in and then abruptly stops, it is probable that the tantrums will be extinguished rapidly (unless they are being reinforced by other workers' attention).

The Premack Principle

As was stated earlier, reinforcement is functionally defined as a consequence that makes the performance of a certain behavior more likely. Many people mistakenly assume that reinforcement is synonymous with reward; a reward is probably a reinforcement, but a reinforcement is not necessarily a reward. For example, the quality control inspector's behavior is probably reinforced by identifying a defective item, although one can hardly consider spotting a defective item a reward. The Premack principle of reinforcement states that a high-probability behavior (a behavior that is enacted very frequently) can reinforce a low-probability behavior (a behavior that is performed infrequently). This principle is very important for managers, because when utilized contingently it can help managers use work to reinforce work.

Suppose that a salesperson calls on a lot of old clients, but has very few new clients. The number of new clients called upon can be increased if calling on old clients is made contingent on calling upon a specified number of new clients. Basically, it is a matter of doing the least liked work first and the most liked work second. Generally, any behavior (that is not painful or unpleasant for that person) that a person enacts very frequently can be used as a reinforcer. If a secretary uses the copy machine several times a day, then going to the copy machine can be used to reinforce a low-probability behavior such as filing. In order to be effective as a reinforcer, going to the copy machine must be contingent on a specified amount of filing. Common high-probability behaviors include looking at one's watch, drinking coffee, smoking cigarettes, and talking on the telephone.

Vicarious Learning

To learn that a particular behavior will lead to a specific consequence, a person does not have to engage in that behavior and be personally reinforced for doing so; that person can learn vicariously by watching a model's behavior and its consequences. This phenomenon is known as *modeling*. For example, if you observe your friend petting a neighborhood dog and then being bitten by it, you will probably avoid petting that dog even though you were not bitten by it.

You learned through modeling that the probability of being bitten is increased by petting the dog.

Modeling is used extensively in all types of training. When you learn to play tennis the instructor usually first models the different kinds of swings you can use. You observe that one type of swing usually results in hitting the ball over the net and another does not. A sales trainee can learn to give a sales pitch by watching the trainer model a sales pitch. (Trainees will learn more rapidly, of course, if after watching the model they then practice giving a sales pitch themselves and are reinforced for doing so.)

A person does not necessarily even have to observe a behavior/consequence to learn the probable consequences of that behavior. For example, your friend could tell you that she was bitten by the dog after petting it. Based on this information, you would know that you're likely to be bitten if you pet the dog. This is one form of symbolic learning. Through the use of words (*symbols*) and abstract concepts you can learn contingency relationships. Being instructed or reading instructions is another form of symbolic learning.

Superstitious Behavior

Superstitious behavior is designed to effect a consequence when there is actually no causal relationship between that consequence and the behavior. Blowing on dice before rolling them probably does not influence the roll, and knocking on wood probably has little influence over future events. The ace pilot who while flying must carry a talisman is engaging in superstitious behavior. The person who pushes the elevator button (provided it is not defective) several times is engaging in superstitious behavior, because pushing a button more than once does not bring the elevator faster.

Superstitious behavior is established through chance. Suppose that the wiring in your car is defective so that you must turn the key several times in order to start the car. If you turn the key in vain, then bang on the dashboard and the car starts on the next key turn, you might mistakenly assume that banging on the dashboard resulted in the car's starting; in fact, the association between the banging and the starting of the car was an accident. Yet the car did start (*consequence*) after you banged on the dashboard (*behavior*), and essentially this is how superstitious behavior is established.

Superstitious behavior can become very resistant to extinction because it is usually maintained by a variable schedule of reinforcement: Because there is no real cause-effect (*contingency*) relationship, the desired consequence occurs occasionally by chance. Superstitious behaviors that are maintained by negative reinforcement are extremely resistant to extinction. Ace pilots carry charms so that they will not crash. Each time they fly while carrying the talisman and don't crash (a *negative stimulus* that is withheld) their charm-carrying behavior is negatively reinforced. Only if a pilot were to crash several times while carrying the charm would that particular behavior be extinguished.

Cognitive-Symbolic Processes

Individual behavior patterns are largely influenced by cognitive mediation. Thus, although rats may respond in a very predictable fashion to the presence of an antecedent cue and to the subsequent consequences, people's behavior is affected by their *perception* of the cue and by their anticipation of the consequences. Feelings, physical sensations, thoughts, fantasies, or visual images can function as antecedent cues, as behaviors, or as consequences in the same manner as overt actions do. For example, a sexual fantasy may function as an antecedent cue that elicits sexual behavior, as a positive reinforcer for the behavior of looking at attractive people, or as a behavior itself.

Cognitive-symbolic processes play an important role in self-instruction and in self-reinforcement. One person may respond to a particular antecedent cue such as an insult by instructing himself to count to ten; another person may reinforce herself by thinking positive thoughts about herself. Self-reinforcement is an important component of self-esteem, and it plays an instrumental role in maintaining what could be called self-directed behavior. The department self-starter probably uses a lot of self-instruction and self-reinforcement.

Cognitive-symbolic processes can influence a person's perceptions of an antecedent cue. If you offer to take an employee who is a vegetarian for a steak dinner, he or she may respond with hostility rather than with the expected appreciation. The employee may have used various thoughts and images to change the invitation from a positive to a negative event. Such internal processes can also influence people's perceptions of consequences. You may intend to reinforce an employee by using praise, but if that person thinks, "I know he's just saying that to get me to write the report," then the reinforcing power of the praise is negated.

Because of the existence of cognitive-symbolic processes, modification of complex work behavior can be difficult; these internal processes *can* be modified, however. Research has demonstrated that when they are defined as behaviors, they do function in accord with the laws of learning.

Response Frequency

No doubt you have noticed that throughout this chapter there have been numerous references to probability (i.e., a behavior is *more or less* likely) and frequency. Measurement is at the heart of behavior modification: *What* people do or *how* they do it is not as important as *how often* they do it. Only when you measure the frequency of response can you determine if a behavior is increasing, decreasing, or remaining the same. Knowing this is essential to determining whether a consequence is functioning as a reinforcer or as a punisher (recall that these are defined in terms of whether appearance of the behavior is more or less likely), or whether a behavior is in the process of extinction. Likewise, counting behaviors helps to determine if a particular antecedent cue has stimulus control over a particular behavior. Finally, measuring response frequency is an essential step in both monitoring and evaluating a behavior change strategy.

Conclusion

Organizational behavior is inextricably connected with the environment and is controlled by what precedes and what follows it. The first step in solving employee problems is pinpointing the problem behavior and analyzing how it functions within the environment. The problem behavior is changed by systematically altering one or more of the controlling environmental events. The next chapter discusses techniques for altering the environment.

NOTES

1. John B. Watson, *Behaviorism* (Chicago: Phoenix Books, 1957), pp. 158–164.
2. Table adapted with permission from Michael Mahoney and Carl E. Thoresen, *Self-Control: Power to the Person* (Monterey, Calif.: Brooks/Cole, 1974), pp. 49.
3. For an in-depth discussion of the dangers of punishment, see Fred Luthans and Robert Kreitner, *Organizational Behavior Modification* (Glenview, Ill.: Scott, Foresman and Company, 1975), pp. 117–123.

SUGGESTED READINGS

Bandura, Albert, *Principles of Behavior Modification*. New York: Holt, Rinehart and Winston, 1969.

Hilts, Phillip J., *Behavior Mod*. New York: Bantam Books, 1976.

Luthans, Fred, and Kreitner, Robert, *Organizational Behavior Modification*. Glenview, Ill.: Scott, Foresman and Company, 1975.

Skinner, B.F., *Science and Human Behavior*. New York: Macmillan, 1962.

2

Behavior Management

UNTIL recently supervisors have not had a reliable methodology for changing employee behavior. This chapter will discuss how to develop, implement, and evaluate a behavior change program and what specific techniques to use in such a program. The underlying premise is that undesirable or antiproductive behaviors are learned and maintained by events in the environment. Change is accomplished by arranging environmental conditions that promote unlearning undesirable behavior and learning desirable behavior.

Behavior change programs based upon behavior modification technology always follow a systematic procedure. There are five basic steps:

1. Specify the problem behavior.
2. Observe current levels of the target behavior.
3. Intervene.
4. Evaluate.
5. Maintain.

Specify the Problem Behavior

In this step the target behavior to be modified is determined. The target behavior can be some undesirable behavior that you want to reduce or eliminate, or some desirable behavior that you want to increase. Desirable behaviors in an organizational setting are those that eventually lead to the accomplishment of predetermined organizational objectives; undesirable behaviors are those that directly or indirectly detract from or inhibit organizational objectives.

We have already discussed how behavior is learned and unlearned or modified, but we haven't yet defined behavior itself. Contrary to popular opinion, the definition of behavior goes beyond visually observable actions. Research has demonstrated that internal or covert behavior operates by the same principles and can be modified by the same techniques as external or overt behaviors. Sharon Bower's[1] definition of behavior is one that is easy to understand and remember. AMPS stands for the four different modes of responding.

A = Actions
M = Mental Pictures
P = Physical Sensations
S = Sentences

Actions are movements you can observe in others and yourself. These include body movements, posture, gestures, and facial expressions. *Mental pictures* are fantasies or images in the imagination. *Physical sensations* are bodily sensations—such as pain, tightness, tingling, and heat—that signal how we feel. *Sentences* are things we say aloud (*overt*) or silently (*covert*).

Although actions and spoken sentences are the only behaviors we can actually observe in others, we often make guesses about others' internal behaviors by observing how people act and by listening to what they say. We can, however, directly observe internal behaviors in ourselves, and when it is appropriate we can ask employees to observe their internal behaviors. For example, a salesperson might avoid the action of calling a particular client on the phone because of the physical sensation of tightness in the throat (one of a class of behaviors commonly called anxiety). Or a management trainee may sulk in a planning meeting in response to negative thoughts or silent sentences (one of a class of behaviors commonly called self-consciousness or lack of confidence). Generally, however, most behavior change programs in organizations are aimed directly at observable behavior such as actions or speech.

The four parts of behavior are dynamic—that is, if you change one, then the others usually change as well. Norman Vincent Peale, among others, attests to the power of positive thought on actions. Likewise, a subordinate who learns to feel relaxed (*P*) in an evaluative situation will generally have a better self-image (*M*), make more positive self-statements (*S*), and perform more effectively (*A*). A behavior change program may target any one of these behaviors for intervention in order to change any or all of the others.

AMPS, however, is only the beginning of a definition of behavior, because it merely explains the types of behavior. In our daily lives we use numerous abstract words—such as immature, hostile, capable, feminine, independent, motivated—to stand for classes of behavior. Words of this kind do not work in a behavior change program. Consider the following example from one of my workshops: Georgia says, "Otto is an older salesman with a lot of experience. The problem is that he is continually challenging my authority." This sounds pretty bad, but do we really know what the problem behavior is? What is meant by "challenging my authority"? What does Otto actually *do?* Is it Otto's expression or something he says? Or does Otto go over Georgia's head with requests and complaints? This description doesn't tell us.

Thus, the first task is to translate abstract and vague descriptions into words that stand for specific observable behaviors. In general you can ask, "Is there a distinct beginning and end to the behavior—that is, can it be *counted?*" ("Count-ability" and accountability are essential components of a behavior change program.) "What must the person *do* in order for me to say that the behavior has occurred?" And finally, "Can it be reliably *observed* (including self-observation)—that is, can it be heard, or seen, or felt, or smelled?" When you can answer all of these questions either affirmatively or in terms of very specific occurrences, then you will have identified a behavioral event.

But the task is not yet complete. Going back to the problem with Otto, we see that Georgia's description implies that Otto's undesirable behavior exists independently of the environmental setting. It does not specify the situation in which the behavior that challenges authority actually occurs. *When* does Otto challenge Georgia's authority? To complete the description of the problem it is necessary to think of the behavior in combination with the situation in which it occurs (*behavior-in-situation*).[2] Let's look at an improved description of the problem with Otto: "During the weekly staff meeting, Otto—an older, experienced salesman on my staff—frequently makes negative (uncooperative, disapproving, defeatist) comments about my program." Here we have:

Behavior:	Making negative comments about program
in	
Situation:	Staff meeting

Is "making negative comments about program" a behavior? Let's ask the questions: Can the comments be counted? Yes, a comment has a beginning and an end. What must Otto do before I can say that a negative comment about my program has occurred? He must make a statement that is negative—connoting disapproval, predicting failure, or advocating noncooperation. In a controlled laboratory experiment, the operational definition of negative comments about a program would be far more precise, and only specified kinds of statements would be permitted to count. As a practicing manager you don't need to go to that length, but you do need to be able to determine whether or not each of Otto's comments is negative about the program. The answer to the final question is helpful here: Can a negative comment about the program be reliably observed? Yes, two or more people listening to Otto could probably agree whether one of his specific comments about the program was negative. We can now say that the problem has been specified—Otto's negative comments about the program in the weekly staff meeting.

Once you have identified the behavior-in-situation, you are confronted with the question: Is this behavior performance-related? If the behavior has no impact on the accomplishment of organizational objectives, then using company time to change it would be inefficient and wasteful. Thus, it is important to be sure that the behavior is related to the employee's own performance outcomes or to the performance of other employees to such an extent that it influences accomplishment of company objectives. If Otto's sales performance under the new program is exceptional and his negative comments do not appear to influence the sales performance of others, then Otto's behavior is probably not performance-related. On the other hand, if Georgia responds to Otto's negative comments with "self-doubts" (*silent sentences*) and these self-doubts result in her making defensive remarks to Otto (*spoken sentences*), then Otto's behavior is performance-related in that it has an adverse effect on Georgia's performance. Under these circumstances it would be an appropriate target behavior to consider for a behavior change program. (Of course, Georgia might also consider a self-change program in which she alters her self-doubting silent sentences and defensive remarks to Otto in the staff meeting.)

Identifying the target behavior is not always as easy and as obvious as it is in the case of Otto. Suppose a supervisor says, "Meredith is too aggressive." You already know this description is inadequate because it tells you nothing of the circumstances in which Meredith is aggressive or even what is meant by "aggressive." Suppose that in trying to clarify these points the supervisor says, "I don't know what situations she's aggressive in—she's always aggressive!" The way to solve this is to think of specific examples and to observe. For example, the supervisor says, "Today, when another secretary asked her to copy a flier she said 'no' loudly and stomped out the door." And the next day the supervisor observes Meredith reply sharply, "Get it yourself!" when a file clerk asks her to pick up an extra cup of coffee at the canteen.

By looking for and collecting examples, you can quickly identify specific behaviors in specific situations: When asked to do a favor, Meredith tends to refuse in an ungracious manner. Write down several examples of the target behavior. Describe fully the situations and analyze what they have in common. When the behavior occurs in many situations, it may be that the situations have something in common, such as Meredith's rudeness when she is asked to do a favor. If you cannot identify a common thread, you probably have several different problem behaviors.

Often the problem is that someone is *not* doing something. For example, a manager might say, "Jack doesn't approach and greet customers." Here again, begin by observing and writing down examples of behavior-in-situations—only this time specify the situations in which you want the behavior to occur. Jack is doing something else when the manager wants him to approach and greet customers—that is, Jack is actively performing a behavior incompatible with approaching and greeting customers, such as talking to another sales clerk. To have a complete description of the problem, it is necessary to specify the situation and what desirable behavior is not occurring as well as what undesirable behavior *is* occurring. Jack's supervisor should specify the situation in which he wants the behavior to occur—when a customer enters the store—and then observe what happens instead of the desired behavior.

Another problem difficult to identify is an absent or inadequate *outcome,* such as an uncompleted report or unfilled sales quota. An outcome is not a behavior, but it is dependent on the performance of a chain of behaviors. Therefore, problem identification requires you to pinpoint the chain of behaviors necessary to produce the desired outcome. The location of the problem is the point in the chain at which the worker is not performing the behavior necessary to move to the next link.

When you know the chain of behaviors necessary to produce the desired outcome, problem identification is simplified: You need merely observe the person carefully step by step through the task until you identify the breakdown. But managers often supervise people whose work is outside their expertise. This is particularly true in professional and technical areas. In these situations you can ask the subordinate, observe a model, or seek expert advice.

Ask the subordinate. Is is usually a good idea to begin with the assumption that employees know what steps are necessary to complete their assigned tasks and that they are aware of the obstacles they are experiencing. (After all, they were employed because they had the requisite skills and experience.) Subordinates may feel hesitant to express the difficulty, but by using the information-gathering techniques described in Chapter 4, you can help them talk about the problem. This sets the stage for enlisting their cooperation in correcting the outcome problem, but more importantly, it is a good opportunity for you to help your subordinates assume responsibility for their own work behavior. Rather than changing the behavior of the subordinates, you can use this as an opportunity to teach them to change their own behavior.

Consider Charles, the program director in a radio station. His problem is simple—he procrastinates. It takes him twice as long as necessary to finish the schedule of upcoming programs, and this creates problems for all the other departments as well. (For example, sales can't sell programs, because they don't know what's going on the air or when.) Completing a schedule or a report is not a behavior; it is an outcome of a chain of behaviors. Thus, to say that Charles procrastinates does not focus on the problem behavior that results in delayed schedules.

During the coaching session, the station manager asked Charles about each step necessary for completing the program. Charles said, "It's not that I put off the scheduling per se. It's that I have trouble with Rosemary. I need to get a projection of the topics of her editorials, but I have so much trouble asking her for them that I find myself sending memos. She doesn't respond right away, and this causes a delay." Further investigation revealed that Charles found it very difficult to give Rosemary a directive, because she would question his directives. Consequently, he would respond by sending the directive in memo form. Thus, the behavior-in-situation turned out to be not Charles's procrastination but giving Rosemary a directive (*behavior*) when she asked questions (*situation*).

Observe a model. When the target person cannot identify the breakdown in the chain of behaviors and you do not have sufficient expertise to identify the behavior links necessary to produce the outcome, then you can observe a model. This involves identifying another person whose performance leads to a successful outcome and observing the step-by-step behaviors in which the model engages to produce a quality outcome. Then observe the target person and, using the model's chain of behaviors as a criterion, look for a breakdown. For example, if a couple of your salespeople are not reaching their quotas, you might go out into the field with your top performers to observe their sales presentations. Then you could observe the less skilled salespeople in action while looking for the behaviors present in the stars' performance but absent in the less successful presentations. The discrepancy would illuminate the missing links in the behavior chain.

Seek expert advice. When it isn't possible to actually observe a model, consult with a model. In this case, the model is the expert who knows how to perform each behavior necessary for a successful outcome. After the expert delineates the necessary chain of behaviors, observe the target person's behavior, looking for the broken link. Returning to the sales example, you might ask a consultant who has expertise in selling to describe the critical selling steps and their order. You would then observe and compare the below quota salespeople's presentations to the sales expert's description.

After the target behavior has been broken down into discrete behavioral events, a *functional analysis* must be made (see Chapter 1) to determine the ABCs—to observe the target behavior in order to discover the antecedent cues that evoke the behavior and the consequences that maintain it. This relationship gives you a schema of how the behavior functions and of how to determine which points of intervention offer the best potential results.

Observe Current Levels of the Target Behavior

One mistake supervisors often make is to begin intervening before they have adequately observed the target behavior *as it is.* Once we have become aware of a problem, it is very difficult to withhold instituting a change, but careful observation is an essential step in a successful behavior modification program. In addition to making a specific definition of the target behavior, you must analyze how the behavior is controlled and then establish a baseline from which to measure the success of the intervention. These three tasks can often be performed simultaneously, but for clarity of discussion they are presented here as discrete steps.

Discovering Consequences

Identifying consequences of the target behavior can give an important clue to how to modify that behavior. Generally, behaviors that occur often—be they desirable or undesirable—are maintained by positive consequences, and behaviors that occur infrequently are maintained (or suppressed) by negative consequences. Try to think of positive consequences as "turning on" something good (*positive reinforcement*) or "turning off" something bad (*negative reinforcement*), and negative consequences as turning off something good (*positive punishment* or *extinction*) or turning on something bad (*negative punishment*).

Because consequences have such a heavy influence on how often a behavior will occur in the future, identifying them becomes the next step in specifying the problem. The best way to identify a behavior-consequence pattern is through observation. Note and write down what happens *after* the behavior: Is there anything that seems to be turned on or off after the behavior? Is there a pattern or recurring event? Is there more than one consequence? When Georgia observed what happened after Otto made a negative comment, she discovered a curious thing: Her own behavior was a consequence—she consistently responded with defensive comments. If we hypothesize that Otto perceives Georgia's defensiveness as positive, we can say Otto's negative behavior is maintained by the positive reinforcer of Georgia's defensive commenting. Often there is more than one consequence: Georgia found that Otto's negative comments were often followed by positive attention from the other salespeople (such as chuckling and knowing looks). The attention from others was probably a more powerful reinforcer than was Georgia's defensiveness. Had she stopped observing as soon as she had identified one consequence, she might have failed in her change program.

See if you can identify the consequences in the following situations:

1. A claims adjuster trainee handled five claims. Three claims had missing information, and two claims were complete. The supervisor commented on the thoroughness of the two completed claims.
2. The previous supervisor of the typing pool allowed those typists who completed their assignments rapidly to take discretionary time. The new supervisor stopped the practice, and insisted that all typists look productive at all times.
3. A new employee completed the first assignment promptly by the deadline, and handed it to the supervisor. The supervisor made no comment.
4. William submitted to the planning committee a proposal that contained several cost-effective changes. In William's presence,

his supervisor spoke to the department director and made positive comments about the proposal.

5. Bob spent several evenings and most of the weekend putting together an outline for a new sales promotion. His supervisor responded by pointing out three major weak points.

6. Alice completed the quarterly report a day early and gave it to her supervisor. The supervisor gave her an additional assignment to complete during the extra time she created.

Now compare the consequences you identified with those I identified.

1. Completing claims was reinforced by a positive comment. Not completing claims was being extinguished by the absence of a response.

2. Rapid typing was punished by the new supervisor. The supervisor has turned off something good: discretionary time.

3. The employee's on-time behavior was being extinguished by the supervisor's lack of response.

4. William's suggestions were reinforced.

5. Bob's conscientious work was punished.

6. Alice's rapid work was punished, unless Alice perceives extra assignments as positive, that is, as an opportunity to get ahead.

The easiest kind of intervention is one in which you alter the consequences. But in order to do that, you have to be able to provide a new consequence for the target behavior. Unfortunately, it isn't always possible to separate the reinforcement from the behavior—this happens when behaviors consume the reinforcer. For example, smoking is reinforced by inhaling the smoke; overeating is reinforced by ingestions of food; too many drinks at lunch, by the drinks themselves; talking on the phone, by the verbal responses. With such consummatory behaviors you can easily identify the consequence, but rarely change it. Thus when the target behavior is consummatory you will need to look to the *antecedent* for a clue as to how to modify that behavior.

Identification of the consequences can also become obscured by intermittent reinforcement and avoidance behaviors. In these cases, understanding antecedents will also be essential to understanding how the target behavior functions. Some behaviors are *resistant to extinction* because they are maintained on an intermittent schedule of reinforcement. In other words, the behavior goes unreinforced many times, but will continue as long as there is an occasional reinforcement. Intermittent reinforcers are difficult to identify. If the target behavior is reinforced only one time in ten, you would have to observe the behavior 30 times just to obtain three examples of the consequence—and reliable conclusions cannot be drawn from only three examples. Obviously, such lengthy observation is not generally feasible.

The consequences of avoidance behavior are even more difficult to identify. An avoidance behavior is performed to avoid some punishing consequence. If it is successful in avoiding punishment (*positive consequence*), the avoidance behavior will be more likely to occur again in the same situation (*antecedent*). Obviously, if the punishing consequence does not occur, it cannot be observed. Sometimes, by imagining what would happen if a person were to perform differently in a certain situation, we can guess at the consequence that is being avoided. If one of the possible consequences turns out to be punishing, this suggests that the target behavior is an avoidance behavior. For example, when the radio station manager asked Charles what would happen if he were to ask Rosemary directly for the projection, Charles said, "She'd just ask a bunch of questions and make me defend every decision I made!" Because Charles stated this in a way that suggested it was punishing to him, his manager could suspect that Charles's procrastination was tied to his avoidance of directing Rosemary.

Discovering Antecedents

When a stimulus is presented each time a behavior is reinforced, that antecedent stimulus eventually gains the power to evoke the behavior. Likewise, when a behavior is repeatedly punished in the presence of a particular stimulus, that stimulus soon becomes associated with punishment and signals to the person that punishment is imminent. If the person avoids punishment, the stimulus can become an antecedent that signals future avoidance behavior. Each time the person avoids the punishment, the antecedent becomes more powerful in its ability to evoke avoidance behavior. Because antecedents can become very powerful in turning behaviors on and off, it is important that these cues be identified.

To discover antecedents, the events that occur just *before* the target behavior must be identified and recorded. Once several examples have been collected, a common theme can usually be identified. Consider Melody, who makes personal calls during work time. Through observation, her supervisor discovered that Melody frequently made a phone call after she finished typing an assignment. Here the antecedent that evoked the consummatory behavior of making phone calls was probably a finished assignment.

When you have difficulty identifying what occurs just before the target behavior, a complete description of the situation can often reveal the antecedent. When Georgia wrote a complete description of the situation in which Otto's problem behavior occurred, she discovered the antecedent: "Whenever I mention my innovative program in the weekly staff meeting, Otto makes negative comments about the program." This description suggests that the antecedent of Otto's negative commenting is "mention of the innovative program." And indeed, when Georgia carefully observed and recorded each instance of Otto's negative comments in one staff meeting, she confirmed this: Each mention of the innovative program was followed by a negative comment by Otto. Here is Georgia's functional analysis of Otto's behavior.

A	B	C
Antecedent	*Behavior*	*Consequence*
Mentioned new responsibilities in innovative program	Otto questioned necessity of the innovative program	Told Otto why innovative program is necessary
Discussed sales promotion under innovative program	Otto said promotion wouldn't work	Told Otto I had a lot of experience
Discussed procedures for keeping records in innovative program	Otto said old method was a lot better and cheaper	Told Otto that I am the manager

Establishing the Baseline

One way in which behavior modification differs from other approaches to managing people is the *baseline*. The baseline tells how often the target behavior is occurring now—before intervention. It is a method of accountability and evaluation. The baseline helps to monitor the program and rapidly detect an ineffective intervention. Consequently, it is cost-effective, and is also an essential step in a successful behavior change program.

Making the functional analysis and gathering baseline data frequently overlap, because both require careful observation. However, the type of observation differs. Antecedents and consequences are identified by recording descriptions of events. To establish the baseline, *count* how many times the behavior occurs and record that number.

To obtain an accurate and reliable baseline, the target behavior must be clearly specified. If your description of the target behavior is vague or ambiguous, you will find out quickly. Gathering baseline data involves counting each occurrence of the behavior-in-situation. For example, Georgia counted each time Otto made a negative comment in the staff meeting about the innovative program. At the end of the meeting, she recorded the number of negative comments on a graph (Figure 4). In this way she could determine the frequency of Otto's negative comments over time.

Sometimes the concern with the target behavior is not a matter of how often it occurs but the duration of the occurrence. Suppose the problem with Melody's personal calls was not that she made them but that she talked for an average of 15 minutes. Here, her supervisor would record the length of the calls. Generally, count either the number of separate times people perform the behavior or the amount of time they spend performing the behavior.

Figure 4. Georgia's graph of Otto's negative behavior.

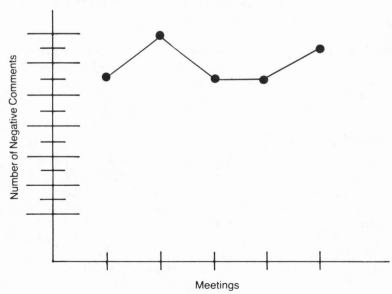

The most common difficulty encountered in gathering baseline data is being able to decide whether or not the behavior has occurred. This can be avoided by pinpointing the target behavior precisely enough so that you can give a simple yes or no answer: Yes, Melody is talking on the phone; or no, she isn't. Yes, Otto made a negative comment about the program; or no, he didn't. Suppose Otto says, "I think we should reconsider each step of this program in light of the new developments in the market." Is this to be counted as a negative comment or not? Any answer besides a definite yes or no should alert us to an incompletely defined target behavior. Georgia would reduce the effectiveness of her team and would limit Otto as well if she employed a change program that decreased the frequency of Otto's problem-solving comments along with his negative ones. Before Georgia can continue collecting baseline data, she needs to return to the first step of specifying the problem behavior. When she can clearly define a negative comment about the program, she is ready to resume collecting the baseline data.

There are times when it is not necessary to observe directly, because the information has already been collected. Institutional sources of behavioral data include payroll records for absenteeism, time cards for tardiness, and log records for speed of response (such as in police calls). Whenever possible, utilize such records—it saves time.

Some natural questions are, "How do I count?" and "What tool do I use?" There are a number of methods, the most obvious and traditional of which is the tally. Each time you observe the target behavior, make a check on a piece of paper or on a 3″ × 5″ index card. At the end of the day or of the meeting, count up the checks and transfer this data onto your graph. A second tool you can try is the golf counter. The best is the type you wear on your wrist—it looks like a watch. These are particularly effective, because you can use them without interrupting your activity or diverting your attention. The point is to count. The method you use doesn't matter as long as you get accurate data, so devise a method that is easy and that works for you.

The best approach is to have the subordinates in question count and record their own behavior. For example, chronically late employees can record their time of arrival each day, packers on an assembly line can count the number of boxes correctly packed, a secretary can record the length of each personal phone call. An advantage of self-recording is that it gives employees immediate feedback on their behavior and involves them in all stages of the change process. It is important that you reinforce employees for collecting data on their own behavior.

There is no set length of time for collecting baseline data; you need to keep counting until the data is stable—that is, until you can see a consistent trend. If the target behavior occurs several times a day, then most likely a week-long baseline would suffice. When there is a lot of variation from day to day, a longer baseline period will be needed. The purpose is to establish how often the behavior occurs. This counting should continue until you feel you understand the pattern of the target behavior.

If the target behavior occurs regularly, the actual time involved gathering baseline data can be shortened considerably by using a *time sample.* A time sample is similar to an opinion poll: Just as those conducting the poll cannot interview everyone in the country, you probably cannot count every occurrence of the behavior. Opinion polls solve the problem by selecting a sample of people and talking to them. With a time sample, you count the occurrence of the behavior in a few short time periods each day. For example, Georgia might select two five-minute time periods in each meeting to count Otto's comments.

How the sample is selected is also important. If an opinion poll were to base its conclusions solely on the opinions of Californians, the results might not be representative of the country as a whole. The time sample, too, must represent the whole time period covered. This is best done by randomly selecting the time periods. Georgia could assign a number to each five-minute period in the meeting, put them into the proverbial hat, and select two at random to use as her sample.

Behavior modification techniques are not crisis techniques; they are foundation-building techniques that require careful analysis before using them. Grounded in the scientific method, behavior modification is an approach in which you become an applied behavioral scientist solving a problem. Each behavior change program is a unique challenge, because no two people are alike. What one person finds reinforcing, another does not. What provokes one person has no impact on another. To be an effective behavior manager, you need to understand and respond to each person as an individual. In part, you can accomplish this by observing, analyzing, and counting. By understanding each supervisee's uniqueness you can develop a change program suited to his or her individual needs. By continuing to collect data during the intervention and through comparison with the baseline, you can obtain an immediate indication of the effectiveness of the change program. And such data can be used as concrete evidence of your effectiveness as a manager. If comparisons reveal that the data are moving in the desired direction (if the frequency of undesired behaviors decreases and that of desired behaviors increases), you can rely on your program. If the trend begins to plateau or to reverse, this signals that it is time for troubleshooting. Finally, baseline comparisons are a good indicator of how long to continue in the intervention phase and of when to move to the maintenance phase of the change program. When the frequency of the target behavior reaches a predetermined goal, it is a signal to implement techniques that will maintain the behavior at that frequency—in other words, it signals that the intervention phase is complete.

Intervention Strategies

All behavior modification intervention strategies have the common goal of changing the *frequency* of the target behavior by increasing desirable behaviors or decreasing undesirable ones. Throughout the intervention the occurrences of the target behavior are counted and charted in order to determine the effectiveness of the intervention. Strategies not resulting in the desired increase or decrease can be quickly identified and either modified or discarded.

Before selecting an intervention strategy, it is necessary to identify a desirable behavior to be increased. When the problem behavior is undesirable, translating it into desirable behavior will deemphasize punishment and focus attention on positive behavior change techniques. If the target person knows how to perform the desired behavior but is not doing so, consider using one of the contingency management strategies described below. If the target person is not aware of the behavior necessary to perform, you will need to use the shaping technique to teach the employee how to perform the desired behavior.

A number of ethical concerns should be considered as you are developing a program to alter another person's behavior.* Primary are the immediate and possible long-term effects upon the target person. A secondary consideration is the potential impact of the intervention and the resulting behavior change upon others in the environment. Whenever possible the target person should be included in each step of the change program. Not only does this assist in resolving some of the ethical issues, but it speeds up the change process and increases chances of success as well as assisting the person in learning how to manage his or her own behavior.

Behavior management is not a crisis intervention approach;

*For a fuller discussion of this point, please refer back to the preface.

rather, it is aimed at long-term problem solving and problem preven-
tion. By inviting the employees' active participation in contingency
management, you solve the problem at hand at the same time that you
teach them how to work and how to solve their work problems. Over
the long run you will be relieved from close monitoring and crisis
intervention and will be free to invest more in functions such as decid-
ing, planning, coordinating, and directing.

Contingency Management Strategies

Rearrange the Contingencies

This is the simplest intervention. Contingencies describe the behavior-consequence sequence. "If you work eight hours, then I will
pay you $40"—this statement describes the contingency relationship
between work and pay. The "then-consequence" is contingent on the
"if-behavior": Receiving $40 is contingent on working eight hours.

A functional analysis (identifying the ABCs) is performed in part
to discover the current contingencies, or the "if-then" relationship
between the behavior and the consequences. "If Otto makes a negative comment about the program, then I will pay attention to him."
Rearranging the contingencies means altering the if-then relationship
so that the then-consequence follows a *different* if-behavior. For example, "If Otto makes a problem-solving comment, then I will pay attention to him; if he makes a negative comment about the program, then
I will ignore him." Here, Georgia has rearranged the contingencies so
that positive attention follows problem-solving comments but not negative comments. This strategy does not require adding anything new
to the environment. It does not require new programs or bonuses or
more money or more attention; the existing reinforcers and punish-
ers are simply rearranged.

Contingency rearrangement is most frequently employed with undesirable behaviors that occur often and that are reinforced by a
positive consequence. A desirable behavior is identified and substituted into the if-then statement. Usually the desirable behavior selected is one that is *incompatible* with the undesirable behavior. Two
behaviors are said to be incompatible when they cannot be performed
simultaneously (see Chapter 1). Examples of incompatible behaviors
include: talking, being silent; sitting at desk, walking around; making
a positive comment, making a negative comment; being on time,
being late.

Rearrangement of contingencies is also appropriate when the if-
then sequence is out of order. Consider Jim's example: "Charlie has a

really bad attitude, so I thought if I gave him a few breaks he'd shape up and be more committed. But it doesn't work. Last week he wanted to take off a couple of hours early. I said it was OK with me if he got his sales log in the next afternoon. Well I didn't see that log for four days!" This is a then-if sequence. In such situations the contingencies need to be rearranged: The consequence must follow the behavior if it is to effectively increase that behavior. The consequence of getting off a couple of hours early must be made contingent on a completed log sheet.

The final situation in which contingency rearrangement is employed is when a low-frequency desirable behavior is followed by no consequence or a negative one. For example, if Ralph is on time, then his supervisor Sam says nothing. Or if Betty makes a suggestion, then her supervisor Varner criticizes the suggestion. Ralph's on-time behavior is being extinguished, and Betty's suggestions are being punished. Here, the then-consequence needs to be changed from negative to positive.

Identify Existing Reinforcers

Once again observation is the primary tool. The necessity of detailed and systematic observation cannot be overemphasized. The points of observation are the consequences following behaviors that the target person performs often (high-probability behaviors) and activities or behaviors that the person chooses to engage in during discretionary time.

The technical definition of a reinforcer is "an event that increases the future probability of the behavior it follows." Therefore, those behaviors the target person performs frequently are usually followed by a reinforcer. Of course, sometimes the reinforcer may be the avoidance of punishment. For reasons discussed earlier, negative reinforcement is difficult to observe. Furthermore, it is not suggested that supervisors employ negative reinforcement in rearranging contingencies. That is, an if-then statement such as "If Betty makes a suggestion, then I will not criticize her" is less desirable than "If Betty makes a suggestion, then I will make an appreciative comment." The use of negative reinforcers (withholding punishment) promotes working to avoid punishment and generally results in the need for constant close monitoring of the employee. This obviously reduces the time supervisors have available for other management functions. It also deprives employees of satisfaction in their work.

The task is to identify positive reinforcers that currently exist in the target person's environment and to insert them into the if-then statement. Thus, identify several behaviors the person performs often, and look for positive consequences. Just as in identifying the problem behavior, other high-probability behaviors should be clearly defined. Keep a record of each behavior and its consequences.

For example, Ralph's supervisor identified two of Ralph's high-frequency behaviors: telling jokes and talking to the secretary. Through observation, the supervisor noted that Ralph's joking behavior was usually followed by statements of the secretary indicating that Ralph was funny and clever, and Ralph's talking to the secretary was usually followed by her rapid completion of his work. This suggests that hearing that he is funny and clever and seeing rapidly completed typing are reinforcing to Ralph.

Betty's supervisor identified making agreeing statements and volunteering to do busywork as high-probability behaviors. For Betty, the consequence of agreement was usually a statement attesting to her competence, and volunteering to do busywork was followed by comments indicating her indispensability. Betty's supervisor can consider these as possible reinforcers for Betty. Now Ralph and Betty's supervisors have some possible consequences to insert into the if-then contingency statement: "If Ralph is on time, then I will tell the secretary to make his work high priority." "If Betty makes a suggestion, then I will comment on her competency."

The second source of existing positive reinforcers is the high-probability behaviors or activities themselves. These may be actual work activities or leisure activities, but they must be activities or behaviors over which the target person has some discretion. Except for those who perform repetitive menial tasks, most employees have choices of which assignments they will work on at any given moment. Brian, for example, is a secretary. He types memos, letters, short reports, and long reports; copies material; and files papers. Brian has considerable discretion in choosing when he will perform each of these tasks. Suppose that Brian generally types memos, letters, and short reports first, leaving filing and typing long reports until last. For Brian, typing memos, letters, and short reports can be considered high-probability behaviors. Likewise, Brian's supervisor might observe that Brian drinks eight or nine cups of coffee each day and during breaks he usually makes personal phone calls. These can be considered high-probability leisure behaviors.

The Premack principle of reinforcement states that a high-probability behavior can reinforce a low-probability behavior. Thus, Brian's supervisor can consider any of Brian's high-probability behaviors as potential reinforcers to insert into an if-then statement. If Brian tends to put off typing long reports and filing, his supervisor can assist him in being more productive by rearranging the contingencies and using work to reinforce work. The contingencies are rearranged so that high-probability work behavior follows low-probability work behavior. For example, if Brian types a long report, then he can type five letters. The Premack principle is one of the most valuable and potent tools for supervisors. Once again it is not necessary to add anything new to the environment to increase performance.

When observing consequences of employee behavior, supervisors all too frequently discover to their dismay that there are few positive reinforcers in operation. This is common—most work environments are not very reinforcing. Rarely are supervisors deliberately punitive; they become punitive through frustration. Punishment gets immediate (although temporary) results, and the vicious cycle of being punished by the supervisor and working to avoid that punishment becomes entrenched.

There are two situations when contingency rearrangement is difficult to use. First, when the target behavior is one in which the reinforcer is consumed by the employee, it is not usually possible to rearrange the contingencies, because the reinforcement cannot be separated from the behavior. The employee who drinks too much at lunch and the one who makes frequent personal phone calls are examples: Each sip of the cocktail is immediately reinforced by the alcohol, and the friend's response reinforces the personal call. Second, when the target behavior is intermittently reinforced, it is resistant to extinction. Because intermittent reinforcers occur so infrequently, it is difficult to identify them so that they can be rearranged.

Contingency Addition

Managers who find themselves in environments with few existing reinforcers—or who desire to alter behaviors that consume the reinforcer or that are intermittently reinforced—can employ the intervention strategy of *contingency addition.* In this strategy new reinforcers are identified and inserted into the if-then statement, or the frequency of administering existing reinforcers is increased. To employ contingency addition, the supervisor needs to identify potential reinforcers.

Incentive programs, bonuses, fringe benefits, and promotions are traditional contingency addition strategies. All too often, however, these programs prove costly and ineffective because they are not granted contingently or because they are not genuine reinforcers. To be effective in increasing and maintaining behaviors, the reinforcer must be desired by the target individual and must be *contingent* on the performance of a particular behavior. An annual bonus and a dental plan given to all employees are rarely effective, because they are not contingent. When they are granted contingently, too often the employee actually receives the bonus so much later than the performance of the behavior that it will be virtually ineffective as a reinforcer. Furthermore, benefits and bonuses may not be desired by the target person. Because they are not refused does not mean they are actively desired.

Often supervisors and managers believe that they know what is reinforcing to employees. In a recent study, supervisors and employees were asked to rate the importance of ten factors in motivating employees.[3] The results revealed that supervisors had a very different idea about employee motivators than employees did. Employees rated "appreciation or deserved praise" as first, "feeling 'in' on things" as second, and "understanding personal problems" as third in importance. Supervisors considered these factors to be the least effective motivators (eighth, tenth, and ninth, respectively) and, on the other hand, rated as very potent motivators "good wages" (first), "promotion" (third), and "good working conditions" (fourth). Employees rated these factors as considerably less important (fifth, seventh, and ninth, respectively). A recent survey conducted by *Psychology Today*[4] on its readership underscores these findings. Of 18 job factors explored, readers rated the following as the six most important: (1) chances to do something that makes you feel good about yourself; (2) chances to accomplish something worthwhile; (3) chances to learn new things; (4) opportunities to develop your skills and abilities; (5) the amount of freedom you have in your job; (6) chances you have to do things you do best. Those factors that have been traditionally assumed to be potent motivators fell low on the list. For example, job security rated eleventh, amount of pay rated twelfth, fringe benefits rated sixteenth, chances for promotion rated seventeenth, and physical surroundings rated eighteenth. Clearly, managers and supervisors have a very different idea of what is reinforcing to employees than what actually is reinforcing. Money and fringe benefits are not the powerful motivators they have been assumed to be, and therein lies the problem. Supervisors too frequently assume that they know what is reinforcing. No wonder so many finely conceived incentive programs have failed! The solution to this dilemma is to observe and to ask questions.

The task is to discover what *is* reinforcing to the target person and then to insert it in the if-then statement. The primary difference between the strategies of rearranging contingencies and of adding contingencies is that in the first, only those reinforcers currently in operation are used, whereas in the second *more* of the existing reinforcers as well as *new* reinforcers are employed. In general, contingency addition does not require additional expense; rather, it involves additional attention, additional opportunities for recognition and skill development, and additional privileges (generally more of those privileges that already exist).

Potential reinforcers are identified in the same way as existing reinforcers, but the emphasis is on the manager's asking the employee. Usually employees are keenly aware of what they want and what they find reinforcing. For one employee, it may be more or longer breaks; for another, it may be more input into decisions; for yet another, it may be the opportunity to work on tasks that will eventually lead to greater skills. Michael Maccoby's intensive interviews with top-level executives revealed many of their potential reinforcers, such as more autonomy, opportunities to build an effective team, and a chance to feel like a winner.[5] Many of the most powerful potential reinforcers are already available to supervisors and do not need formal organizational approval or reorganization. Some of the most useful ones are listed here.

Special Attention Reinforcers

Praise
Praise in front of others
Special work assignments
Reserved parking space
Choice of office
Selection of own office furnishings
Invitation to higher-level meetings
Choice of work attire
Social contacts with others
Solicitation of opinions and ideas
Choice of work partner
Flexible job duties

Company Time Reinforcers

Time off for work-related activities
Time off for personal business
Extra break time
Extra meal time
Choice of working hours or days off

Monetary Reinforcers

Promotion
Paid days off
Company stock
Company car
Pay for sick days not taken
Pay for overtime accumulated
Tickets to special events
Free raffle or lottery tickets
Extra furnishing for office
Gift certificates
Dinner for family at nice restaurant
Personalized license plate
Personalized gifts
Desk calculator or computer
    terminal
Business cards
Expense account

Participation

Voice in policy decisions
Help set standards
Be a representative at meetings
More responsibility
Opportunity to learn new skill

Of course not all of these will be reinforcing to any one person. Select a reinforcer tailored to the person (by observing and asking), and insert it into the if-then statement. For example, as a consequence of making a suggestion, Betty's supervisor might make a comment about its creativity to his own supervisor in Betty's presence. Or the radio station manager might take Charles out to lunch if he negotiates with Rosemary about getting the projection on time.

Extinction and Punishment as Contingent Consequences

Contingency management is routinely employed by most managers, but unfortunately the contingencies are often punishment or extinction. "If you are late, then I will dock your pay," or "If you make a typo, then I will criticize you" are examples of if-then statements in which the then-consequence is punishment. Contingency extinction is characterized by statements such as "If you are on time, then I will ignore you," or "If you correct all the typos, then I will say nothing." Of course, such contingencies are rarely conceptualized, but the observant eye reveals their operation.

A much more effective approach is to think of a desirable behavior to be increased rather than an undesirable behavior to be decreased. Think of what you want the target people to *do* rather than what you want them to *stop* doing. Just making this simple change in your way of looking at the problem will assist you in becoming more reinforcing. Once the problem behavior has been translated in this way, use a combination of reinforcement plus extinction as the contingent consequences. For example, "If you are on time, then I will make a friendly good morning greeting; if you are late, then I will say nothing." Extinction is almost always preferable to punishment. (Extinction or the reduction in the frequency of a behavior occurs when the behavior has no consequence.) Thus, the best strategy is to ignore or extinguish the undesirable behavior and to reinforce an incompatible desirable one. If done systematically, this strategy will effectively increase the frequency of the desired behavior and avoid the negative side effects of punishment.

Many managers have difficulty accepting this approach. A frequent response is, "He gets paid to work. Why should I have to reinforce him?" This viewpoint advocates extinguishing desirable work behavior. Considering the paycheck in terms of the principles of reinforcement, we see that it is not given for doing efficient work, but rather for putting in a specified number of hours. Other supervisors feel, "She *knows* she's supposed to be on time—I just can't say *nothing* when she comes in late!" It is easy to get caught up in "she shoulds" and "he knows" and fears that if the smallest error goes unmentioned it will spread like a malignancy. But innumerable studies have demonstrated that long-term behavior changes are most effectively accomplished through positive reinforcement plus extinction.

It becomes easier to understand when you view the target person in the context of the environment and ask the question: "What environmental consequences are maintaining this undesirable behavior?" Sometimes it is the very response meant to be a punisher. In a low-reinforcing environment, negative attention can become reinforcing. In other situations, the negative attention is perceived as positive ("Boy, did I get her goat that time!"). The best testimonial is experience. By abandoning punitive consequences and substituting extinction plus reinforcement, for example, you will decrease the amount of avoidance as well as the frequency of nonproductive emotional reactions (such as anger, fear, and crying) that are so common a side effect of punishment.

In some instances a manager may feel that commenting on substandard performance is essential. When necessary, confront the undesired behavior in a way that is not punitive—that is, avoid evaluation or criticism. Begin by *describing* the substandard performance, then *express* your concern about bringing the behavior up to standards and *ask* for suggestions to improve performance. Finally, *negotiate* a contingency contract. For example, you might say the following to a salesman who has failed to meet his quota: "Ben, you closed seven deals last week. I am concerned about this, because the quota is sixteen. What suggestions do you have for increasing your sales?" Use any reasonable suggestion as a starting point for negotiating a change plan.

There are times when punishment might be the most appropriate consequence, but these instances are few. If the undesirable behavior is a threat to people or to property (such as driving a forklift too fast around the yard), punishment in the form of a reprimand would be appropriate. But punishment should always be used in combination with reinforcement. Punish the undesirable behavior of driving the forklift too fast, and reinforce the desirable behavior of driving the forklift slowly. Punishment usually results in immediate cessation of the punished behavior, but punishment does not teach or encourage a desirable behavior. Once the forklift driver stops speeding, how he does drive is left to chance. And punishment does not result in a lasting reduction in most cases. By using it in combination with reinforcement, you create a hiatus in the performance of undesirable behavior. This is your opportunity to use your reinforcing skills to promote the more appropriate behavior.

Contingency Contracting

A contingency contract is an agreement between you and the target person in which the behavior to be performed and the contingencies that will evoke the desired behavior are explicitly stated. Involving the cooperation of the target person has many advantages. When the target person knows the contingencies, the change process is accelerated. Change programs almost always involve an alteration in current contingencies. The target person who is not aware of the program may become confused when the contingencies suddenly change. Contracting can help eliminate this confusion: By working out the contract with the target person, you have access to valuable feedback. By listening and incorporating the feedback, you can enlist cooperation and frequently a genuine commitment.

Many supervisors use informal contracts or agreements in their coaching sessions, but too frequently these fail to produce the desired change. "If you improve your attitude, then you'll get ahead around here" is one example. Such a contract does not specify exactly what behaviors are expected. The target person may have a very different set of behaviors in mind from those the supervisor intended. Likewise, it does not specify exactly what the contingency is. What does it mean to get ahead? Promotion, more money, or more privileges? Disappointment and confusion can be avoided with the contingency contract.

The first step is to pinpoint the "if" portion of the contract. Three elements should be included in pinpointing: (1) specific behavior (*what*); (2) the situation where the behavior is to be performed (*where, when, with whom*); and (3) the amount of the behavior expected (*how much, how long*). There should be no ambiguity in any of these elements. The second step is to determine the "then" portion of the contract. An appropriate reinforcer must be identified and agreed on. Here, too, it is important to be very specific: If the contingency involves a response from you, then state explicitly what you agree to do. If the contingency is an activity, clearly describe that activity as well as the amount.

High-probability behaviors are ideal reinforcers for contingency contracts in the organizational setting. That is, behaviors the target person is already performing can be used as reinforcers. These generally include work activities and leisure activities. For example: "If you make one call to a new client, then you may make five calls to old clients." In this contract, a high-probability work behavior is contingent on a low-probability work behavior. In effect, through contingency contracting, the manager teaches the target person to better manage work behavior. Or: "If you type six letters without errors, then you may make one five-minute personal call." This contract employs a high-probability leisure behavior as the contingent reinforcer. Note that the amount of the activity in both cases is clearly indicated.

The contract must be fair, and the behavior expected should be one that the target person can reasonably perform.[6] Contracts that require people to perform behaviors they don't know well or that require a substantial increase in frequency generally fail, whereas contracts that specify a small increase in the frequency of a familiar behavior are more successful. Likewise, the contract must be honest. Contingencies should be carried out immediately and within the terms of the contract. If for some reason the agreed upon contingencies cannot be delivered, negotiate a new contract with the target person. A series of short-term contracts (a week or a month long) is generally better than a long-term one (six months or a year). The duration of the contract should be definite, not open-ended—the expiration date reminds you to review progress and revise the contract's terms. The contract's terms should be clear, in writing, and be signed by you and by the target person. This not only adds to clarity, but emphasizes the commitment on both sides.

Contingency contracting can be a powerful management tool in promoting self-directed work behavior. By using the contracting method to solve behavior problems, you can simultaneously teach employees to manage their own behavior more effectively. The ideal goal is a setting in which all employees develop and carry out contracts with themselves and with others. You can teach and reinforce employee self-directed behavior by gradually shifting the determining role from yourself to the target person. This involves moving from manager-controlled contracting to employee-controlled contracting. In manager-controlled contracting, you determine the amount of the task required and the amount of the reinforcer to be given. When the target person performs the task, you deliver the reinforcement. As the target person begins to understand the process, begin to give that individual the responsibility for determining behavior and consequences and for delivering the reinforcer. If you do this systematically and consistently, you can increase the frequency of self-directed work behavior. The reinforcer to you is a more productive team and more time for other aspects of your work.

TOKENS

Tokens are objects that take on reinforcing value because they can be exchanged for a tangible reinforcement. Money is a token, for example: The coins and paper have no inherent reinforcing value, but can purchase an unlimited variety of reinforcers. There are several advantages to tokens. First, because they can be converted into a variety of reinforcers, they allow for individualized reinforcement. For example, a company might give employees points for being on time, and such points can be accumulated and exchanged for items in a mail-order catalogue. Points allow all target people to select reinforcements of their own choice.

A second advantage is that the tokens or points bridge the delay between the time people perform the desired behavior and when they actually receive the reinforcement. The Christmas bonus is in theory supposed to reinforce quality work in the past year, but because the bonus comes so long after the performance of the work behavior, it has limited reinforcement power. In contrast, points can be given almost immediately for a variety of contracted desirable work behaviors, and these points can then be accumulated and exchanged for the bonus. In this system, even though the bonus comes only once a year, its reinforcing value extends throughout the year.

Furthermore, those who have exhibited superior performance earn more points. This makes the bonus truly contingent, because you simply insert a specific number of points into the if-then statement: "If you complete the report on time, then you will receive three points." This allows you to use the same reinforcer—the points—with several people as well as to reinforce several different behaviors of one person.

It is not necessary that a token or point system be company-wide; it can easily be established in a single office or division or with a single person. Points can be exchanged for any potential reinforcer, such as extended lunch hours or additional breaks. The token system also works well in conjunction with the reinforcement menu discussed below. A final advantage is that tokens can be used to increase a behavior slowly by gradually requiring more and more performance of the behavior to earn a token or point.

REINFORCEMENT MENU

This flexible tool can be used in conjunction with points in implementing a contingency contract. You and the target person identify several desired reinforcers, assign each a point value, and list them in menu form. When the target person has successfully performed the contracted behavior, the points are exchanged for one of the reinforcers on the menu. The menu provides an easy method of using a variety of reinforcers. Target people can select the most powerful reinforcers for themselves at that time. In addition, it allows for more than one behavior change program.

Consider the following system worked out between Roger, a management trainee, and Louis, his supervisor. "Roger did quality work, but he also took a lot of breaks and was often late in the morning and at lunch," said Louis. "I met with Roger for a coaching session. We discussed the problem. I expressed my expectations and explored reinforcers. Roger said he was primarily interested in learning the skills necessary to move into management. He said he wanted more direct supervision from me, and had had a hard time pinning me down. I didn't know this before. He continued to state that he liked to have flexibility in his time. I told him he *had to* arrive on time in the mornings, and he said that that was a real problem for him. I agreed to help him develop his management skills and suggested that the first area he needed to work on was to contribute more in the staff meetings. Roger agreed, but said it was difficult for him to speak out in groups. We carefully pinpointed each behavior expected, set up a point system, and agreed on a menu. Each day Roger was on time in the morning, he received one activity point. For each 15 minutes of task performance he received one point. And for each problem-solving comment made in the weekly staff meeting he received two activity points." Here is the menu that Roger and Louis developed:

Points	Rewarding Activity
5	Five minutes leisure reading at desk
5	Five-minute break
10	Five minutes added to lunch hours
10	Five minutes off early on Friday
10	Ten minutes reviewing learning tapes
10	Ten minutes studying in library
15	Ten minutes skill supervision (by appointment)
100	One day off for training seminar

This example illustrates how the same point and menu system can be used in several behavior change programs. Louis could assist Roger in increasing on-time behavior, in developing group leader skills, and in managing his time better. The reinforcers were of two kinds, those that allowed for leisure activities and those that encouraged professional growth. The leisure activities were those that Roger was currently enjoying noncontingently and that were causing Louis concern. The opportunity for development was something that had been promised but was not really forthcoming. By making the expectations and contingencies explicit, Louis was assisted in carrying out his responsibilities to Roger and Roger was confronted with having to assume responsibility for his choices. He could choose an immediate pleasurable activity or he could work toward a desired goal. In this process Roger had an opportunity to become self-managing.

The effectiveness of the reinforcement menu has been empirically validated in a variety of educational and therapeutic settings, but virtually no research has been conducted on its use in the organization. Many of the supervisors in my workshops, like Louis, have employed variations of the menu with positive results. Thomas Gordon says that effective leaders are those who can simultaneously meet their own needs and the needs of their employees. Contingency contracting is similar to Thomas Gordon's "no-lose method of conflict resolution"; the difference is that the contingency contract employs learning principles systematically.[7]

Certainly the goal of meeting the needs of both supervisor and employee is essential. The contract that fails to meet one or the other's needs will probably fail to change the problem behavior. Carrying out the terms of the contract would not be reinforcing to that person. Many supervisors react to contingency contracting as "bribery," but it can just as easily be viewed as a structured method of setting up a win-win interaction. The structure reduces trial and error and facilitates success.

When introduced on a department-wide basis, the same point system can be utilized for all employees, yet each can have a tailored reinforcement menu. In this way it can simultaneously be used as a corrective device with problem employees and as a maintenance device with those performing on target. After all, if you reserve it only for correcting problem behaviors, you may inadvertently be reinforcing problem behavior. That is, employees who exhibit too many undesirable behaviors or too few desirable ones may be reinforced for their undesirable behavior by the special attention and increased reinforcement, whereas those performing satisfactorily receive none of this. The example with Louis and Roger illustrated how to use reinforcement menus to maintain on-target behavior. Very simply Roger received one point for each 15 minutes of task performance.

Used on an ongoing department-wide basis, the menu can be a preventive measure. Consider the new staff member. This person has probably just left an environment that had dramatically different contingencies, and rarely are the daily operating contingencies explained to the new employee. Instead, upon entering your department, this person must decipher the contingencies through an unspoken trial-and-error process. Suppose that in the last position this person held, he or she was reinforced for autonomous work and independent decision making. Naturally this individual would probably exhibit this behavior in the new environment, your department. But if you prefer to review decisions and monitor work a bit more closely, you may view this employee's behavior as "getting out of control" and respond negatively, which would probably surprise the new person.

There is no way to predict how such an individual might respond —perhaps even with aggression or withdrawal. At this point it is easy to inadvertently set into action a negative vicious cycle, one that could have been avoided by having made explicit all your expectations and contingencies. At best there would be a period of confusion and reorganization. The person would be experiencing "contingency shock," because several of the contingencies for his or her behavior would have been rearranged suddenly. Obviously, during such an adjustment period, the new person's work efficiency is likely to suffer.

Many of these problems can be prevented by meeting with the new person and setting up a contingency contract implemented by a reinforcement menu. The new person does not have to try to guess your subtle expectations, and can express his or her own expectations and desired contingencies. With this approach you can establish—from the very first day—open communication as well as a foundation for resolving problems. It provides a method of emphasizing the interrelationship of management and employee and of demonstrating genuine concern for the new person.

Another advantage of using the reinforcement menu on such an ongoing basis is that it provides a means of additional reinforcement: The menu can be expanded. Instead of being allotted (or assumed) on a random and noncontingent basis, privileges can be contingently linked to improved performance. By working out menus with employees, you have the opportunity to expand your own reinforcing repertoire. Many employees will suggest reinforcers that you may never have considered, but will find acceptable. In the process of negotiating contingencies, employees can be encouraged to question the standards and to provide feedback. Even when they do not agree with the standards, they are more likely to cooperate when they know that their reactions had been considered. Their feedback also provides an opportunity to reexamine and possibly alter outmoded or unrealistic standards. Finally, having such an ongoing system in effect makes more complex and sophisticated change programs easy to implement.

Stimulus Control

Contingency management modifies behavior by changing the *consequences*. There are two strategies, stimulus control and desensitization, that focus on the *antecedents* as the locus of change. Although these techniques have been demonstrated to be effective in changing adult behavior in a variety of settings, few systematic studies have been conducted in the workplace. Nonetheless, it is an asset to understand the antecedent strategies and have them available in your management skill repertoire.

Antecedents acquire a powerful influence on behavior by being present when it is reinforced or punished. The antecedent becomes a cue that informs the person of the probable consequence of a behavior. The presence of the supervisor can be a cue which signals that looking busy will have positive consequences and loafing will have negative ones. Rarely does a person deliberate over such questions; the antecedent is perceived and the behavior is performed without thought. The antecedent becomes so powerful a cue that it controls the behavior.

Work behavior can be brought under stimulus control by arranging the conditions in such a way that a particular work behavior becomes associated with a particular antecedent cue. Consider Bill's problem. One of Bill's responsibilities was to write proposals. In his previous position he wrote many of them, and had little trouble. But in his new position he arrived each morning with a strong determination to write, only to find that he had difficulty getting started and could work on the proposal for only a few minutes. He entered his office and sat at his desk with the intention of writing. But while sitting at the desk he engaged in several other behaviors, such as answering his mail, talking on the phone, reading the paper, reviewing resource material, eating lunch, and chatting with peers. Many of these behaviors were reinforced, so that sitting at his desk had lost much of its power as an antecedent to proposal writing.

Bill's supervisor assisted by giving him a new antecedent for writing—moving him to the conference room, where Bill did nothing but write. If he began to daydream he simply left, and eventually writing came under stimulus control—that is, entering the conference room would evoke or signal writing. Therefore, Bill should find it easier and easier to write in the conference room.

Of course, it is essential that the writing in the conference room be reinforced. Most likely the act of writing itself and seeing the words on the paper, as well as the feelings of accomplishment they evoke, would be reinforcing, but it would be wise for Bill's supervisor to insure reinforcement with contingency contracting, such as "If I write in the conference room for 30 minutes, then I may answer the mail." In this contract, writing (*behavior*) in the conference room (*antecedent*) is reinforced by the high-probability behavior of answering the mail (*consequence*). A word of caution: Bill should not attempt to begin by going into the conference room and trying to write for two or three hours; he should start off by requiring himself to write for only a short time. The length of time can be gradually increased. This is called *shaping* and is discussed later in this chapter.

The lack of stimulus control can create problems in all areas of the company. In small offices, for example, employees frequently engage in a lot of socializing. This reduces the stimulus control power of the office, so that the socializing can eventually become a real threat to productivity. Socializing can be controlled without punishment by designating a specific area for its occurrence and then setting a time limit on breaks. In general, arrange for a situation or a signal to be associated with the behaviors that you want to encourage. It is easier to establish an association between a new antecedent and a desired work behavior than it would be to attempt to revitalize an antecedent that has become contaminated by its association with several undesirable behaviors.

Creating Stimulus Generalization

There are times when you do not want the performance of a behavior restricted to one situation. Training is a prime example: Time and money would be poorly invested if skills learned in training workshops were not generalized to the entire work environment. Yet all too often this important step is neglected. Let's examine this problem more closely.

Stimulus generalization occurs when a behavior that has been learned in the presence of one antecedent is performed in the presence of other, similar antecedents. The more similar the subsequent antecedents are to the original one, the more likely the behavior will be performed. Training sessions should therefore employ mock settings and situations that simulate as much as possible the work setting in which the behavior is to be performed. Whenever possible, training should move out of the workshop into the target setting: The more the training approximates the target setting, the more generalization can be expected.

Homework assignments can be a valuable tool. For example, in the first session of my communication skills workshop, I teach questioning techniques for gathering information and for maintaining an interaction. During the workshop session, participants practice the techniques in behavioral rehearsal exercises. Then, as a homework assignment, they are given data sheets and requested to conduct a "shyness poll"—that is, they interview three people about their experiences with shyness. In addition to learning first hand that most people have felt shy, they practice their new interviewing skills in a situation outside the workshop setting. As they do their assignments, stimulus generalization begins to occur, because they are performing the behavior in the presence of a new antecedent. If the behavior meets with positive consequences, then they are more likely to perform the behavior again outside the workshop.

Any training can include assignments that require participants to perform the behaviors that they have just learned in their work settings. For example, participants in sales training could be asked to tape record an actual presentation, and in the next session (or individually) the trainer could review the tapes and give valuable feedback. In short, training is incomplete if it ends in the classroom. To be effective, the training must be structured to move from the classroom into the target environment.

Feedback

Feedback as a managing technique grew out of communications theory. It is not a behavioral technique in the purest sense, but is frequently incorporated as a vital link in organizational behavior modification programs.

Feedback is information to a work unit (individual, group, organization) about its performance. In and of itself, feedback is neutral; the way in which the information is dispensed and how it is interpreted by the target person can make it reinforcing or punishing. The supervisor who uses feedback to berate a subordinate for substandard performance is translating it into a punitive consequence; needless to say, this is counterproductive, and should be avoided. The individual who evaluates feedback in terms of progress toward a goal is translating it into a reinforcing (or punishing) consequence. Here are some guidelines for an effective feedback system:

1. *Feedback should be related to a goal.* When combined with goal-setting, feedback provides guidance and direction so that both manager and subordinates know when they are performing up to standard and when they need to improve. Goals and behavioral objectives for achieving them can be assigned or individually negotiated during contingency contracting. Likewise, feedback is a particularly useful adjunct to the shaping technique (to be discussed next) in which successive approximations of the desired goal behavior are reinforced. Monitoring the feedback quickly tells when the current goal has been reached and when a new behavioral objective should be set.

2. To have the most impact, *feedback should be directed at the person or group that has direct control over actual performance.* In most cases this would mean the employee and immediate supervisor. Feedback that indicates improvement can be particularly reinforcing to employees when they are committed to the goal. This will tend to foster more improvement. By the same token, feedback tells the supervisor when to reinforce. Feedback is also error-correcting, because it points out when additional efforts are necessary to correct declines in performance.

3. *Collect feedback on the appropriate behavior.* If the goal is to increase the quality of typing, for example, collecting feedback on the quantity of letters and reports typed per day may be counterproductive, because employees could use the information as an impetus to increase speed at the expense of quality. If quality is a priority, then feedback should be collected on the quality of each unit produced.

4. Like reinforcement, *feedback should be timely.* Obviously, an employee can't correct a mistake six months after the fact. From reinforcement theory we know that the most rapid learning takes place when feedback is immediate and continuous. The best way to shorten the gap between performance and feedback is to have employees collect data on their own performances. The data collected not only provides immediate information, but it can be used as the baseline and evaluative data for a behavior change program. In addition, it takes from the manager the responsibility for monitoring performance and puts it on the employee. Such self-monitoring can be the first step in teaching self-directed behavior to employees. Finally, self-monitoring can be continued as a maintenance technique after the intervention phase.

5. *Stress the positive, not the negative.* Express feedback in terms of how closely it approximates the desired goal. Feedback should be information on the frequency of the desired behavior—for example, number of sales made, length of up time of equipment, number of invoices completed correctly. Information on successes or improvement tends to be more reinforcing than information on failures and setbacks.

6. *Present feedback graphically.* A graph is like a picture—it depicts movement. At the end of each day the data for that day can be recorded on a graph. Whenever possible, display the graph so that others can see it. In this way the employee's peers can provide reinforcement by commenting on improvement. When the target is a work group, posting of the graph is essential.

Shaping

Behavior change programs depend heavily on reinforcement that follows the behavior to strengthen that behavior. But if the behavior never occurs, reinforcement cannot help you. The subordinate must first perform the behavior so that the intervention plan can reinforce it; you cannot expect people to carry out a behavior that they do not know how to perform. A behavior that a subordinate does not now possess must be learned, but new and complex behaviors rarely emerge spontaneously. To help a subordinate learn a new behavior, begin by reinforcing the behavior that is the closest approximation of the desired behavior.

One of the most common reasons for failure in behavior change programs is the lack of shaping. In fact, any change program that calls for an increase in a behavior should use some shaping. Too frequently, however, managers reinforce only perfected behavior, and this greatly decreases the chance that the behavior will ever occur. To effectively teach a new behavior, you must reinforce approximations that may be *much* lower than the desired behavior and proceed step by step until you reach the goal.

Some managers resist using shaping because they believe employees "should" perform at certain standards and do not "deserve" to be reinforced for performance that is below that standard. Managers who have this attitude impede learning, because they don't reinforce important progress toward meeting the standard. To help employees learn a new behavior, even if it is one they should already know, begin at whatever level at which they are currently performing and slowly but steadily move toward the goal, reinforcing them as they progress.

This is an additional reason for having a good baseline: Baseline tells us the *current* level of performance, and this is where the shaping process should begin. Reinforce the target person for performing at the baseline level or slightly above it. Call this step one. When the target person consistently carries out the behavior at that level, move upward one small step. Now the target person must perform at step two to gain the reinforcer previously given for step one. Shaping continues in this manner until the target person reaches the goal.

The shaping process can never begin at too low a level, and the steps can never be too small. Whenever you are in doubt, begin at a lower step or reduce the size of the steps. Make it *easy* for the target person to perform the desired behavior. This is important because it increases your chances of success. The first steps especially must be very small and easily attainable. You want to create a movement. Success in mastering the first steps can be reinforcing in and of itself, and can add to the momentum. Once the target person is moving, the later steps can be progressively larger. Frustration and failure in beginning steps can act as a brake, making progress a slow, laborious process that is hardly reinforcing.

Behavioral objectives. As with other intervention strategies, each step in shaping should be defined precisely and unambiguously. Behavioral objectives are the precision tools that tell you when one step has been successfully achieved and when the next step should begin. Each step should be stated in terms of an objective. By following the guidelines discussed earlier, clearly pinpoint the behavior in such a way that it can be counted. Specify the situation where the behavior is to occur and the amount of the behavior required. Consider the following objectives:

1. "For one week Arlene will work more independently." An objective stated like this one will surely result in failure. What is independent work? Because the behavior is not clearly defined, it will probably lead to erratic reinforcement of a variety of behaviors. Furthermore, on what is Arlene to work independently and for how long? Is one instance of independent work sufficient to satisfy the objective?

2. "For one week Arlene will make more suggestions for solutions." This objective is an improvement. A statement that suggests a solution can be counted—you know what to reinforce. But the objective fails to specify the circumstances (are suggestions as to where to go to lunch to be reinforced?), and of course it does not indicate how many suggestions are needed.

3. "For one week, when Arlene asks me to assist her with one of her assignments, she will make at least two suggestions for solutions to her problem." This statement meets all the criteria for a behavior objective.

A good objective tells you exactly what to reinforce, and precise objectives help the target person know when to act and what to strive for. When the target person participates in the development of the program (and this should occur most of the time), each objective can be converted into a contingency contract that specifies the objective in the "if" portion and the reinforcement in the "then" portion: "If you make two suggestions for solutions to your problem when you ask me for assistance on your assignments, then I will listen to each suggestion and comment on its merits."

The shaping continuum. A tentative series of steps should be determined at the outset of the program. The following schedule was developed to improve the performance of a quality control checker in training:

Baseline: 18 defective units passed per day
   Goal: 2 or fewer defective units passed per day

Step 1.   For one week 17 or fewer defective units passed per day
Step 2.   For one week 15 or fewer defective units passed per day
Step 3.   For one week 12 or fewer defective units passed per day
Step 4.   For one week 8 or fewer defective units passed per day
Step 5.   For one week 4 or fewer defective units passed per day
Step 6.   2 or fewer defective units passed per day

Be flexible and ready to change the schedule. Steps planned on paper may seem easier than they really are, or the size of steps may need to be reduced. The target person may have to work on one step for several time periods, or may have to return to an earlier step if some setback occurs. There is a rule of thumb for solving these problems: Do not move up a step until the previous objective has been met.

The schedule with the quality control checker is designed to shape behavior by increasing the amount of the target behavior (number of defective units spotted). Many schedules are built along a time continuum: Each subsequent step in the shaping requires that the target person perform the behavior for a longer time than the previous step that was to be reinforced. Bill, the man who couldn't concentrate on his proposal writing, could follow a schedule that at each step increased the amount of time he was supposed to spend writing.

Schedules can also be developed around the chain of behaviors necessary to produce the goal behavior. A schedule for Arlene could specify a chain of behaviors as follows: (1) analyze the problem, (2) generate solutions, (3) implement solutions without assistance. Of course, each step should be broken down into a series of very small substeps. The best way to identify the shaping steps necessary in a chain is to begin with the goal behavior and, working backwards, identify each behavior that is necessary to the subsequent step. For example, to implement solutions without assistance, Arlene must first generate solutions. To generate solutions, she must first analyze the problem, and so forth. Then each of these behaviors can be shaped through a series of small steps.

Plateaus. The plateau is a common occurrence in the course of a shaping schedule: The target person may make excellent progress and then stop suddenly. The easiest way to prompt new movement upward is to reduce the size of the steps. When this is not feasible, continue the plan for a week or more. Increasing the reinforcement might also help. If all attempts fail to produce movement, the target person may have reached an upper limit, and you should consider terminating the plan.

Modeling. Most frequently, shaping begins at the baseline frequency. But sometimes in a chain of behaviors, the target person will not know how to perform the first step, no matter how easy it may appear to be. Using a model can solve this problem. Modeling is learning indirectly through others' experience. By observing or hearing about another's performance, we learn vicariously what behaviors will be reinforced or punished. Models include live and filmed demonstrations of behavior, pictures and descriptions in books, and oral reports. Viewing a live or filmed model is best because we can observe exactly how the behavior is performed, the exact sequences of chains of behavior, and the consequences of each.

Even when the target person is not actively involved in the shaping program, you can still employ models to encourage the manifestation of step one behaviors. Suppose that you have decided to shape a subordinate's assertive behavior, but the subordinate is not aware of your program. (Programs move faster when the target person is actively involved and committed—and they are more ethically sound.) In this case you can reinforce another subordinate's assertive behavior in front of the target person. Through observation, the target person will learn assertive behaviors and their consequences, but may still not manifest them. Such people may need to be prompted with an antecedent: "Ann, I'd be interested in your opinion on this topic." Then reinforce any assertive response. Even if the target person says, "Gee, Rich, I really don't know," you can redefine it as an assertive response and reinforce that: "I'm glad you could say that. Maybe we should take a second look before coming to a conclusion. What questions do you still have, Ann?"

Some models are better than others. As a general guideline, the model should have credibility and status in the target person's eyes. Less learning occurs when the model's credibility is discounted, but some learning still occurs. But the more real and believable the model, the better. The model should also have the target person's respect, and it is best if the model is a member of the target person's current group or of the group to which the person aspires.

Models can be used in any of the intervention strategies. We learn not only how to perform the behavior from a model and what consequences to expect, but also what situation to perform it in. The important thing to remember is that modeling is occurring constantly. When you reinforce one subordinate's behavior, you increase the probability that that subordinate—and all those watching—will perform that behavior in the future. And when you punish an employee, you set an example, and observers are less likely to engage in the undesirable behavior. But punishment can produce counterproductive side effects, which means that any or all of those who learned from the example are more likely to sabotage, steal, engage in angry outbursts, become overly anxious, or withdraw.

Behavioral rehearsal. In behavioral rehearsal, the target person rehearses the role or behaviors that he or she wishes to learn, and is reinforced for practicing each link in the chain of behaviors. It is vital that you use shaping during the rehearsal—that is, give detailed feedback on what the target person did well and a minimum of "constructive criticism." Focus on successive approximations of the desired behavior rather than on the undesired behavior.

Antecedents are an important consideration in behavioral rehearsal. Whenever possible, gradually make the rehearsal setting more and more like the target setting. If this is not done, the target person may learn to perform the behavior in the rehearsal setting but not outside it (*stimulus control*). By making the setting increasingly realistic, you are creating stimulus generalization.

Shape one class of behaviors at a time during the rehearsal. For example, in teaching assertive behaviors, first shape the words, then the voice quality and control, then the body movements, and finally all of them together. Try it—it's easy, it's free, and you can shape up your management skills when you participate in the rehearsal.

Evaluation

Evaluation is not a separate activity that occurs after the termination of the plan; it is an ongoing process in behavior change programs. Through constant monitoring and counting, the current behavior frequencies are compared with the baseline. As long as the desired behavior steadily increases, the program continues. When a plateau or drop in target behavior frequency occurs, the program should be critically reviewed and revised. By charting Otto's behavior (Figure 5), Georgia can easily evaluate her intervention. Because the frequency of Otto's negative comments about the program has dropped, she can conclude that her intervention has been successful.

Maintenance

All behavior change programs should contain a precisely stated goal. The goal can specify a behavior, such as being on time or mak-

Figure 5. Georgia's graph of Otto's negative behavior before and after her intervention.

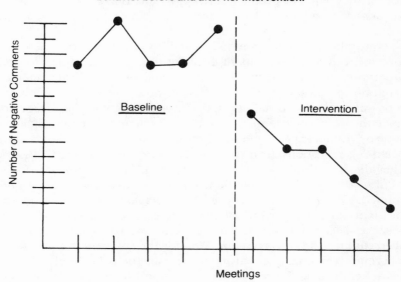

ing problem-solving comments, or it can specify an outcome, such as a completed proposal or a successful sale. It is important that the goal be quantitative: How many sales? How many days on time? Without a numerical statement you cannot determine when the goal has been reached. The behavior occurring at the desired frequency is the signal for termination of the intervention phase. *Maintaining* a behavior at the desired frequency is the final step in the behavior change program.

Change programs in which the contingencies were rearranged become self-maintaining as long as the new arrangement of contingencies stays in effect. Suppose that you want to reinforce your staff's prompt arrival at meetings. You might rearrange the existing contingencies (waiting or avoiding waiting) by starting on time instead of starting late and thus reinforce promptness. This behavior change will probably stay in effect as long as the contingencies remain the same—that is, as long as you start the meeting on time. Some change programs have built-in contingencies that reinforce the desired behavior. These programs could be considered self-maintaining. For example, a salesperson's improved skills will be continually reinforced by increased sales. But with interventions that require additional or new reinforcement, building in natural reinforcers becomes an important step. For example, if Arlene's supervisor stops reinforcing her for independent problem solving, Arlene is likely to begin asking for assistance again. Arlene's supervisor needs to develop natural reinforcers as a maintenance procedure.

Natural reinforcers generally fall into two categories: self-reinforcement and reinforcement from others. For example, Arlene's supervisor could encourage Arlene to implement a self-management program to teach herself to use self-reinforcement ("I just made a good suggestion!"). In addition, the supervisor could encourage others in the work environment to reinforce Arlene's suggestions. This is done by *reinforcing the reinforcer.* For example, positive remarks about Arlene's suggestions from her peers could be prompted ("Lorrie, what did you think of Arlene's suggestion?") and then reinforced ("I'm glad I asked your opinion, Lorrie, because you made a good point."). To do this you simply set up a behavior change program that has as its target behavior increased mutual reinforcement among peers. Collect baseline data on your staff and use appropriately applied contingent reinforcement. Monitor the frequency of peers' mutual reinforcement. This barometer reveals the cohesiveness of your team. Reinforcing the reinforcer is an important technique for building a team. Once this has been achieved, the demands on you are reduced, because the team maintains itself and can actually energize you. If you read between the lines in Michael Maccoby's analysis, you will see that this is a technique unique to gamesmen.[8]

Another necessary maintenance strategy is to alter the frequency or schedule of reinforcement. Reinforcement of each instance of the behavior (*continuous reinforcement*) is important in increasing a behavior, but intermittent and unpredictable reinforcement is most effective in maintaining a behavior at a high frequency. But don't make an abrupt switch (that would be contingency shock); slowly stretch or fade out the reinforcement. If a feedback system was used as part of the intervention, continue it into the maintenance phase. Employees can use the feedback to prompt self-reinforcement.

Another tool in maintenance is the antecedent. Whenever possible, build stimulus control into your program. Arrange for antecedents in the environment to prompt the behavior. Reinforce peers for prompting one another, and don't let the antecedent become contaminated. If you want the office to retain stimulus control over work behavior, make sure that socializing occurs only in the social area. Clearly defined rules and limits adhered to fairly and consistently maintain stimulus control. "Smoking in the social area only and never by anyone in the stockroom"—such a rule is a statement of stimulus control. Rules do not have to be rigid, but they must be consistent. And it is the consequences of rule-following or rule-breaking that reveal consistency. Rules and norms can maintain work-oriented interactions. "People work together around here." This creates an expectation. If cooperative work is subsequently reinforced, the expectation can become a maintaining antecedent. In a similar manner, goals can maintain high productivity. Goals become a maintaining antecedent when goal attainment is consistently reinforced.

The Target Person: You or the Subordinate?

A behavior is not an isolated event; it occurs in an ongoing chain of antecedents and consequences. And a behavior is not merely a behavior—it also functions as a consequence to the behavior that precedes it and as an antecedent to the behavior that follows it.

A functional analysis revealing that your behavior is an antecedent or consequence of a subordinate's undesirable behavior indicates that you must change your behavior to change the subordinate's behavior. When Georgia discovered that it was her responses to Otto's negative comments that were maintaining his behavior, she had to change her behavior to eliminate the negative comments. A self-management program can help you effect the desired change easily, and this is the subject of the next chapter.

NOTES

1. Sharon A. Bower and Beverly A. Potter, *Instructor's Manual for Asserting Yourself: A Practical Guide for Positive Change* (Reading, Mass.: Addison-Wesley, 1976), p. 21.
2. Behavior-in-situation is adapted from "behavior-in-a-situation" developed by David L. Watson and Roland G. Tharp, *Self-Directed Behavior: Self-Modification for Personal Adjustment* (Monterey, Calif.: Brooks/Cole, 1972), pp. 63–64.
3. G.L. Wenzee, "Motivations as Employees, Supervisors See Them," *Motivation Training Manual* (404 Riley Road, Austin, Texas 78746, 1970), p. 7.
4. P.A. Renwick and E.E. Lawler, "What You Really Want From Your Job," *Psychology Today*, Vol. 11, No. 12 (May 1978), pp. 53–65.
5. Michael Maccoby, *The Gamesman* (New York: Simon and Schuster, 1976).
6. For a detailed discussion of the dos and don'ts of using contingency management, consult Lloyd Homme and Donald Tosti, *Behavior Technology: Motivation and Contingency Management* (San Rafael, Calif.: Individual Learning Systems, 1971).

7. Thomas Gordon, *Leader Effectiveness Training? The No-Lose Way to Release the Productive Potential of People* (New York: Wyden Books, 1977).
8. Michael Maccoby, *The Gamesman* (New York: Simon and Schuster, 1976).

SUGGESTED READINGS

Connellan, Thomas K., *How to Improve Human Performance: Behaviorism in Business and Industry.* New York: Harper and Row, 1978.

Laird, Dugan, "Why Everything Is All Loused Up, Really," *Training in Business and Industry* (March 1971), pp. 52–55.

Luthans, Fred, and Kreitner, Robert, *Organizational Behavior Modification.* Glenview, Ill.: Scott, Foresman and Company, 1975.

Melvin, G.H., "Want Better Performance? Accentuate the Positive," *Supervisory Management* (April 1972), pp. 2–11.

Miller, Lawrence M., *Behavior Management: The New Science of Managing People at Work.* New York: John Wiley, 1978.

"Performance Audit, Feedback, and Positive Reinforcement," *Training and Development Journal,* Vol. 26 (November 1972), pp. 8–13.

"Productivity Gains From a Pat on the Back," *Business Week* (January 23, 1978), pp. 56–62.

Watson, D.L., and Tharp, R.G., *Self-Directed Behavior: Self-Modification for Personal Adjustment.* Monterey, Calif.: Brooks/Cole, 1972.

3

Self-Management

YOUR own behavior has an impact on those around you. Things you do and say (or don't do and don't say) can function as antecedents that evoke—or as consequences that maintain—the behavior of someone else. The more you understand the interrelationship between your behaviors and the behavior of subordinates, the more you can manage others by managing yourself. For example, if Jack is 20 minutes late, what should you do and say? If Jan produces a quality report, what should your response be? When you get down to basics, your primary and most powerful managing tool is your own behavior.

Managing Others by Managing Yourself

Many traditional management theories have failed to produce the desired results because they have tended to view employee behaviors as isolated events, and have thus overlooked their relationship to the environmental setting. These theories often point to internal needs, motives, and conflicts as the sole determinants of a person's actions. (Jack is late because he is immature and rebellious; this implies that Jack's lateness is his personal problem. And Jan's productivity is caused by her maturity and discipline.) On the other hand, when you expand your vision to look at those behaviors in their environmental context, you may conclude that within that environment there are events that foster and maintain Jack's lateness and Jan's productivity. You, of course, are part of your subordinates' environment—it may be that your actions or nonactions are the very events that evoke or maintain the behaviors you would like to eliminate. In other words, one way of changing the behavior of those around you is to change your own behavior.

The relationship between the consequences of employee behavior and the likelihood of that behavior's recurrence is becoming widely known. When you discover that your response to an employee is reinforcing an undesirable behavior, the solution seems quite simple: Stop reinforcing the undesirable behavior and start reinforcing a desirable one. The problem is that it is not always easy to simply stop and start reinforcing; it requires changing your responses, or more specifically, changing your behavior. The existing literature on the application of behavior modification in the organization often fails to emphasize that much of the manager's behavior is evoked or maintained by the behavior of employees.

Consider this example. Craig has an open-door policy—he encourages his staff to drop in his office to talk about their work. The problem is that Bruce drops in once or twice a day to talk about matters unrelated to work. The manager before Craig had alienated the staff with his contradictory actions: One of the many complaints was that he encouraged them to go to him with problems, yet when they did he was either critical of them or "too busy" to listen. Craig was new in the position and knew that the staff was sizing him up. In his eagerness to be seen as different from his predecessor, he was reluctant to speak with Bruce about his socializing.

The functional analysis revealed that it was Craig's active listening (nodding and saying "uh, huh") that appeared to be reinforcing Bruce's socializing. The solution seemed obvious: Ignore Bruce's social talk and respond positively to any work-related talk—that is, change Craig's behavior so that he responded differently to Bruce. The problem was that Craig found this very difficult. "I don't understand it. In spite of my good intentions and efforts, I catch myself once again listening to Bruce's chatting." Sometimes Craig ignored the social talk; at other times he listened. His intermittent attempts to change his own behavior had a bad effect on Bruce because Craig intermittently reinforced Bruce and thus made the social talk more resistant to extinction. Craig solved this problem by making his response to Bruce the focus of a formal self-management program. The functional analysis of his own listening behavior was as follows:

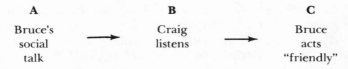

A		B		C
Bruce's social talk	→	Craig listens	→	Bruce acts "friendly"

Upon studying the analysis, Craig expressed frustration. "It's an impossible situation. The social talk is irresistible, so I always listen. In fact, I feel very uncomfortable ignoring Bruce—it's rude. The only solution is to get Bruce to talk about work. And that's why I'm trying to stop listening to his chatting!" I suggested that he look more closely at *all* the antecedents of his listening. Craig did this and discovered his thoughts were another antecedent.

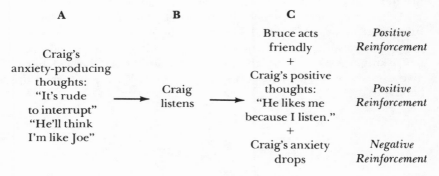

A		B		C	
Craig's anxiety-producing thoughts: "It's rude to interrupt" "He'll think I'm like Joe"	→	Craig listens	→	Bruce acts friendly	*Positive Reinforcement*
				+	
				Craig's positive thoughts: "He likes me because I listen."	*Positive Reinforcement*
				+	
				Craig's anxiety drops	*Negative Reinforcement*

From this more complete analysis, Craig developed an effective self-management program in which he altered the anxiety-producing thoughts that prompted listening. When he noticed an anxiety-producing thought while Bruce was socializing, Craig used self-instructions (discussed later in this chapter) to block out the unproductive thought and to direct his responses to Bruce. Once Craig modified his own behavior Bruce's talk quickly switched from social to work-related topics.

Let's look at another example. Ruth had a lot of trouble getting her secretary, whom she shared with two others, to do her work promptly. In fact, Ruth found it was often easier to type short things herself. Each time she asked that something be typed, Betty made excuses. Conducting a functional analysis, she discovered that almost every time Betty made excuses, Ruth either did the work herself or in some way altered her directive. This suggested that she was unknowingly reinforcing the very behavior that she wanted reduced. The solution to the problem seemed quite clear—rearrange the contingencies so that making excuses was ignored and deferential acceptance was reinforced. Ruth immediately set out to do this. She asked Betty to type a letter and predictably Betty made an excuse. Ruth ignored the excuse and did not alter her directive.

At that point, it appeared to be working, since she was getting fewer excuses, but another problem developed: Betty's work was often late, so that Ruth had to ask for it. She did not like her work late and did not like asking for it. She was getting frustrated and angry. About two weeks after beginning the intervention phase, she asked that a report be pulled from the files by 11:00 A.M. for an important luncheon conference. At 11:15 the folder was still in the locked file and Betty was out of the office with the key. When Ruth finally found Betty, she exploded. Betty made an excuse, and Ruth threatened to fire her. Ruth looked and felt incompetent as a manager.

What happened? What went wrong? Ruth did not complete the functional analysis. She had identified the consequences of Betty's giving excuses but not the antecedent. The antecedent turned out to be "asking." Asking Betty to perform required tasks caused her to give excuses and *then,* by altering her request, Ruth reinforced this behavior.

A		B		C
Ruth asks	→	Betty makes excuse	→	Ruth alters request

Sometimes it is more efficient to alter or remove the antecedent that evokes the behavior. Thus, Ruth could have been more effective in reducing Betty's excuse-giving behavior by intervening at the antecedent point—the way in which Ruth herself gave directives. By making her *own* behavior the target of the change program, she modified Betty's excuse-giving behavior. Ruth focused her attention on the way in which she gave directives, which served as the antecedent of Betty's giving excuses. When she conducted a functional analysis, she had difficulty identifying the antecedents of her own behavior until she began observing her own thought processes and discovered that each incident of making a tentative directive (see Chapter 5) was preceded by considerable physical tension and many negative thoughts.

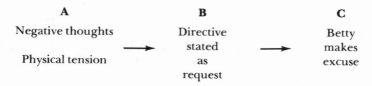

A		B		C
Negative thoughts		Directive stated		Betty makes
	→	as	→	excuse
Physical tension		request		

On the basis of this information, Ruth developed a multidimensional self-management program. She taught herself the desired behavior of giving authoritative directives. Using the shaping procedure, she developed a series of small steps in which she gradually increased the difficulty of the directive. Simultaneously, she employed thought-stopping to replace the negative thoughts with positive self-statements, and physical relaxation to eliminate the tension (see later in this chapter). Finally, Ruth continued ignoring all Betty's excuses.

When she conducted the functional analysis, Ruth was able to collect baseline data on the actual frequency of Betty's excuse-giving and on her own behavior of making requests. She used a wrist counter to monitor the actual number of requests made. After each encounter with Betty, Ruth tallied the number of Betty's excuses on a file card that she kept in her desk. During the baseline phase, Ruth felt that collecting data was irrelevant. She was busy and impatient to deal with the problem with Betty. Later, however, she acknowledged the importance of establishing the baseline, and observing the concrete evidence of the change in Betty's behavior built up her confidence. In her annual performance review, Ruth used the data she had collected to demonstrate the development of her supervisory skills.

When first introduced to operant conditioning and reinforcement principles, managers often balk at the idea of ignoring an undesirable behavior: "How can I ignore errors in the monthly report? It must be perfect." "She's paid to do that work. I can't just listen to her excuses and say nothing." This is an understandable concern—it is difficult to ignore errors and transgressions, especially when we find them personally irritating. One solution is to alter the antecedent that evokes the undesirable behavior in the first place because this way you can head off that behavior before it happens. It is often your own actions that trigger the undesirable behavior, and then your response reinforces the employee's response to you. Granted, antecedents can be difficult to identify, but you should always make a concerted effort to do so. And whenever your own behavior is the focus of a functional analysis, look for antecedents and consequences in your internal as well as external environment.

The important point to remember is that whenever you discover that your own behavior is evoking or maintaining the employee's undesirable behavior, the most effective intervention will involve altering your behavior in some way. Your behavior is controlled by the same principles discussed in Chapter 1. For this reason, it is just as difficult for you to change your own behavior on command as it is for the employee to change on command. Recognize that your behavior is controlled and that it will be difficult to change, but by using the principles and techniques discussed in this book, you can begin to manage your own behavior. All the analysis and data collection may seem unnecessary or even academic, but it will add to your success in managing yourself and others.[1]

Specify the Problem Behavior

All behavior change programs start with this essential step. As with subordinates, the problem behavior to be modified can be an undesirable behavior that you want to reduce or a desirable behavior that you want to increase. In a self-management program, however, it is not necessary to restrict yourself to behaviors that occur only in the work setting; you can choose to increase or decrease any of your behaviors. The problem behavior can be an overt action observable to others, or it can be an internal behavior that only you can observe. In Chapter 2, it was shown that there are four modes of behavior (AMPS)—actions, mental pictures, physical sensations, and sentences.[2] Any of these kinds of behavior can be the target of a self-management program.

Specifying the problem behavior to be modified involves two essential steps: identifying the behavior and identifying the situation in which the behavior occurs. To identify your own problem behavior, use the same guidelines described in Chapter 2, and define the behavior specifically enough that you can *count* each occurrence—that is, you must be able to determine when it is and is not occurring. If at any given moment you observe yourself and can give a definite "yes" or "no" answer to the question, "Is the behavior occurring now?" then you will have clearly defined the behavior. And once again, it is important to specify *when* the behavior occurs. This can be in a specific setting such as at the coffee machine, in the sales meeting, or in your office, or it can be when specific factors converge, such as when you feel rushed, when you are speaking to a person in authority, or when you are making a request. When you have unambiguously stated the behavior-in-situation, you are ready to move on to the second step in your self-management program.

Observe Your Behavior

The observation phase has two major steps: determining what factors are controlling the problem behavior, and establishing a baseline for evaluation. Conduct a functional analysis to identify what happens just before and just after the behavior. Controlling events, antecedents, and consequences are not limited to the external environment; internal events are also part of your overall environment.

So observe your actions, mental pictures, physical sensations, and sentences as well as the actions of others that occur before and after the problem behavior.

For example, Ron's problem behavior was remaining silent at policy review meetings. In observing his behavior (each time he wanted to speak up but remained silent instead), he discovered that his own internal behaviors were causing his silence. Ron's functional analysis revealed that the physical sensations of tension evoked silence (or inhibited speaking up), and that through his negative self-statements about his silence he punished himself for not speaking up. When Ron expanded his functional analysis, he discovered that negative self-statements also preceded the physical tension. He was indeed trapped in a self-imposed vicious cycle of tension and negativity, with each triggering the other, making it next to impossible for him to speak calmly and coherently in the meeting.

At other times the behavior of other people can function as an antecedent to our own internal behaviors. When someone criticizes us, most of us experience a variety of negative internal behaviors. In short, it is important to observe all of your behaviors as well as those of others. Such a careful analysis helps point to the most effective intervention point. Record your observations. After you have collected several examples, it will be easier to see a pattern.

Once you have completed the functional analysis, begin counting each occurrence of the behavior with a time sampling procedure. You can use any of the methods suggested for collecting baseline data on subordinates' behavior, but the important thing is to do this systematically and to record your data each day on a graph. Continue the baseline counting until you believe that you have a good picture of the overall frequency and pattern of the problem behavior. In general, this will usually take a week to ten days. However, when the problem behavior occurs less frequently, you'll need to count for a longer period of time.

Impatience is a frequent error of self-management. Once the problem behavior has been identified, managers sometimes rush into an intervention before carefully observing the problem behavior and those factors that control it. Such impatience is hard to resist, but you must do so if you don't want to set yourself up for failure. You may have overlooked an important controlling factor (such as physical tension) and thereby attempt to implement an inappropriate intervention. Such a failure is discouraging, wastes valuable time and energy, and can validate the belief that you can't change.

The baseline is very important for evaluation. Changing behaviors, especially entrenched bad habits, can be a long process. By comparing your current level of performance with the baseline level, you can see gradual progress. Without the baseline comparison, you might conclude that the intervention isn't working when it actually is. In addition, the baseline comparison can quickly reveal ineffective interventions that should be reworked or discarded.

Intervening Directly

Sometimes you will want to modify the problem behavior directly. For example, Ron could use a contingency contracting procedure in which he makes an agreement with himself to make at least one comment in the next three meetings and then reinforces himself for doing so. At other times you might decide to modify the problem behavior indirectly by changing another behavior that is controlling the problem behavior. For example, Ron might make his physical tension the target of his self-management program. The *problem* behavior is the behavior that you ultimately want to change (and the behavior that you continue to monitor throughout the intervention); the *target* behavior is the behavior that you attempt to modify directly with the goal of eventually modifying the problem behavior. Sometimes, of course, they are one and the same.

The purpose of the functional analysis is to reveal what factors control your problem behavior and to assist in determining the most efficient intervention point. This point may be the antecedent, the consequence, the behavior itself, or all three. It must be emphasized that every individual is unique, and functions in a unique environment that has a unique effect on behavior. Behavior technology delineates general principles of behavior control and change, but as a manager of behavior—be it a subordinate's or your own—you must make a leap from the general principles and techniques to an individualized behavior management program. For example, a would-be carpenter can be instructed to use various tools on various types of wood to produce various results. But the carpenter must tailor the woodworking techniques to the specific project at hand. Any of the intervention strategies described in Chapter 2 can be used in a self-management program. The important thing is that you tailor it to your unique needs and that you follow it consistently.

Discipline in self-management is often a problem. It is easy to procrastinate in carrying out a specific action or in administering a consequence. Being systematic and consistent is essential—your success depends on it. Don't tackle your most troublesome behavior in your first project; select a fairly simple problem, one that is only mildly troublesome and does not pervade your entire life. A project that involves making a positive comment when a subordinate completes work on time is probably easier than one that is designed to help you act more assertively. Success in your first project will help you be successful in later ones, so set yourself up to succeed.

The contracting techniques described in Chapter 2 can help you do this. Negotiate a contract with yourself for each phase of your project. In the contract, specify exactly how much of what behavior you require of yourself and what you will give yourself for successful accomplishment. Write this down—seeing your agreement with yourself in writing will help you feel more committed to the change you seek. Be reasonable with yourself; in fact, be overly reasonable: Each contract should require only a small change and cover a short period of time. (An agreement that extends only two days is a lot easier to carry out than one that lasts a month.) You can write as many contracts as you like—as long as you fulfill them. As you succeed in meeting the terms of your contracts with yourself, your ability to keep future agreements will increase. In other words, self-contracting is a way of developing discipline.

One of the advantages of self-management is that it allows a much broader range of reinforcers: You don't have to restrict yourself to activities that exist in your work environment or that are in any way related to your work; you can use a variety of social, leisure, and personal activities as reinforcers for changes in your work behavior. It's a good idea to write down all your reinforcers in a menu form. Don't forget the intangibles—a relaxing fantasy as well as the physical state of relaxation itself can be very reinforcing. Comments like "I did a good job," or "I knew my idea would set some minds spinning," or "I caught myself that time—I can see I'm making progress" can be surprisingly powerful. Remember, the sooner you receive the reinforcement, the better. When the reinforcement is not available until some time later, consider using a token system (described in Chapter 2) to bridge the time gap. Self-reinforcement is also helpful in this regard—you can compliment yourself immediately after performing the desired behavior, and grant the designated reward later on.

Be especially careful not to deprive yourself. To be effective, you should receive *more* reinforcement than you were receiving before you began the self-management program—receiving less reinforcement is tantamount to self-punishment. If you find that you must deny yourself reinforcement because you didn't fulfill the terms of your contract, then you are probably asking too much of yourself, and you should rewrite the contract in such a way that it will be easy to fulfill. A problem behavior is not a sin; it's a habit—and habits are hard to break. If your strategy for breaking the habit results in less reinforcement, you'll only undermine yourself. It's important to make self-management as easy and as pleasurable as possible.

Throughout your self-management program, continue to collect data on the frequency of the problem behavior. If your behavior does not show a consistent change in the desired direction, go back to the beginning and review each step. Perhaps there is a consequence that you overlooked and that is maintaining the behavior you are trying to eliminate. Perhaps you are trying to move too fast and are requiring too much of yourself. Or perhaps the reinforcement is too far removed from the actual occurrence of the behavior. Redesign your strategy and begin again. And if, after a few attempts, there is still no change in the problem behavior, then perhaps it is time to go to a consultant. If you cannot find a management consultant who has expertise in behavior modification, you might look for a behavioral psychologist. Most behavioral psychologists can help you set up a self-management program. On the other hand, if your data indicate that the problem behavior is changing as you'd like it to, then pat yourself on the back—this is concrete evidence of your effectiveness as a manager.

Evaluate and Maintain the Behavior Change

The final step in self-management is maintaining the behavior change. Here, too, all the principles and techniques for managing others apply. When you are satisfied with your change, then change your reinforcement schedule from continuous to intermittent. By reducing the frequency and consistency of reinforcement, you can make the behavior resistant to extinction. Of course, the ideal situation occurs when people or events in the environment reinforce your change. For example, as you become more specific in giving a directive, your subordinates' performance often improves. But you should know that there will be times when those in your environment will attempt to prevent you from changing. Change can be disconcerting and uncomfortable. Other people lose reinforcement when you change, and they may make active efforts to push you back into your old behavior. If it looks like this sort of resistance could be a problem in your self-management program, then plan a strategy for dealing with it.

Defeating the Peter Principle by Managing Yourself

Harry had an outstanding record in hospital supply sales. When the regional sales manager position opened, he was selected to fill it.

Harry worked hard and put in long hours, but despite his efforts sales dropped. Managing a sales team spread across four states was a very different task from selling equipment. Eventually sales picked up slightly, but Harry did not fulfill the company's expectations as a star performer. He did fulfill his worst fears, however: He had reached his level of incompetence.

Situations like Harry's—being promoted into a position that requires skills you don't have—provide a fertile area for the behavior modification approach to self-management. What should you do if this happens to you? First of all, preserve your self-esteem by recognizing that you are in a tough spot: You are being expected to do a good job at the same time that you are learning how to do it. It will take more than talent to do this; you will need determination and resiliency. Prepare yourself for this difficult task by learning how to manage stress, how to control defeatist thinking, and how to purposefully teach yourself the skills you need.

To teach yourself, you must identify what behaviors you need to learn. This can be done in a variety of ways. Watching colleagues who have the skills you desire is important. Training workshops and how-to books can be helpful. But to be effective, the behaviors you identify as necessary must be incorporated into your management repertoire. When you attend a training workshop or read a how-to book, tailor the general guidelines to your specific situation. This will involve trial and error: Repeat what works and drop what doesn't. In other words, rather than becoming attached to a particular managing action, consider it a trial and then look to the consequences to determine whether you should repeat it, refine it, or drop it. This is where you can use self-management tools, such as shaping and self-contracting, to practice and learn the new behaviors. And don't forget to liberally reinforce small successes to build your confidence.

However, there are some behaviors that result in a reinforcing consequence that you do not necessarily want to repeat. As was stated in Chapter 1, any consequence that involves the cessation of a negative event is reinforcing and encourages repetition of the behavior involved. This is not always productive. If someone is chronically tardy and your actions result in a reduction of that tardiness, we could consider this to be a productive negative reinforcement. On the other hand, there are times when negative reinforcement can box you into incompetence.

To understand this potent danger, consider Harry's case again. As the new regional sales manager, Harry was understandably anxious about his performance. Michael (a bright, aggressive, and ambitious salesman) proposed a new marketing strategy. The problem was that the stress of adapting to his new job outweighed Harry's objectivity. Consequently, he responded by half-listening, and offhandedly dismissed Michael's proposal as unfeasible. Harry's response was counterproductive—he failed to encourage Michael's enthusiasm and creativity; in fact, he stifled it. But the immediate hidden consequence for Harry was the elimination of a demand upon his already overextended time and energy and a brief reduction in his growing anxiety or tension level.

Michael Maccoby interviewed hundreds of successful corporate leaders. One of his startling findings was that about half reported high levels of chronic anxiety. They cited three sources of tension: (1) worry that important projects would not succeed; (2) worry that they lacked essential knowledge about their jobs; and (3) worry that they would lose control and look bad or do something wrong.[3] Anxiety of this sort is dangerous, especially when a manager takes punitive or counterproductive measures to gain a brief reduction in tension. Such an individual is in danger of becoming incompetent because the punitive behavior can easily become an entrenched habit.

What is the solution when unrelenting anxiety stresses the body and undermines performance, and when attempts to reduce stress can lead you right into the Peter Principle trap? A solution is to first become aware of your stress and then to learn to manage that stress.

Self-Management of Stress

In the last decade, stress has become a problem of increasing concern to industry. Numerous medical and psychological studies have established an intimate relationship between chronic stress and life-threatening health problems. For example, there is little doubt that stress is a contributing factor in heart disease, and there is evidence suggesting that it may be a factor in cancer as well. Space restrictions prevent a detailed discussion here of the nature and causes of stress,[4] but few managers would disagree that their jobs and responsibilities generate excessive stress or tension. In their comprehensive study of decision making, Irving Janis and Leon Mann maintain that the process of making *any* consequential decision is stressful.[5] Decision making, of course, is central to the manager's job. Drs. Holmes and Rahe demonstrated that adjusting to change—whether good or bad—causes stress, making a person more susceptible to disease.[6] We all know that negative changes such as job loss or relocation are stressful, but the Holmes and Rahe study reveals that adjusting to *positive* changes such as a promotion or salary increase can also be stressful. It is hoped that organizations will begin to evolve less stressful work modes and environments. Perhaps "health maintenance days" will replace sick leave, or maybe companies of the future will consider health spas with exercise rooms and hot tubs to be as essential as cafeterias. But in the meantime, stress is a very real problem for most managers.

Of course, the antidote for stress and tension is relaxation, but the problem is that most people don't know *how* to relax. In fact, many people experience such chronic, habitual tension that they don't even realize they're tense but actually believe they are relaxed! As an experiment, raise your eyebrows so that you create wrinkles in your forehead, and hold this position for just one minute. This is rather difficult to do—in fact, you will probably find it mildly painful. If you were to continue this experiment for an hour, you would probably develop a splitting headache! Now observe others around you—you'd be amazed to see how many people do manage to maintain this expression all day. Were you to ask any of them, they would probably be unaware of their chronic frowns, because their tension feels normal. Most people—and that probably includes you—become aware of tension only after it has reached an extreme degree.

Relaxation combats the effects of stress, but it is useless to admonish yourself to relax; you must first learn how. After you have mastered the skill of relaxing, you must use it if it is to become an effecitve stress antidote. Stress management involves changes in all four AMPS modes of behavior: You must teach yourself new actions, new mental pictures, new physical sensations, and new sentences. This will take time and effort, and you'll need to practice the following exercises until you achieve mastery. On the average, it takes two to four weeks of daily practice to learn this skill. But don't let that scare you—the amount of time necessary each day is minimal, and the eventual benefits will make you feel better and will assist in preserving your health and peace of mind. It is best to begin your training at home. After you have learned the basic skills, extend them to your work environment.

Your first objective is to learn what tension and relaxation feel like in each muscle group. This is a necessary step and is easily accomplished. You must learn to recognize tension in its initial stages so that you can eliminate it before it gets out of control. To do this, you need to sharpen your self-perception and stress-detection mechanisms. One of the best ways to do this is to alternately tense and relax the various muscle groups. Study the physical sensations when the muscle is tense. What exactly does tension in this muscle feel like? Relax the muscle. Study the different physical sensations that relaxation produces. By contrasting the tension and relaxation, it becomes easier to distinguish them.

To illustrate, make a fist tight enough so that you feel a *slight* increase in tension (don't tense so hard that it hurts), and hold this for five to seven seconds. Study the physical sensations of tension in your knuckles, your fingers, and other parts of your arm. Then remove the tension by *quickly* opening your hand and relaxing the muscles. Study the changing sensations. Try this exercise several times. Your objective is to become aware of the different physical sensations.

The purpose of the tension-relaxation recognition exercise is to illustrate the basic procedure for physical relaxation training. By purposefully tensing muscles, you can study where your muscles get tight and what that feels like to you. As you release the tension, you can study what that feels like as well. By using the same tensing-relaxing procedure with all your major muscles, you can learn to identify tension throughout your body. Think of this as a means of developing your early detection system. To accomplish this, you will need to focus your attention conscientiously on the physical sensations of tension and relaxation in your muscles.

The Muscle Groups[7]

There are four major muscle groups, each composed of several smaller muscle groups. The following list describes each group and how to tense the muscles.

1. *Hands and Arms*
   a. Dominant hand and forearm: Make a fist with your dominant hand.
   b. Dominant biceps: Bend your dominant arm at the elbow, and point your fingers toward your shoulder.
   c. Nondominant hand and forearm: Make a fist with your nondominant hand.
   d. Nondominant biceps: Bend your nondominant arm at the elbow, and point your fingers toward your shoulder.
2. *Head and Face*
   a. Forehead: Raise your eyebrows toward the top of your head or knit your eyebrows to create a frown.
   b. Cheeks and nose: Squint your eyes and wrinkle your nose.
   c. Jaws: While clenching your teeth, press your lips together and pull back the corners of your mouth.
   d. Lips and tongue: While pressing your lips together, push your tongue into the roof of your mouth.

e. Neck and throat: While pushing your chin into your chest, apply a counterforce by pressing your head backwards into the back of your chair.

3. *Upper Body*

a. Shoulders and upper back I: Raise your shoulders toward your ears.

b. Shoulders and upper back II: Arch your back and push your shoulder blades together.

c. Chest: Take a deep breath and hold it.

d. Stomach: Suck in your stomach toward your spine, or push your stomach out as far as you can.

4. *Lower Back*

a. Buttocks: Flex your buttock muscles and push them into your chair.

b. Thighs: Press your heels into the floor or straighten out your legs and tense your thigh muscles.

c. Calves: Point your toes down toward the floor or point your toes up toward your head.

d. Feet: Curl your toes as if you were burying them in sand. (To avoid cramps, tense these muscles slightly for about three seconds.)

Rules for Practice[7]

1. Select a quiet setting and arrange not to be interrupted. Unplug your phone and put a "do not disturb" sign on your door.

2. Make yourself as comfortable as possible before beginning the exercise. Sit in a comfortable chair that supports your head, or recline on a couch or bed.

3. Work on the major muscle groups in any order you prefer. It is important, however, to tense and relax *all* the muscles in any one group before moving on to the next one.

4. Hold the tension in the muscles for 5–7 seconds. Experience the relaxations for about 20–30 seconds.

5. Be careful not to tense your muscles too hard. If you do this, you will have difficulty learning to detect the first signs of tension. Use a sufficient amount of tension to notice a distinct sensation—but don't tense the muscles any more than that.

6. Actively reduce the tension by quickly releasing your hold on the muscles.

7. Study the physical sensations of tension and relaxation. Concentrate on the contrast between tension and relaxation.

8. Breathe evenly and smoothly. Inhale during the tension phase and exhale at the beginning of the relaxation phase.
9. Throughout the exercise instruct yourself silently. During the tension phase, speak to yourself rapidly; during the relaxation phase, speak slowly and soothingly.
10. At the moment of relaxation, think of your antistress command.
11. Practice with your eyes closed.
12. When distracting thoughts come into your mind, simply notice that you have become distracted, and return your attention to the sensations in your muscles.
13. Let yourself enjoy the physical sensations of relaxation and of smooth, even breathing.
14. Practice twice a day for 20 minutes. Schedule an appointment with yourself and insist that you keep it. Reinforce yourself for doing so.
15. Practice consistently and conscientiously.

What to Say to Yourself

What you say to yourself during your practice sessions is an important part of relaxation training. In a training workshop the leader would guide you through the exercise, telling you at each point what to do. But as your own trainer you need to instruct yourself. As you will see later in this chapter, self-instruction is a very powerful change technique. Talk to yourself, perhaps this way: "I'm going to begin by making a fist with my right hand. Tense my fist and forearm. Good. Feel the tension building up. Study the sensations of tension. Feel that tension and now . . . Relax (antistress command) . . . just let the tension dissolve. Good. How does relaxation feel compared with tension? Better, huh?"

Many people prefer to use tape-recorded instructions. This method is effective, but it has its drawbacks—you can become a passive listener, for instance. If you listen passively to instructions, you will find it more difficult to make the transition from your practice session to actually using relaxation to counteract stress. And you can hardly take out your tape recorder in the middle of a tense meeting or a performance appraisal, so try actively instructing yourself. If after several practice sessions you still want recorded instructions, then make a tape for yourself or purchase a prerecorded instructional tape. When you instruct yourself (or make your instructional tape), don't worry about the exact wording; make up your own instructions, and instruct yourself the way you like to be instructed.

Your Antistress Command

In Chapter 1 we reviewed how, through classical conditioning, words can come to evoke physical and emotional responses. For example, when children are slapped, they usually experience unpleasant physical sensations or emotions. If the word "bad" is repeatedly paired with the slap, simply hearing "bad" will result in the same emotional response. Use this same conditioning principle in your relaxation training. When you think a specific word just at the moment you relax yourself, the word will become associated (paired) with the physical sensations of relaxation. Eventually just thinking the word will help you to relax yourself in tense situations. This is why I have called it your antistress command.

In the example, the word "relax" is used as the antistress command. Of course, you can choose from a wide variety of words, such as "calm," "slow down," and "rest." Or you might prefer to make up a new word. Once you have settled upon a word or sound to use as your antistress command, say it to yourself consistently just at the moment that you release the tension and begin to relax.

When to Practice

Learning to relax takes time, patience, and practice. Building the relaxation exercises into your daily routine is crucial. It will be difficult to develop your skill if you practice sporadically. The best times to practice are in the morning before work, during lunch (if you can arrange to be undisturbed), and in the evening, especially just before retiring. Go through the entire exercise during each session. After you have completed the exercise, review your bodily sensations. If you notice residual tension in any muscles, such as the neck or shoulders, work on these areas a little more. It is a good idea not to go on to any of the next steps for about two weeks, because you need to develop a firm foundation for actually using your new relaxation skills to reduce stress in your life. Doing these exercises twice a day may at first seem unfeasible; however, most of us are "too busy." Challenge this reason. Ask yourself if you can afford to continue experiencing stress. What about the very real potential health hazards of stress, as well as its debilitating effects upon your daily performance?

It is important to make a real commitment to yourself and to set aside the time just as you would for any other crucial project. A self-contract can help you with the commitment. Develop an if-then statement for yourself and write it down. Make your contract for a short period of time. When you have succeeded in achieving one objective, write another contract for yourself. In this way you can build and keep your commitment. Avoid the all-or-nothing New Year's resolution; a self-contract covering two or three days will help you reach your goal. Write your contract in an "official" manner. List your if-then statement and the time when you will practice each day, then sign your name at the bottom. Try posting it on a door or mirror at home. Seeing it a few times a day will remind you of your agreement with yourself. Here is a sample:

> After I, John Anderson, practice my relaxation exercise twice a day for three consecutive days I can purchase a new casting fly. I will practice for 20 minutes before breakfast and before dinner.

_____

(Signature)

Date_____

Altering Stress-Producing Thoughts

When learning any complex skill, most people go through the steps mentally as they carry them out. For example, when you were learning to drive you may have thought something like this: "OK, here comes a corner. I've got to slow down. First, I'll take my foot off the gas and brake slowly. Now I have to shift down. OK, I can do that. Take my foot off the brake and slowly push in the clutch. Now shift from third to second. Slowly—I don't want to go into reverse. Good, I did it. Now foot off the clutch. . . ." As you became more skilled you probably abbreviated the self-instructions to: "Corner. Brake slowly. Clutch in. Shift to second. . . ." As you mastered the skill, the instructions dropped out. You shifted down automatically when you saw the corner. This behavior probably feels natural now. In the same way that we learn helpful self-instructions and behaviors, we can learn unhelpful ones. In an abbreviated form you may be thinking such things as "Jones is late and I'm too busy. Now I'm going to get tense" or "I'll never make it through today" or "It's too much—I can't take it anymore."

Our thoughts, images, and other mental activities race on almost constantly. Some claim that nirvana is simply the cessation of thought, although only a select few will ever experience anything resembling this kind of bliss. The content of our unrelenting internal monologue has a powerful impact on our physical sensations (emotions) and on our actions. To illustrate, close your eyes and for about 60 seconds relive a situation in which you were dissatisfied with your behavior or with the behavior of someone else. As you do this, notice your AMPS: What are your Actions? Mental pictures? Physical sensations? Sentences? Most people who try this experiment report that they first notice many silent negative sentences, such as "If only I had . . .," or "She should have . . .," or "He had the nerve to . . .," followed by the same unpleasant sensations (such as knots in the stomach or tightness in the neck) that they experienced when they actually lived through the encounter. Some people also report negative mental pictures, such as "I could see them all sitting across from me like judge and jury—I was condemned!" which then triggered unpleasant sensations or emotions. This experiment reveals the close relationship between thoughts and fantasies, emotional responses, and our subsequent actions. We can easily become a victim of our own negative internal behaviors.

It is difficult to act the way we want to when we're experiencing tension and are engaging in stress-producing thoughts or fantasies. Our movements, our voice control, and our decisions can be seriously impaired. It becomes a vicious stress-producing cycle in which our failures and disappointments trigger more debilitating internal behaviors. Unfortunately, just as with driving the car, our negative thoughts become abbreviated and so subtle that we are often entirely unaware of them. To successfully use your relaxation skills, you need to identify and change your tension-producing self-instructions.

Keeping a Thought Diary

Observe your "silent sentences," and each time you catch yourself thinking a tension-producing thought, write it down in your diary. Your diary can be a small pad or file card that you keep on your desk or carry in your briefcase. Just collecting these negative instructions will probably be very enlightening. Don't try to observe all your thoughts about everything; start off by listing and recording what you say to yourself about your tension, your ability to learn to relax, and your relaxation exercises.

Generating Helpful Thoughts[8]

Take a piece of paper and, in one column, list your negative thoughts about your ability to relax and to cope with stress. Try to write down the exact words you said to yourself. Then, across from each negative thought, write an appropriate countermanding thought, which should be positive, optimistic, and realistic. For example:

Stress-Producing Thought	Helpful Thought
"This exercise is stupid. Nothing is happening."	"Be patient and give it a chance."
"I'll never learn to relax!"	"If I keep practicing I can learn to relax."
"This training takes too long. I don't have the time."	"I can make time for what's really important to me; this is important."
"I'm tense. I can't relax."	"If I do the exercise I can relax a little bit. Then I'll be less tense and that's good."
"I've always been high strung. I can't change."	"That's just a bad habit. I can learn a new, better habit."
"I don't have the self-discipline."	"I just need to agree to practice for two days. Then I can decide to do a little more."

Putting It All Together

By the time most people become aware of their stress, it is out of control. The strategy for managing stress described here requires immediate intervention early in the cycle, before it gets out of hand (see Figure 6). This is why I have emphasized learning to identify slight tension in the muscles and to recognize stress-producing thoughts. The more finely tuned your detection system becomes, the more effective you will be in managing your stress. The strategy is based on operant conditioning principles and the ABCs described in Chapter 1. This is the model you will use to actually reduce stress in your day-to-day life.

In this case, the behavior you want to increase is that of relaxing your muscles. If you've been conscientiously training yourself to relax, then you should be able to perform the desired behavior at point B. What you need to do is to establish antecedents to trigger your relaxing behavior at point A. The antecedents in this strategy are awareness of tension in your muscles and hearing yourself thinking stress-producing thoughts.

The diagram on page 88 shows the self-management strategy.

Figure 6. Out-of-control stress cycle.

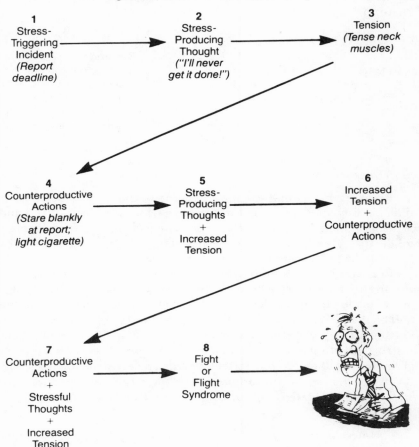

As soon as you become aware of tension or stress-producing thoughts, or both (A), actively instruct yourself to relax, and begin to consciously relax your muscles (B). Follow up with a positive statement about your ability to relax or to cope with the situation (C). The more you practice this, the easier it will become and the more successful you will be. The experience of relaxing is inherently reinforcing (because it adds a pleasurable feeling and removes unpleasant tension), and reinforced behavior increases in frequency. Eventually it will become habitual to relax in response to stress triggers, and it will feel "natural."

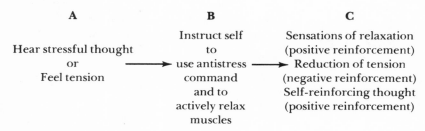

A	B	C
Hear stressful thought or Feel tension	Instruct self to use antistress command and to actively relax muscles	Sensations of relaxation (positive reinforcement) Reduction of tension (negative reinforcement) Self-reinforcing thought (positive reinforcement)

Self-Instructions

Breaking habits and learning to control undesirable behavior is difficult. Engaging in the new desired behavior often feels forced and artificial at first. This is where self-instructions help. Instructions are a guide that greatly assist in the early stages of learning a complex behavior like driving a car or managing stress.

Consider how most of us learn to play tennis. The ball comes over the net and we quickly think, "Run left. Backhand. Easy, swing!" We've made our first volley. As we become skilled, we can see the ball and be there. We are one with the ball, the racket, and our opponent. During a fast volley, our internal speech is momentarily silent. Self-instructions at this moment would be counterproductive. Don't worry about having to talk to yourself all the time. Self-instruction is a *behavior change technique*—you can use it to change the way you cope with stress triggers.[9] Here is a list of sample instructions.

Antecedent *Stress-Triggering Cues*	Behavior *Self-Instruction*	Consequence *Self-Reinforcement*
Detecting tension (Tense neck muscles)	"My neck feels a little stiff. Hey, that's what that book said to look for. My sign to relax. I'll try my antistress command . . . Calm . . . Better try it a couple of times . . . Calm . . . Calm . . . Calm . . ."	"Let's see. I *do* feel more relaxed!"
(Tense dia- phragm)	"There's that knot in my stomach. OK, time to relax. Take a deep breath . . . Slow down and relax . . ."	"I'm really getting better at this."

Detecting a stress-producing thought (Worry about a confrontation)	"Jones is not going to like it when I tell him I blew it again. I know he's going to be furious and I'm going to . . . Wait! These are stressful thoughts. This isn't going to help. I'll handle the whole thing a lot better if I'm relaxed. The important thing is to relax. OK, a deep breath and . . . Relax . . . That's right, just let the tension go. Again . . . Relax . . . Good. Now let me concentrate on a constructive plan of action."	"Boy, I can think better now that I've gotten hold of myself!"
(Worry about completing work)	"I don't know what I'm going to do. I'll never get this done. I'll be here all night and the whole weekend, too! Hold on now. There I go again, talking myself into a frenzy. Use the command . . . Slow down . . . just . . . Slow down . . ."	"That's better. At least I won't get a headache—and I can think better when I'm calm."
When stress has gotten out of control (Stressful thoughts, tension, counterproductive behavior)	"That interview was terrible! I'm shaking all over. Where *are* my cigarettes? Try the command . . . Relax . . . Relax . . . Relax . . . Still tense. Well, I can't expect immediate results."	"At least I'm becoming more aware of how I do this to myself. And *that* is progress. Next time I'll be able to catch myself sooner."
When anticipating a stressful event (The staff meeting)	"I always get uptight in these meetings. I'm going to prepare myself to nip it in the bud. I'll relax right now and when I walk in and sit down I'll. . . . With a plan I'll know what to do."	"Good, I feel a lot better. I'm really learning how to control myself."

Present the instructions to yourself in a way that you like to be instructed. It's like giving yourself a pep talk, except that instead of saying, "Come on, I can do it," tell yourself *what* to do. And then, of course, follow your instructions—you'll notice that each of the sample instructions is followed by a self-reinforcing statement. In the early stages we learn fastest when we receive a lot of reinforcement. Actively look for what you've done right, then point it out to yourself. For the time being, forget the constructive criticism—it's often a stress trigger. As you become more skilled at relaxing yourself, the experience of relaxation itself will become a built-in reinforcement. Then you won't need to consciously instruct yourself or to reinforce yourself. But in the beginning, indulge yourself. The tension habit is tenacious: It takes concerted effort and a lot of reinforcement to break it.

Practicing Stress Management

Practice is essential to putting all the pieces of any complex skill together. Stress management can be practiced in the theater of the mind. Use your fantasies and your mental pictures. In your imagination, *see* yourself becoming aware of tension in your neck muscles, for example. Then, *hear* yourself intervening with your stress-reducing instructions, and *feel* yourself relaxing. Finally, *hear* yourself saying self-reinforcing sentences.

In a sense, during this mental rehearsal you are giving yourself "meta-instructions": "If I feel tense or think a stressful thought, then I will actively relax myself." The response is fast. In a tense situation you don't always have the wherewithal to stop, observe, and decide to relax. With mental rehearsal you can speed up the relaxation response time.

What to Practice

Looking back at the sample instructions for managing stress, you see there are four types of antecedents: tension in the muscles, stress thoughts, times you did not manage stress as successfully as you wanted to, and those in which you anticipate experiencing stress. Mentally practice managing stress in the presence of each of these antecedents.

There are two general types of mental rehearsals: mastery practice and coping practice. Mastery practice is essentially what comes to mind when you think of positive thinking: "I am a good salesperson" and "I am getting better and better" are examples of mastery practice. Coping practice, however, is more effective in managing stress. Whenever you learn a new skill, you invariably experience frustration and setbacks in the beginning. Prepare yourself for this by mentally rehearsing what you will say to yourself and what you will do when this happens.

When you first begin to practice, you may find it helpful to write down your instructions. Pick a specific situation in which you frequently experience stress. (For example, if you often experience tension in your forehead, the antecedent would be "tense forehead.") Now write down exactly how you will tel' yourself to relax. This instruction is the behavior you'll deliberately enact when you notice the tense forehead (antecedent); the pleasure of relaxation will be the positive consequence.

By deliberately practicing this sequence, you will learn that a tense forehead is an antecedent or a signal to relax. Imagine that you are a thermostat. When your early detection system senses tension in your forehead, your stress management system responds by instructing you to relax your forehead muscles, thereby lowering the tension level. To learn to do this, follow the small-step procedure. First, make sure you learn the instructions themselves. If you skip this step, you may end up ad-libbing and become even more tense. Then deliberately tense your forehead and use the instructions so that you can learn the behavioral sequence. Finally, practice in real life.

To practice coping with stress that has gotten out of control, select a past situation in which this has happened. Write down the instruction you would have liked to have given yourself at the time, then begin to relive the situation in your mind's eye and practice managing stress. Go easy on yourself. Begin with mildly stressful scenarios, and shape your ability to manage stress in small steps. As you develop skill, increase the stressfulness of the rehearsal scenarios.

When to Practice

The end of your relaxation exercise session is the best time to do your mental practice. Don't rush yourself—begin your fantasy work only after you have learned to achieve a deep level of relaxation. When you're relaxed, it is easier to focus your attention, and you become more suggestible. Practicing while completely relaxed becomes a mildly hypnotic suggestion.

Follow the same tensing and relaxing process you used when you learned to relax muscles. Allow yourself to experience a mild stress-producing scenario. Then mentally practice coping with it. For example, deliberately tense your neck muscles while picturing yourself having trouble closing a sale, then mentally hear your self-instructions while you relax your neck muscles. Or think of one of your habitual stress-producing thoughts while picturing yourself trapped in a traffic jam, then hear your self-instructions and see yourself relaxing in your car. When you can do this easily during your home sessions, slowly extend your mental rehearsals into your daily life. Mentally rehearse while commuting, when you're waiting on "hold" or riding the elevator, or during a solitary lunch. Consider taking relaxation breaks and skipping the coffee: Close your office door, turn off the lights, close your eyes, relax all your muscles, and enjoy the relaxation at the same time that you make stress management a natural part of your daily life.

The final step is actually confronting the stress trigger. Don't overdo it; set yourself up to succeed. Begin practicing stress management in situations that are mildly stressful. And remember, not all tension is bad: In a real-life situation, tension alerts us to dangers and prepares us to deal with the situation. The goal is to *control* tension, not to eliminate it entirely. You are learning to manage your stress. When it threatens to get out of control, actively reduce it to a manageable level. Controlled tension can be used to help you. It can be used as a motivator that prods you through projects you don't like. Debilitating tension interferes with your performance.

To get results, you need to master the skills at each step. So, when thinking of the parable of the tortoise and the hare, become the tortoise. It takes consistent and systematic effort: Don't race through the training, but master each step before going on to the next. Slow down and relax!

Controlling Mental Torture and Other Stress-Producing Fantasies

At one time or another, all of us inflict mental anguish upon ourselves. We punish ourselves with nagging admonitions to improve, berate ourselves with guilty thoughts, and endlessly replay scenarios in which we come out the loser. These are, of course, our own thoughts and images, yet they seem to perform independently and to take on an existence of their own. Just as you can learn to control the tension in your muscles, you can control mental tension by learning to shut out stress-producing thought processes. The procedure is relatively simple, but learning to use it once again requires consistent effort.

The basic principle is obvious. Think of something relaxing. Despite the sophistication and complexity of our brains, few of us can think of more than one thing during a particular moment. This means that while we are mentally abusing ourselves, we cannot focus our attention on important decisions or on more creative and productive thinking. It also means that if we deliberately engage in relaxing and pleasurable fantasies, we close out our destructive, nagging thoughts. Learning to control what you think begins with identifying what you enjoy thinking about, practicing these thoughts, and then using them when you want to relax your mind.

Learning to Use Your Fantasies

Until recently, fantasizing has been dismissed as useless day-dreaming. With the discovery of the right-left brain dichotomy, however, interest in right-brain activities such as fantasizing became legitimate. There is an impressive body of research into the functions of mental imagery. One consistent finding shows that mental practice can often substitute for actual physical practice of a skill! In other words, scientific experiments have revealed that if you imagine yourself skiing well your performance on the slopes is likely to improve. By the same token, when you replay failure experiences in your mind, you are actually practicing and learning behavior you probably prefer to forget. The important point is that mental rehearsal has a direct impact on your performance.

Like analytic thinking, mental imagery can be developed through specific exercises. But more often than not, this form of cognitive development has been ignored or downgraded. If this has happened to you, then you will need to teach yourself. Not only will this ability prove helpful for stress management, but it will increase creativity and problem solving as well as your enjoyment of many aspects of life.

The first step in imagery training is to be an active participant in your mental scenarios. A simple experiment will help you understand what to do. Close your eyes and imagine the following scene for 15 seconds: You are on a blanket at the beach on a beautiful summer day. What did you see? Probably the ocean in front of you. But did you add details to make the scene as vivid and as real as possible? What color was your towel? Who else was on the beach? Were there clouds in the sky? Did you hear the waves hitting the beach or the seagulls screeching? Did you feel the heat of the sun and the hot sand on your skin or smell the salt in the air?

Being an active participant means adding enough details to engage all your senses. Close your eyes and imagine the beach scene again, but this time experience the scene with *all* your senses. You may notice that one sense is more real than the others. This merely means that you have developed that mode of imagery more than the others. Did you notice the difference the second time? Details bring the scene to life and make it easier to focus all your attention. Here are some examples of practice scenes you can use to develop each imagery mode.

1. You are sitting in a meadow on a beautiful day. *See* the trees, grass, flowers, bugs, and sky.
2. You are making lemonade. *Smell* and *taste* a cut lemon.
3. You are playing catch with a friend. *Feel* the movement in your muscles as you catch the ball and throw it back.
4. You are skating at a public rink. *Hear* the sound of the skaters and of the children laughing. *Feel* yourself glide around the rink and brush against the other skaters. *See* the other skaters.

Practice these scenes during your next three or four home training sessions after you have completed the relaxation exercises. Each time you practice, add more details to the scene. Your goal is to involve yourself actively. Use the details to help you see, feel, smell, taste, and hear in your fantasy.

Your Antistress Scene

Create a list of scenes that are enjoyable and relaxing for you. Many people enjoy images of a beautiful day in the park or of a favorite spot in the forest. The scene doesn't have to be realistic; it can be pure fantasy. A participant in one of my stress management workshops liked the image of riding the air currents over Big Sur on a magic carpet. Don't rely on improvisation; write down your antistress scene and include as many sense-stimulating details as possible.

The next step is to practice your personal antistress scene. Once again, begin at home after relaxing. Add to your scene, making it as vivid as possible. Practice the antistress scene until it becomes a familiar, soothing ally. Then you can call on it to combat your mental stress. Practice during your daily routine until you have made this scene part of your spontaneous behavior. Periods of "dead time" (riding the bus, waiting for an appointment, or standing on line) are a perfect opportunity to do this.

Using Your Antistress Scene

Your goal is to purposefully call to mind your antistress scene in order to disrupt stress-producing thoughts and images. Of course, the major hurdle is stopping the thoughts long enough to switch on your antistress scene. A method called *thought-stopping* can help. A simple experiment demonstrates how this works: Call up a stress-producing image and dwell on it for about 10 seconds, then pause for a moment and shout out "Stop!" Now repeat the experiment, only this time silently say "Stop!" If you are like most people, you will have probably lost your train of thought temporarily. This momentary disruption is what you want: You have created a brief blank period during which you can switch your attention to your antistress scene. You must do this purposefully, because if you don't, worrisome thoughts will probably return. The more you have rehearsed your antistress scene, the easier the switch will be.

When you first begin using thought-stopping during your practice sessions (and later during your daily routine), the stressful thoughts may intrude on your relaxing scene. Expect this—old thought habits are difficult to break. As soon as you become aware of the unwanted thoughts, shout "Stop!" again and return to your antistress scene and experience it actively.

Mentally Preparing for a Stressful Event

As I mentioned earlier, research studies have shown that mental rehearsal has an impact on performance. Consider the person who, in anticipation of an important promotion interview, imagines all the blunders he or she could make. Not only do such individuals generate stress (which is certain to be inhibiting), but they also mentally rehearse just those behaviors they least want to perform. With this in mind, you should mentally rehearse behaviors that maximize your chances of performing the way you want to. This kind of rehearsal is called the *coping fantasy*. Prepare yourself for stressful events by purposefully overcoming setbacks and performing adequately in your fantasy scenarios. For example, candidates for promotion should imagine themselves as being relaxed and making impressive responses to difficult questions during the interview. They should hear specific troublesome questions and hear themselves making actual responses.

Whenever you face a pending stressful encounter, use the thought-stopping procedure to close out images of failure. Then switch to a scene in which you cope with the event and perform the way you want to. Here, too, active participation is important. Hear the words you want to say and see the actions you want to perform.

Inoculating Yourself Against the Stress of Unavoidable Losses and Setbacks

Every day, managers face decisions that involve potential costs and risks. Anticipating these losses, making a commitment, and then coping with the losses when they do materialize creates stress. The more critical the decision and the greater the potential loss, the more stress the decision maker is likely to experience.

Many managers cope with decision-related stress by refusing to think about unpleasant decisions that promise to bring future losses. They procrastinate or pass the responsibility for the decision to someone else. When these options are not available, they select the most acceptable solution and exaggerate its positive aspects. By doing this, they reduce stress temporarily, but later it will only become more intense when the feared negative consequences materialize. Too late the decision maker sees what could have been done to prevent or offset a serious setback. Irving Janis and Leon Mann, two decision-making researchers, call this postdecisional regret.[10] Ruminating over what you should have done creates stress and undermines self-confidence and esteem. In using your fantasies, you can develop foresight, by doing the following:

In the theater of the mind, project yourself into the future and imagine the positive and negative consequences of each decision alternative. When doing this you will probably notice an increase in tension. Use this helpful tension now to motivate yourself to seek out more information and better alternative actions that you can perform. Bring the postdecisional regret into the present *before* the decision.

For example, at 82, Frank's father found that his health was declining rapidly, and it was obvious that he would soon die. Frank found this thought intolerable and avoided thinking about it. "He's a tough old bird. I know he'll get better. He'll pull through. He always does. There's nothing to worry about. I'll see him at Christmas." When Frank's father died five weeks later, Frank was distraught. For months he regretted his inaction. "If only I had gone home for my vacation," he thought. "I could have gone to Hawaii any time. I could have told him how much I appreciated all he did for me. Why didn't I write to him? He was alone and had only my letters to look forward to." Frank's depression interfered with his work dramatically, and he nearly lost his job. If Frank had projected himself into the future when he had first learned of his father's illness, he might well have made different vacation plans. And had Frank allowed himself in his fantasy to become familiar with the inevitable loss of his father, he would have been able to cope better with the event when it actually happened.

Often people make poor decisions because they are not sufficiently motivated to seek out better alternatives. As soon as they find an acceptable choice, they seize upon it without forethought about the possible negative consequences. Then, when faced with the real consequences of poor decision making, they are tempted to renege on their commitment and reverse the decision. For instance, although Sally liked her job and her co-workers, she was impatient for promotion. When she began considering other positions, she received an immediate offer at a substantially higher salary. Elated, Sally accepted. She didn't think much about the fact that she would have to relocate. "I've always wanted to see the world. I've lived in this town all my life. Living in a big city will be exciting!" she told herself. But soon after starting her new job, Sally suffered intense regret. She was alone and friendless in a strange city and felt alienated from her new co-workers. In desperation she asked her old employer if she could return to her former position, but it had already been filled. Had Sally used mental imagery to explore her new job, she might have decided to continue her search until she found a suitable position in her home town.

This kind of "stress inoculation" procedure can improve the quality of your decisions and help you to adhere to your commitments. The procedure is particularly effective for any decision requiring you to suffer a short-term loss before you reap the long-term gains that constitute the main incentive for adopting that course of action. For example, Sally could have prepared herself for the social isolation she was about to experience by mentally rehearsing for it and developing a concrete plan of action to build a new social circle. By already experiencing in her mind the kinds of problems that would face her, she would have been more able to cope with the loss of her friends and probably would have suffered considerably less stress.

Of course, there are times when you must make a decision you don't want to make. By mentally rehearsing the consequences you can develop a plan of action for coping with unavoidable losses. A voter-mandated property-tax reduction meant that the community health center that Josette directed would suffer a dramatic drop in operating capital. Josette felt that she had no choice but to terminate several free services and to authorize staff salary cuts. She anticipated an outcry from clients and staff, and inoculated herself by mentally anticipating how she would handle them. She worked out a plan for presenting the cuts to the staff and community and for dealing with their anger. She then rehearsed this plan mentally. She reported that while she found the confrontations very unpleasant, she did not experience the magnitude of stress she had suffered in the past when she had to make other disagreeable announcements.

When you try this procedure, don't overdo it—remember, immunization is achieved through small doses. Restrict your stress inoculation session to only a few minutes, and at the end of each session use the thought-stopping procedure and your antistress scene to reduce your purposely induced stress.

Managing Anxiety and Fear

Unmanaged fear can interfere with performance and career advancement. Most of us retreat rather than confront fear, and in so doing give it more power. Yet it is difficult to do otherwise: Just thinking about a fearful confrontation is frightening, but unmanaged fear is constricting. It can interfere with and at times even prevent performance and career advancement.

Bill, for example, turned down a unique and attractive promotion. Why? Because as Western Regional Director, he would have to fly regularly to Hawaii, Japan, and the Philippines. Bill was afraid of flying—he experienced anxiety at the mere thought of a flight. Bill's unmanaged fear took precedence in his decision. Avoidance of flying was more important than the substantial salary increase, the opportunities for travel, and the increase in responsibility and prestige he would have gotten with the promotion.

As was shown in Chapter 1, anxiety and fear are learned respondent behaviors that occur in direct response to some stimulus. Through a process of pairing or classical conditioning, the person learns to react anxiously to a formerly neutral stimulus. It is important to realize that anxiety is learned, because that means it can be unlearned as well.

Consider this representation of the genesis of the fear of flying:

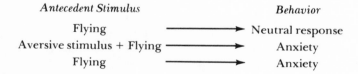

Antecedent Stimulus		*Behavior*
Flying	⟶	Neutral response
Aversive stimulus + Flying	⟶	Anxiety
Flying	⟶	Anxiety

Anxiety is learned through a process of association in which a neutral stimulus is paired with an aversive one. The aversive stimulus can be anything. With flying it might be an actual frightening experience in the air, or reading or hearing about air disasters, or taking a trip to an unpleasant place, or having to sit in flight next to someone whom you wish you could have avoided. The aversive stimulus can be anything that causes you to worry or to feel anxious. When you fly through a storm, for example, any stimulus present can become associated with the anxiety evoked by the rough flight. Merely being in a plane, thinking about the plane, and seeing the interior of the plane can later create anxiety during routine flights.

This process is insidious because of higher-order conditioning: Once a person, a thought, a place, an activity, or any stimulus that is not inherently frightening assumes stimulus control or the power to evoke anxiety, it also becomes capable of infecting other neutral stimuli that are present when you become anxious. For example:

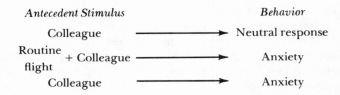

This model illustrates the way in which fear becomes contagious. A person who is afraid of flying will experience anxiety on routine flights, and any stimulus present during the flight can then become associated with flying and will assume the power to evoke anxiety.

For instance, Bill, who turned down the promotion, still had to fly occasionally. One time he and the sales manager, Murphy, flew to Los Angeles to participate in critical planning for overseas marketing of a filtration system. Before the trip Bill had had good rapport with Murphy, and except for Bill's intense anxiety, the flight was uneventful. After that, however, Bill noticed he felt mildly apprehensive around Murphy. It didn't occur to him that it was a hangover from the flight across the country. Rather, he began scrutinizing Murphy, looking for something to explain his anxiety. Of course, he discovered lots of things about Murphy that he found irritating: the way Murphy dressed, the way he interrupted, the way he laughed. Bill noticed something else, too—he lost interest in marketing the filtration system. Working on anything related to it became an effort, and as an explanation for his negative reaction, he began to look for flaws and shortcomings in the project itself. It never occurred to Bill that this negative reaction began with the anxiety from the flight that became associated with Murphy and the project.

Fear is insidious in another respect—it promotes avoidance behavior. Turning off anxiety is negatively reinforcing. Whatever we do to avoid or turn off anxiety, we are likely to do again. So you can see that anxiety becomes a trap: If you grit your teeth and confront it, the anxiety you experience may intensify your fear as well as infect any neutral stimulus that may be present. And if you try to avoid it, you insulate the fear and teach yourself a lot of counterproductive avoidance behaviors.

Desensitization

Desensitization is a systematic method for breaking the association between the antecedent stimulus and anxiety. It is aimed at eliminating the power of the feared stimulus—such as sitting in an airplane—to evoke anxiety. The association is broken by engaging in a behavior that prevents you from feeling anxious in the presence of the feared stimulus. There are many behaviors incompatible with anxiety—that is, behaviors that cannot be performed simultaneously with anxiety. (A discussion of incompatible behaviors can be found in Chapter 1.) These behaviors include eating, sexual responses,* problem solving (thinking about complex ideas), assertiveness, following instructions (focusing attention on something other than the feared stimulus), curiosity, and relaxation. The basic strategy behind desensitization is to gradually increase exposure to the feared stimulus while engaging in one of the incompatible behaviors. The procedure described here uses relaxation and self-instruction.[11]

The desensitization procedure requires that you remain relaxed as you gradually approach the feared stimulus. This process can be performed mentally, but whenever possible choose some real-life technique. There are three reasons why this is desirable. First, changes in real-life behavior typically lag behind changes made in fantasy. Second, imagination can rarely duplicate real-life experiences with all the sights, smells, sounds, tastes, and sensory richness. The success of desensitization depends on reconditioning the full array of stimuli that control the anxiety. Most importantly, real-life techniques allow for the learning of new behavior. For example, Frank becomes very anxious whenever he has to speak before a group, and avoids doing so whenever possible. Even if he were to suddenly get rid of his fear, he would still lack the skills necessary to give a dynamic, persuasive speech. The negative feedback he might receive could result in his relearning his fear. Therefore, whenever anxiety is accompanied by a deficiency in the skills necessary to function in the feared situation, you should work on getting rid of your fear and begin to practice the new behaviors required.

---

*It should be noted here that eating and sexual responses are often associated with anxiety because they are so frequently used to reduce anxiety. When an anxious person eats, for example, anxiety will be temporarily reduced. If this occurs frequently, a person could develop a problem with overeating.

Shaping results in a gradual approach to a particular situation, and thus helps you learn new behaviors while desensitizing your fear. Frank could use shaping to overcome his fear of public speaking. He might begin by reinforcing himself for speaking to two or three close friends on a topic he knows well. Then he could gradually increase the difficulty of the topic, the number of listeners, and the threat level of the audience. In this way he would teach himself speaking skills while he reduced his fear of speaking.

But there are times when it is not possible to use shaping techniques. Suppose Frank has to give a speech at a convention scheduled for two weeks from now. The time factor would make shaping unfeasible, so he could use fantasy desensitization to reduce and control his anxiety. When you cannot arrange your daily life so that you can gradually move up real-life shaping steps, fantasy techniques can be used to reduce your anxiety about higher levels of performance. There are five steps in desensitization:

1. Listing the feared situations.
2. Arranging the feared situations into a hierarchy.
3. Training yourself to relax.
4. Developing a relaxing scene.
5. Step-by-step reconditioning.

LISTING THE FEARED SITUATIONS

The first step is to identify the situations that evoke anxiety. Bill's nervousness, for example, was not limited to flying itself; he found the takeoff and landing particularly uncomfortable. He experienced anxiety when talking about a trip requiring flying, as well as when others talked about their flights. Packing, leaving the house for the airport, approaching the terminal, boarding the plane—all made Bill nervous. One way to cope with this problem is to write down each situation (related to the general fear) in which you experience anxiety. It is important that you include even those situations in which you experience only mild anxiety. Work on one fear at a time.

DEVELOPING YOUR HIERARCHY

A hierarchy is a ranked list of 10 to 20 situations that evoke anxiety. Order the situations you identified from the least to the most anxiety-producing. Don't worry about logic in your ranking—use your subjective experience of anxiety as your ruler. Think of your hierarchy as a kind of shaping ladder. Make sure the spacing between steps is about equal so that your progress up the hierarchy will be smooth. A step that is too big will cause you trouble—you will have difficulty exposing yourself to it while remaining relaxed.

The size of your steps can be checked with the SUDS technique. SUDS is shorthand for *subjective units of discomfort.* Assign a score of zero to a situation that would produce no anxiety whatsoever and a score of 100 to a situation that would produce panic or terror. Steps in your hierarchy should be no larger than 5 to 10 SUDS. If you have a large step in your hierarchy, break it into smaller steps by thinking of intermediate situations.

Developing a good hierarchy is crucial to the desensitization procedure. Make sure that you include the entire range of situations related to the general fear you are desensitizing. For Bill, an airline ad on TV might be mildly anxiety-provoking. Such mild situations are important in the beginning stages of desensitization. They are the first small steps in the ladder that will lead you out of your fear trap.

Ruth experienced considerable anxiety when she had to give a directive to anyone who was older than she. Betty, her secretary, was older than Ruth's mother. Each time Ruth contemplated giving Betty a directive, she experienced anxiety and found ways to avoid giving the directive. Here is Ruth's hierarchy:

1. Looking at a memo that requires giving Betty a directive.
2. Making a list of things to do for the day, some of which require directing Betty.
3. Directing Betty to give a specific message to people who call on the phone.
4. Passing Betty's area and seeing her idle.
5. Directing Betty to type rather than write out phone messages.
6. Looking at a draft of a report that must be typed.
7. Directing Betty to do routine photocopying.
8. Buzzing Betty on the intercom to call her into the office.
9. Entering Betty's area to give a directive.
10. Directing Betty to do a routine typing task.
11. Directing Betty to do a lengthy typing task.
12. Directing Betty to complete a task before going home.
13. Directing Betty to retype a letter containing an error.
14. Repeating a directive when Betty makes an excuse.
15. Directing Betty to be prompt in the morning.

LEARNING TO RELAX AND DEVELOPING A RELAXING SCENE

The next step is to learn to relax. (Follow the procedure described in the stress management section.) Your goal is to be able to recognize when you feel tense and to be able to relax your entire body. The success of your desensitization depends in large part on your ability to relax.

The procedure for developing a relaxing scene is the same as the one described for managing stress (your antistress scene). In fact, you can use the same relaxing scene to desensitize anxiety and to manage stress.

STEP-BY-STEP RECONDITIONING

To desensitize yourself, relax completely, then vividly imagine a situation from your hierarchy. It is important not to rush into the reconditioning stage prematurely. In order to desensitize yourself, you need to be able to identify small degrees of tension. As soon as you feel any tension whatsoever, you must begin to relax yourself completely.

Conduct your desensitization in a peaceful setting—the place where you did your relaxation training is best because it is already associated with relaxation. Each session should take about 20 minutes. Begin by relaxing completely, then imagine the first item on your hierarchy. Use all your senses and actively participate in your fantasy. See yourself confronting the feared situation and doing whatever you can to remain relaxed. You might take a deep breath, give yourself specific instructions, or tense and relax particular muscles. Any or all of these coping behaviors would be appropriate. After about 10 seconds, switch off the fearful scene and switch on your relaxing scene. Monitor your tension at all times, and if at any point you experience *any* tension, immediately switch to your relaxing scene. Continue to enjoy your relaxing scene for about 30 seconds until you are again completely relaxed. Then repeat the procedure by imagining the same situation from your hierarchy. When you can repeat the first hierarchy situation three times while you are completely relaxed, you will be ready to move to the next one. In this way, slowly proceed up your ladder. Begin each new session with the highest item on the hierarchy that you were able to imagine while relaxed.

Real-Life Reconditioning

Desensitizing yourself in real-life situations is like desensitizing yourself in your imagination, except that here you place yourself in the midst of the feared situation. As I said before, real-life techniques are more powerful, but they are also more difficult. Approaching the feared situation in your fantasy is relatively safe, no matter how anxiety-producing it may be, because nothing can actually happen to you. Confrontation in real life, however, is another matter, because you must deal with the actual feared situation.

It is very important that you give your real-life hierarchy a lot of thought, because your success depends on it—a step that is too large could be disastrous. It will be hard enough to place yourself in the feared situation, but if you attempt to move too rapidly up the hierarchy by taking large steps, you are very likely to experience anxiety. This will only strengthen the fear and discourage you from trying again, so take only small steps and proceed very slowly. Make sure you move on to the next step only after you have been able to remain completely relaxed at the former step. The objective is to place yourself in the feared situation while engaging in a behavior that blocks anxiety (a behavior incompatible with anxiety). For example, Bill might eat dinner at the airport several times, or while he's in flight he might look at the pictures in an erotic magazine.

Self-Instructions

Self-instruction can help you in two ways. First of all, when you are actually focusing your attention on following instructions, you can't be too preoccupied with the fear. So keep talking and tell yourself exactly what to do. Second, if you observe your thoughts when you encounter or think about encountering the feared situation, you will probably discover that you are actually giving yourself a lot of anxiety-producing instructions. For example, if you are entering an elevator and know that you fear closed places, you might hear yourself saying, "Oh no, I can't go in there. I'll fall to pieces!" By giving yourself positive instructions, you can block out these detrimental commands. Tell yourself to act, think, and feel the way you want to. Here are some examples of self-instructions that will help you manage fear.

Negative Instruction: "Oh no, I can't face it. I'm tongue-tied."
Positive Instruction: "Stop! I can do it. Just take a deep breath and calm down . . . That's it. Breathing smoothly. Now on the count of three I'm going to raise my hand to speak. One . . . two . . . three." (An example of using thought-stopping and the relaxation command followed by instructions on a specific behavior to perform.)

Negative Instruction: "My heart is starting to pound."
Positive Instruction: "I should expect physiological signs of fear. I'm confronting something frightening to me. It means I'm alert and prepared to cope. Just relax . . . relax . . . relax. . . . That's it. Good." (Most people experience physical signs of tension in situations when they must perform. But overly fearful people take this as validation that they are afraid, and then the fear escalates.)

Negative Instruction: "They're all looking at me. I'm going to make a fool of myself."

Positive Instruction: "Yeah, and I'm looking at them. Now relax and follow your plan. Yes, just relax. . . . There's nothing to worry about. I know exactly what to do. First, I'm going to count all the people wearing red. Then I'm going to count the number of men wearing ties." (Having a plan gives you confidence—you know exactly what you're going to do. It helps you to feel more in control, which in turn helps you control your anxiety. This is also an example of using instructions to divert your attention from the feared stimulus: people looking at you. Counting and multiplying, drawing complex charts, and similar tasks require considerable attention, which is incompatible with anxiety.)

Negative Instruction: "Oh no, there goes the seat belt light. These planes are miserable. I can't stand it. I'm going to freak out!"

Positive Instruction: "Ignore the plane! Look at the stewardesses. First, I'll pick out the one I think is sexiest. Then, I'll have an erotic fantasy. She'll never know!" (Here sexual arousal is used as the incompatible behavior.)

You might begin with fantasy desensitization: Give yourself instructions each time you approach the feared situation on your mental stage. This will give you practice in thinking the thoughts you want to think when you are actually in the presence of the feared situation, because you will have mentally rehearsed how you will act, how you will think, and how you will feel.

A lot of the instructions sound artificial and contrived. Don't worry about this; you won't have to use them forever, although they will be helpful in breaking your old fear habit, and once that has happened, you won't need the instructions.

Building Self-Confidence

Self-confidence is usually high on the list of qualities sought in executives, managers, and supervisors—and rightly so: The confident person seems to perform better and to do so with ease. An implicit requisite of confidence is success: But paradoxically, lack of confidence makes success difficult, if not impossible. So to be more successful, build your confidence. It's like the old adage: The rich get richer and the poor get poorer. Those who are confident succeed in their endeavors and become even more confident; those who lack confidence stumble and barely get by, feeling less able to tackle the next challenge.

What exactly is self-confidence? It is a belief in your ability to accomplish an objective, a feeling of certainty that you can handle the task at hand. What you feel and say to yourself about your ability to perform has a powerful impact upon your subsequent performance. In many ways, your past performance influences what you say to yourself. You can *choose* to focus on successes or failures in your past. People who feel less confident usually overemphasize past failures and disappointments.

Self-confidence is manifested in all four behavioral modalities: actions, mental pictures, physical sensations, and sentences. Positive changes in any one of these modalities tend to prompt positive changes in others.

Building Confidence Through Actions

Goal accomplishment. Take the proverb "Nothing succeeds like success" as your guide—create successes in your life. The shaping technique can help you: Break down long-range objectives into small subgoals, so that each step toward your objective is small enough for you to accomplish with ease. For example, in writing this book I might say to myself: "Today I will write the section on how to build confidence." I sit down to begin and find I can't get started. "This step must be too big," I conclude, so I break the task down further and decide to make an outline. When that's accomplished, I then agree to write the section on goal accomplishment. Completing each small task is an accomplishment. The more I accomplish, the more I believe I can accomplish what I set out to do. I have built up my self-confidence (and have also gotten some work done!).

Begin to build your confidence through achieving small successes. Use the self-contracting procedure to define your small steps. This will clarify exactly what and how much you need to do. Then reinforce yourself when you succeed, so that eventually (or perhaps very quickly) those around you will begin to notice and to acknowledge your successes. ("You seem to get so much done, Bev, I just don't know *how* you do it.") Acknowledgment from significant others is powerful reinforcement: Not only does it encourage us to keep on succeeding, but it also supplies evidence on which to base our confidence. But don't wait for recognition; if you do, it may never come. You gain confidence by accomplishing goals, and the easiest way to do that is through small action steps.

Learning new skills. Lack of confidence is realistic if you lack the skill to do something you want to do. Of course, it is possible to "learn while doing," but it requires a lot of confidence to avoid becoming demoralized by the inevitable errors and setbacks. It's like the dilemma of the job candidate: "All the employers want experience. But how can I get experience when no one will give me a job?" Formal training is one way to solve this dilemma. Why suffer through trial and error and thereby risk undermining your shaky confidence? If you don't know how to manage time (or make a good decision or give a directive or speak assertively), then seek out training. Most community colleges offer a myriad of inexpensive training workshops and courses. When these are unavailable, you can use self-help books. But simply reading or attending a workshop is not enough; use the techniques described in this book to set up your personal training program. When you have the skills necessary to perform, your confidence will grow.

Act "as if" or fake it and you'll make it. Our opinions of ourselves are in large part determined by what we see ourselves doing and how others respond to us. Suppose, for example, that you observe Dean speaking very hesitantly about an idea he has. What conclusions might you draw about Dean and about his idea? What conclusions might Dean be making about himself? How likely is it that Dean's idea will be accepted?

Theater directors emphasize enacting specific behaviors. By acting *as if*, the actor creates a mood and projects emotions. In her autobiography,[12] Liv Ullman describes how she creates a critical moment in the life of Jenny, the main character of Ingmar Bergman's film *Face to Face:*

> Today we shall film the suicide scene. . . . Ingmar gives me loose directions and says, "Now we will see what happens."
> Action.
> I don't know how I will do it. I can hardly take an aspirin without coughing and clearing my throat. Now I have to swallow a hundred pills.

Miss Ullman doesn't try to *feel* like Jenny; she begins by acting as if she *is* Jenny committing suicide:

> Jenny arranges the bedcovers, fluffs up two pillows, and fixes them nicely so that her head can rest on them, pulls down the shade, locks the door, straightens out the covers once more, sits down on the edge of the bed, fills a glass with soda, opens the medicine bottle, puts two, three pills in her hand, swallows with a little difficulty. . . .

Notice how she enacts *specific* behaviors: pulls down the shade, locks the door, swallows the pills one by one.

> Next time there are more in the palm. She stuffs them into her mouth, drinks. Suddenly Jenny's hand begins to tremble so violently that the glass knocks against my teeth—and while *Jenny* is trying to take her life *I* know how it feels.

She creates the *feeling* by acting "as if. . . ."

> Jenny and I are doing it together. I experience it at the same time as I am standing outside, watching. I am living through a suicide . . . it only becomes theater when I turn my face towards the wall and *do not* die.

One way to build self-confidence is to act as if you *are* confident! Of course, at first it will feel awkward and contrived, but just as Liv Ullman created the feelings associated with suicide, you can create the feelings of self-confidence. (Although this particular example is of a suicide scene, the principle of acting "as if" applies to all kinds of behavior, and it is important to stress the generally positive applications of this principle.) Attention to specific behaviors is important. If you command yourself to "act as if I am confident," you won't know what to do. It's better to say, "I'll walk in briskly, smile at Jones, lay my materials on his desk, and then casually light a cigarette."

The first task in acting as if you are confident is to identify confident behaviors. Identify one or two people who project the kind of confidence you desire, and study their *actions.* How do they walk and sit? What do they say? How do they dress? Detail is essential. Observe the posture, gestures, and voice quality. After you have defined several discrete behaviors, deliberately *act.* Don't worry about feeling confident; just concentrate on enacting specific behaviors. Liv Ullman says, "What I do on stage cannot be based on *my* feelings alone, for then I might be fantastically good one evening, but because it was all *my* emotion, I wouldn't know what made me laugh and cry, and I couldn't reproduce it at the next performance."

Once again, use the behavior change procedures described in Chapter 2, and teach yourself confident behaviors in the same way that you would any important project—work on it bit by bit. Through consistent effort and small steps you will learn self-confidence.

Using Mental Pictures to Build Confidence

Your fantasies are a powerful resource for building confidence. Start off by reviewing your past and identifying those situations when you felt most confident, and reenact these situations on your mental stage. This will have a number of positive benefits. First, by mentally observing your performance in that situation, you can identify specific confident actions. Use this data as a guide for what to do in similar future situations. Second, by reenacting your confident performances you are rehearsing the behaviors you want to increase. This mental rehearsal is often as valuable a learning aid as actual practice is. Finally, deliberately observing your self-confidence will help you develop a positive self-image. Don't allow yourself to be seduced into criticizing these past performances: Focus on your successes, relive them on your mental stage, and give yourself the positive reinforcement you deserve. An alternative is to select another person as a role model. Put this person on your mental stage, and observe his or her behaviors carefully. Then imagine yourself acting as if you were this person.

Mentally acting out successful behaviors is a *mastery* fantasy; a *coping* fantasy can help you learn and grow from less successful experiences and prepare you to cope with real problems in the future. The setting on your mental stage can be either a past or anticipated problem situation. Mentally act out the undesirable behavior. What happened? Which of your behaviors produced problems? You will want to reduce the frequency of these. Develop an alternative method for handling the situation, and enact this on your mental stage. What happened? What behaviors worked for you? Which ones didn't work? Continue this process until you can see yourself overcoming the problem, and do not allow yourself to continually reenact failure: You would be practicing the very behaviors you want to eliminate, and would thereby erode your feelings of confidence as well as your self-image. Use the self-instruction procedure to mentally rehearse how you want to act in the future.

Building Confidence Through Relaxation

Excessive tension or anxiety is the enemy of confidence. High anxiety inhibits performance and thinking; on the other hand, moderate tension enhances performance: It makes us physically alert and ready to act. If you are observant, you will probably notice that when you *act* confidently, your tension level is moderate and manageable. You can accelerate this process and increase the quality of your performance by purposefully relaxing yourself, during both your mental rehearsals and your real-life performances. By using the procedure for physical relaxation described earlier in this chapter, you can simultaneously manage stress and build confidence.

Talk Yourself into Confidence

What you say to yourself about yourself is very important. Think of your self-image as being the sum of how you see yourself (your images of yourself) and how you describe yourself to yourself. Unfortunately, in our formative years many of us were subjected to a lot of criticism from parents, teachers, and other children. All too often we believed the criticism and learned to level it silently against ourselves. By doing so we became our own worst enemies. We know our own areas of sensitivity better than anyone. Our own self-criticism can be more devastating than any made by others. Even when the criticism is valid, it does not deserve overemphasis. When you evaluate yourself objectively and set out to correct problem behaviors, self-criticism is productive. But repeating a criticism over and over becomes self-punishment and serves no productive purpose. It is one of the worst things you can do to yourself. Saying positive things to yourself about yourself builds confidence.

Many times we are unaware of our negative thoughts. So the first step is to bring these thoughts into awareness by observation. How often do you say negative things about yourself? Positive things? You can use a golf counter to collect data on your thoughts. Keep a record of how often you criticize yourself and plot this data on a graph just as you would with any other problem behavior. This is your baseline.

You can increase or decrease thoughts or self-statements with the same procedures you use for modifying overt behaviors. For example, you might begin by writing down each negative self-statement. Translate each of these into a positive, productive self-statement, then write each positive self-statement on an individual file card. Think of these positive self-statements as *low-probability behaviors.*

Use the Premack principle of reinforcement to increase the frequency of your positive self-statements—that is, make engaging in a high-probability behavior (such as smoking a cigarette) contingent on your thinking a positive self-statement. Each time you feel like smoking, use this feeling as a cue for reading the positive self-statement on the first file card. Then smoke the cigarette. In this way, the desire to smoke becomes an antecedent cue for thinking a positive self-statement, and actually smoking the cigarette becomes the reinforcing consequence. Other high-probability behaviors include drinking coffee, talking on the phone, and daydreaming (engaging in a pleasurable fantasy). You might attach the deck of positive self-statements to your phone and each time you have to make a call, first read a positive self-statement, then make the call.

It is helpful to include a blank card in your deck. When the blank card comes up, you must generate a new positive self-statement and write it on the card before engaging in the high-probability behavior. This will help you to alter your selective perception. When you know the blank card is there and that you must come up with another positive, you will be more inclined to begin looking for positives. A lot of people are in the habit of ignoring the positives and selectively focusing on the negative features in each situation; people who appear more confident generally look for their successes. The file card technique may sound contrived and artificial, but it is amazingly successful. Try it for a week or two and count the frequency of your spontaneous positive self-statements. They will probably increase, and as they do increase you will begin to feel more confident.

Some people have difficulty generating positive statements about themselves. An exercise called "success stories" can help. Here are some examples of different people's "success stories," the personal strengths that they illustrate, and some positive self-statements that the individuals were able to make after having discovered those personal strengths. After reading the stories here, fill in the blanks and describe a success story of your own, identify the personal strength revealed by that story, and use that strength to make a positive self-statement.

Success	*Strength*	*Positive Self-Statement*
"I went to night school for five years and earned a master's degree."	Persistence	"I can persist in something that is important to me."
"I was afraid to speak in groups so I enrolled in a public speaking class."	Problem solving	"When I have a problem I take active steps to solve it."
"I raised two children."	Dependable	"I can be depended upon to carry out my responsibilities."
"I tried Joe's suggestion and it worked."	Open	"I can be open to others and learn from them."
"I designed a new sales report form."	Creative	"I can be creative in solving procedural problems."
"I tuned up my car."	Competent	_____ _____
"I get to work each day on time."	Reliable	_____ _____

"I saved the department   ——————————   ———————————
$2,000 by getting   ———————————
several bids."

——————————————   ——————————   ———————————
——————————————   ———————————
——————————————

Of course, the things you say about yourself to others are also important. If you present yourself to others as incompetent, lacking in confidence, and a failure, then those around you will see these traits in you (their selective perception) and treat you accordingly.

The way you present yourself is particularly important when you meet someone for the first time, because first impressions can be very difficult to change. In a job interview, for example, talk about what you have done and can do, not what you haven't done. It is astounding how many people say things like, "I don't have a college degree, but . . ." or "I haven't worked in a hotel, but. . . ." The interviewer often doesn't listen after the "but." It is much better to say, "I have a lot of practical experience that you can't get in school," or "I developed a new sales strategy, and this experience would be helpful in the leisure industry because. . . ."

There are many strategies for increasing your positive self-statements. Another method is to select a person whom you view as confident and to ask yourself what you think this person would be thinking in a situation that requires confidence. Write down the exact words. Sybel, a participant in one of my workshops, wrote, "She's the master of her ship. She is confident in her ability and knows she can do what she sets out to do. She refuses to give in to fear or failure. She is realistic and doesn't get discouraged if she doesn't do something perfectly the first time. She learns from each attempt and tries again. She concentrates upon what she has done well in each situation." Now rewrite the monologue in the first person. "I am the master of my ship. I am confident in my ability and know I can do what I set out to do. . . ." Write this on a file card and use the Premack principle of reinforcement. Sybel used driving her car as a high-probability behavior. Each time she got in her car, she read the monologue before starting the car.

Several times I have suggested using self-instructions to facilitate your behavior change. Self-instructions can help you in building confidence as well. Instruct yourself to act "as if" and guide yourself through the exact behaviors you want to enact. Instruct yourself to use coping fantasies, to relax, and to say positive statements to yourself. Use the thought-stopping technique to cut off unproductive thoughts and images. And be a helpful, supportive, and positive instructor. Make self-reinforcing statements to yourself for progress, however small it may seem. Give yourself lots of pats on the back: Not only does it feel good, but it will help you accomplish your goal—a new, confident you.

Other Important Manager Behaviors

It is interesting to know what others consider crucial to successful job performance. In intensive interviews with 250 corporate leaders, Michael Maccoby[13] found the following qualities to be important to them:

Qualities of the Head	*Qualities of the Heart*
Ability to take the initiative	Independence
Satisfaction in creating something new	Loyalty to fellow workers
Self-confidence	Critical attitude to authority
Coolness under stress	Friendliness
Cooperation	Sense of humor
Pleasure in learning something new	Openness, spontaneity
Pride in performance	Honesty
Flexibility	Compassion
Open-mindedness	Generosity
	Idealism

The dismaying aspect of these findings is that the work environment stimulates the development of only some of these qualities. Specifically, Maccoby's research revealed that the qualities in the first column—which he calls qualities of the head—are encouraged (reinforced) by work, whereas those of the heart are not. They remain underdeveloped and dormant.

NOTES

1. For an in-depth step-by-step procedure to change your own behavior consult David L. Watson and Roland G. Tharp, *Self-Directed Behavior: Self-Modification for Personal Adjustment* (Monterey, Calif.: Brooks/Cole, 1972).
2. AMPS was developed by Sharon Bower and is presented here with her permission. See Sharon A. Bower and Beverly A. Potter, *Instructor's Manual for Asserting Yourself: A Practical Guide for Positive Change* (Reading, Mass.: Addison-Wesley, 1976), p. 21.

3. Michael Maccoby, *The Gamesman* (New York: Simon and Schuster, 1976), p. 202.
4. For in-depth information on the effects of stress please consult the Suggested Readings.
5. Irving L. Janis and Leon Mann, *Decision Making: A Psychological Analysis of Conflict, Choice and Commitment* (New York: The Free Press, 1977).
6. T.H. Holmes and R.H. Rahe, "The Social Readjustment Rating Scale," *Journal of Psychosomatic Research,* Vol. II (1967), pp. 213–218.
7. Adapted with permission from Gerald Rosen, *The Relaxation Book: An Illustrated Self-Help Program* (Englewood Cliffs, N.J.: Prentice-Hall, 1977).
8. This exercise was adapted with permission from Tom Coates and Carl E. Thoresen, *How to Sleep Better: A Drug-Free Program for Overcoming Insomnia* (Englewood Cliffs, N.J.: Prentice-Hall, 1977), pp. 79–80.
9. Adapted with permission from David Meichbaum, *Cognitive-Behavior Modification* (New York: Plenum Press, 1977), pp. 166–167. The table format was adapted from Coates and Thoresen, ibid., p. 80.
10. Irving L. Janis and Leon Mann, *Decision Making: A Psychological Analysis of Conflict, Choice and Commitment* (New York: The Free Press, 1977).
11. Techniques for using other incompatible behaviors to desensitize anxiety are described in Manual Smith, *Kicking the Fear Habit* (New York: Dial Press, 1977).
12. Reprinted with permission from Liv Ullman, *Changing* (New York: Alfred A. Knopf, 1977), pp. 255, 276–277.
13. Michael Maccoby, *The Gamesman* (New York: Simon and Schuster, copyright 1976 by Michael Maccoby), p. 185. Reprinted by permission of Simon and Schuster, a Division of Gulf & Western Industries.

SUGGESTED READINGS

The Impact of Stress
Benson, Herbert, *The Relaxation Response.* New York: Morrow, 1976.
Miller, Emmett E., and Lueth, Deborah, *Feeling Good: How to Stay Healthy.* Englewood Cliffs, N.J.: Prentice-Hall, 1978.
Pelletier, Kenneth, *Mind as Healer, Mind as Slayer: A Holistic Approach to Preventing Stress Disorders.* New York: Delta, 1977.
Seligman, Martin E., *Helplessness: On Depression, Development, Death.* San Francisco, Calif.: Freeman, 1975.

Managing Anxiety and Fear
Rosen, Gerald, *The Relaxation Book: An Illustrated Self-Help Program.* Englewood Cliffs, N.J.: Prentice-Hall, 1977.
Smith, Manual, *Kicking the Fear Habit.* New York: Dial Press, 1977.

Self-Change Strategies
Coates, Tom, and Thoresen, Carl E., *How to Sleep Better: A Drug-Free Program for Overcoming Insomnia.* Englewood Cliffs, N.J.: Prentice-Hall, 1977.

Lazarus, Arnold, *In the Mind's Eye: The Power of Imagery for Personal Enrichment.* New York: Rawson Associates, 1977.

Lewinsohn, Peter M., Munoz, Ricardo F., Youngren, Mary Ann, and Zeiss, Antoinette M., *Control Your Depression.* Englewood Cliffs, N.J.: Prentice-Hall, 1978.

Mahoney, Michael J., *Self-Change: Strategies for Solving Personal Problems.* New York: W.W. Norton, 1979.

Shapiro, Deane H., *Precision Nirvana.* Englewood Cliffs, N.J.: Prentice-Hall, 1978.

Silva, Jose, and Miele, Philip, *The Silva Mind Control Method.* New York: Simon and Schuster, 1977.

Sommer, Robert, *The Mind's Eye: Imagery in Everyday Life.* New York: Delta, 1978.

Watson, David L., and Tharp, Roland G., *Self-Directed Behavior: Self-Modification for Personal Adjustment.* Monterey, Calif.: Brooks/Cole, 1972.

4

Managing
Personnel Selection

Personnel selection is a guessing game, an attempt to predict a candidate's future performance from the evidence gathered during the interview. Hiring is the point of greatest control, yet this vital decision is frequently made in a haphazard manner. Companies utilizing the type of evaluation suggested herein are more likely to select individuals who perform well and remain with the company longer. If high turnover is a problem in your company, scrutinize your hiring procedures before reshuffling management or investing in expensive training and communication workshops. You may be hiring the wrong people and expecting management to shape them into the right people.

At the core of the personnel selection process is the interview. Although many professionals such as lawyers, psychologists, and personnel officers spend much of their time interviewing, few use good interview techniques. Good interview techniques provide an efficient method for gathering information when one has little prior information. This chapter reviews the techniques for gathering information in order to evaluate and select the candidate most likely to perform on the job.[1]

General Principles

Efficient interviewing is grounded in several important principles. The more you as an interviewer adhere to the basic principles, the more likely you will be to obtain objective on-target information in a short period of time.

ESTABLISH RAPPORT

A job interview is threatening to every candidate to some degree because you as interviewer have the power to accept or reject that person. Consequently, expect candidates to be at least somewhat uncomfortable and anxious. It is in the best interest of the company that you make efforts to put candidates at ease. Not only will the interview be easier to conduct, but the candidates will be more likely to present themselves well.

Each interviewer has a unique style for helping candidates relax. Some like to begin with a few casual comments. Care should be taken, however, to limit such "social conversation" to only two or three minutes, or the interview can become sidetracked. In general, give your undivided attention and listen carefully to show that you are genuinely interested in the candidate. Take measures to prevent interruptions. Your general demeanor can help. A relaxed but attentive posture and good eye contact will communicate interest and help reduce tension.

DON'T TALK TOO MUCH

The primary objective is to gather as much information as possible in a short period of time about the candidate's skills, experience, and work behavior. When you are talking you are not gathering information. If you find yourself talking more than about 20 percent of the time, this is a signal that you are not using good techniques or that the interview has drifted into a two-way conversation.

MAINTAIN CONTROL

At all times you should be in command of the interview—that is, you should determine what topics are covered. If you lose control, important areas of inquiry can be missed or inadequately covered and the candidate will probably direct the interview away from areas of inexperience, potential problems, or past failures. Such an interview is obviously biased and incomplete. Maintain control by keeping the interview on target. Cut off irrelevant rambling and bring the candidate back to the issue at hand.

Don't Be Interviewed

Gathering information and giving information are two different processes. While interviewing or gathering information, don't be sidetracked into answering questions or giving information. This does not mean that you never answer questions; rather, maintain control and determine when to gather information and when to give information. It is highly desirable for the candidate to ask questions and receive information about the company and the position. The important point is that while giving information you have ceased interviewing. Answering questions whenever they are asked greatly increases the probability of losing control. That is, you are taking the risk that the candidate's question will shift the interview off target or that an area of inquiry might be prematurely terminated.

Don't ignore or abruptly cut off questions, however. This only undermines rapport and denies the candidate's right to evaluate the company. Rather, acknowledge the question and request that it be held off until a later point. For example, "That's a good question, but before I answer it I want to finish discussing your experience. If I forget to bring it up again, please remind me."

Avoid Leading Questions

A leading question is one that implies the desired answer. Even the most naive candidate will realize that an affirmative reply to the question "Are you looking for responsibility?" is probably the "right" one. There is simply no way to objectively evaluate the candidate's response when the question is biased. The question "How do you feel about responsibility?" is an improvement, but once again the interviewer has introduced the issue of responsibility. An astute candidate can use the context of the question to "figure out" the best answer. A better question would be, "What are you looking for in a job?" This gives the candidate no clue as to what you are looking for. If the candidate brings up the issue of responsibility, you can feel more confident in assuming that this is what the candidate is seeking.

Don't Jump to Conclusions

One of the most dangerous things you can do is to jump to conclusions. It is very difficult to recognize when one is actually drawing a conclusion on the basis of inadequate information. Stereotypes are one source. It is easy to assume that young people are irresponsible; that older people are rigid; that women will leave work to have children; that minorities are lazy; that Germans are meticulous; and so forth. These are all conclusions based on predetermined ideas that probably have little to do with the particular candidate being interviewed.

Jumping to conclusions is not restricted to such obvious stereotypes, however. Mark Snyder, a University of Minnesota psychologist, studied 10-minute first-meeting telephone conversations between men and women.[2] Using photographs, Snyder led the men to believe that their female conversation partners were either attractive or unattractive. Snyder found that the men formed preconceived expectations of the women on the basis of the photographs, and after the conversations gave different assessments of the women who they thought were attractive. In both cases the men stated that the "attractive" women were more sensitive, kind, interesting, strong, poised, modest, sociable, and outgoing than the "unattractive" women.

Snyder then had judges who had not seen the pictures listen to tape recordings of just the women and just the men, and then "rate" these people. The ratings indicated that the women who had been presented as attractive actually acted differently from those who had been presented as unattractive! The "attractive" women were rated as more confident and animated and were said to like the men with whom they spoke. The men also acted differently: Those who thought they had spoken to attractive women were rated as more sociable, interesting, independent, bold, outgoing, humorous, and socially adept.

What this study suggests is that stereotypes or expectations not only affect opinions and actions toward others, but the way others act as well. In short, expectations become self-fulfilling prophecies: Others *become* the expectation. And all of this occurs at an unconscious level. The implication for interviewing is that if you believe, for example, that a man would be more appropriate for an engineering position than a woman would be, then not only are you more likely to perceive male candidates as more qualified, but they will be more likely to present themselves better during the interview than would the female candidates! The reason for this is that through your questions and responses, you will be more likely to draw out the qualifications of the men than those of the women.

Another source of assumption is general, vague statements. What does a candidate mean who says "I want a job with potential"? For interviewers, vague statements can be like Rorschach ink-blot tests: You see and hear what you expect. Language itself can lead to erroneous assumptions. A word or phrase may not have the same meaning for you as it does for the candidate. What is meant by "It was a soft job"? It could possibly mean that the candidate worked very little, or that the job was very easy, or that the benefits were good, or that there was little stress. Making assumptions and jumping to conclusions is a subtle process difficult to counter. The first step is to challenge conclusions, and the second step is to get specific information.

GET SPECIFIC INFORMATION

Specific information about experiences, skills, and work habits is essential to selecting the candidate most suitable for the position. Each time a candidate makes a vague or confusing statement or you catch yourself drawing a conclusion, ask questions that will elicit specific information. The more specific the information you gather, the more confidence you can place in your conclusions and decisions. Consider this interview with a candidate for a sales position:

Interviewer: Tell me about your last position. (*Vague inquiry*)

Candidate: Oh, it was a great job! I was an agent for Bold Travel. I set up exclusive tours for special groups like dentists or nurses. With tours, you know, there's always some crisis like an airline strike and I'd have to work around it and pull everything together. (*Interviewer did not get specific information.*)

Interviewer: Sounds like you're good at coordinating. (*Interviewer jumped to conclusions.*)

Candidate: Oh, yes!

Interviewer: Do you enjoy working with people? (*Leading question*)

Candidate: Yes. That's why I want to go into sales. Each person is different and you learn a lot about human nature and yourself, too. You have to know just the right way to approach someone if you want to get the sale.

Interviewer: Why did you leave Bold?

Candidate: Well, there was a shake-up and they let several people go. And that brings me to an important question. What are the chances that this position will last longer than the year advertised? I'm very interested in job security.

Interviewer: There's a good chance. If we expand, then the person in this position will help set up the sales department in the new office. (*Interviewer lost control and is being interviewed.*)

Candidate: That sounds great! When will a decision be made?
Interviewer: We'll know in four to six months. (*Interviewer is being interviewed.*)
Candidate: Where will the branch be located?
Interviewer: In Southern California. Can you relocate?
Candidate: That's no problem.
Interviewer: What sales experience have you had?

This brief example shows how easily an interviewer can accept vague information, jump to conclusions, and lose control of the interview by answering questions immediately.

Effective Interviewing Techniques

Utilization of the following interview techniques enables interviewers to adhere to the basic principles and to gather information rapidly and efficiently.

ACTIVE LISTENING

Active listening is a technique that greatly aids in establishing rapport. A variety of verbal responses such as "uh huh," "yeah," or "hmmm" and nonverbal responses such as nodding the head, smiling, making gestures, and eye contact communicate interest in what the candidate says. Use active listening throughout the interview whenever the candidate is giving meaningful information. Active listening provides feedback to the candidate and says, "You are on target."

REPEAT

The repeat technique is simple. Repeat a key word, or echo it with a slight inflection. For example, if the candidate says, "I'm looking for a job with potential," you can reply, "Potential?" Candidates will almost always amplify their remarks when you repeat the word. Use the repeat to clarify a general or vague word or phrase. Because candidates usually talk in more depth about a repeated word, you can use the repeat to unobtrusively guide or direct the interview. Suppose a candidate says, "My professional ratings were OK." If you say, "Ratings?," the candidate will probably explain what the ratings were and how they were conducted. If you repeat the "OK?," candidates will probably explain what their own ratings were. In addition to clarifying vague or general comments, the repeat can be used to clarify the meaning of technical as well as slang words.

PROBE

Although the probe appears commonplace, it is a technique that many interviewers have difficulty learning to use. Very simply, the probe is an open-ended question that begins with "how," "when," "who," "what," "in what way," or "which." These interrogatives put pressure on the candidate to clarify and elaborate a particular point. For example, if the candidate says, "The conditions at my former job were terrible," you can reply, "In what way were they terrible?" Or, if a candidate remarks, "Managing apartments was a valuable experience," you can ask, "What aspect was valuable?"

Questions that begin with "Do you . . . ," "Don't you . . . ," "Are you . . . ," and so forth, should be avoided because they are closed questions—that is, they elicit a yes or no response. Interviewers who habitually use a lot of closed questions often find themselves doing most of the talking. The interviewer is pressured into continually thinking of more questions which the candidate can answer with a very brief agreement or disagreement. This is inefficient because the interviewer elicits little information from each question. The second and more serious drawback of closed questions is that they are almost always leading questions. Recall that a leading question implies the desired answer.

In using the probe, avoid the interrogative "why" whenever possible. Questions beginning with "why" imply that the candidate should justify his or her feelings and actions, and can put a person on the defensive. This obviously has a negative effect on rapport. If you monitor your conversations and interviews, you'll probably be surprised by how frequently you ask, "Why?" The reason many interviewers have difficulty using the probe is that "why" and "do-you" questions are so habitual in our culture. However, with practice you can become comfortable and adept at substituting open-ended questions.

SILENCE

At first glance, silence hardly seems like a technique for gathering information, yet there are times when it works well. Most people become uncomfortable being silent in the presence of someone they don't know well, and will break the silence by talking. Silence used judiciously at key points can be an effective technique to encourage a candidate to talk. You can best use silence when the candidate is speaking relevantly and then pauses or stops. Resist the tendency to leap in with a question; simply remain silent. The candidate will generally resume talking about the topic at hand. Use active listening in conjunction with silence, and the candidate will get the message: "I'm listening. I want you to go on." The period of silence should be brief, however; otherwise, you run the risk of making the candidate feel uncomfortable. Likewise, silence is not a good technique to use with a candidate who is overly anxious or hostile. Silence under these conditions can escalate the tension, making the interview an ordeal for both of you.

CHECKOUT

There are three checkout techniques, two aimed at the content of the candidate's statements and one aimed at feelings. The *specific checkout*, like the probe and repeat, is a technique for clarifying and getting specific information. Suppose, for example, that the candidate says, "It was a good job." Such a statement can refer to a variety of factors such as salary, working conditions, type of work, co-workers, and ambience.

To use a specific checkout, formulate a hypothesis about one specific factor that the candidate may have enjoyed about the job and then check it out in a tentative manner, such as "Do you mean you liked the people you worked with?" If you're correct, the candidate will agree, and you can then feel confident in your conclusion. Most people find it disconcerting to be misunderstood and will become very specific and detailed in their attempt to have a listener understand what they have said. For this reason, if your checkout is incorrect because you jumped to a conclusion or misunderstood the statement, the candidate will almost invariably correct you with more specific information. "No, it was that I was given complete responsibility for projects from beginning to end."

It is important that the checkout be presented tentatively ("Do you mean . . . ?"). This communicates, "I'm trying to understand what you've said," and will enhance rapport. If you are incorrect in your checkout and neglect to be tentative, the candidate may then feel genuinely misunderstood and become frustrated or even hostile. Few people like to be told what they mean, especially when it is not what they mean. For example, if a candidate says, "I had a personality conflict with my supervisor," and you reply, "So you couldn't get along with your supervisor," the candidate is likely to respond defensively. "Do you mean you couldn't get along with your supervisor?" is less likely to put the candidate on the defensive.

The specific checkout can be used interchangeably with the repeat and probe. Suppose the candidate says, "I am ready to make a real commitment." In this case, a repeat would be "Commitment?," a probe would be "What type of commitment?," and a specific checkout would be, "Do you mean you want to remain with the company until retirement?" The choice of technique is one of style: Each will elicit more specific information and clarify what the candidate has said.

Sometimes a candidate will answer a question with a stream of details. At first, the intended meaning of all the specific details may appear obvious. Yet here, too, there is a danger of jumping to erroneous conclusions. Consider the following: "I was there each morning at 7:15. I only took 15 minutes for lunch and then rarely. I never left before 9:30 at night and then I always took reports home with me. And I spent most of Saturday and some Sundays in the office."

What is the general message of all this detail? The candidate may be saying that he or she had more work than could be completed during working hours or was so involved in the work that it became the main priority in life. A *general checkout* will clarify exactly what the candidate intends. Once again, formulate a hypothesis about the general meaning and check it out tentatively: "Do you mean you had too much work?" If you're correct in your hypothesis, the candidate will agree ("Yes, I was really doing two jobs and there simply was no way to get it all done in eight hours"), but if you've misunderstood, the candidate will correct you ("No, it was that I was so excited about the project that I put it before everything else").

The *feeling checkout* is used to clarify the candidate's feelings. Sometimes the way a candidate feels about something will be implied but not specifically stated. Rather than make unwarranted assumptions, check out your interpretation to insure complete understanding. For example, a candidate might say, "One guy in the unit wore an earring to work and another had a Mohican haircut. One woman talked constantly about the commune she lived in and kept inviting me to nude parties, and my boss didn't talk at all." You might ask, "I get the feeling that you felt pretty different and alienated from the other people you worked with." Once again, the candidate will either confirm your hypothesis ("Yeah, I just couldn't relate to anyone, so I put in my time and counted the hours till I could escape each day") or correct you ("No, actually I found them quite interesting and I sure had a lot of funny stories to tell my friends").

At other times there may be a discrepancy between what the candidate is saying and the message that is being communicated nonverbally. For example, suppose that while saying, "Oh, it was a really great job—it was everything I was looking for," the candidate is frowning or clenching a fist; the nonverbal message communicated here negates the verbal communication. Here, you could use a feeling checkout, such as "I get the feeling that you were ambivalent about the job despite the fact that it was all that you were looking for."

Finally, a feeling checkout is an excellent technique for helping an anxious candidate relax. You might say, "I sense that you feel somewhat uncomfortable being interviewed." When a person is given the opportunity to express feelings in a situation, it generally helps dissipate the feelings and simultaneously communicates concern and acceptance. But be careful about how you present feeling checkouts: It is antagonizing to be told how one feels, even when it is accurate. Most people have witnessed a situation in which a person literally screams, "I'm NOT mad!" in response to "You're mad, aren't you?" To summarize, checkouts are a means of clarifying and counteracting the tendency to jump to conclusions. Rather than assuming, keep the conclusion as a hypothesis and present it to the candidate tentatively to be either confirmed or corrected.

THE SUM-UP TECHNIQUE

Timing is a problem that faces all interviewers: How do you determine when a topic has been adequately covered? Moving too rapidly from one topic to the next can have negative consequences. You may have missed pertinent information and be evaluating the candidate on a partial picture of his or her ability and experience. Under these circumstances, candidates will probably feel cut off, not having been given the opportunity to present themselves fully. On the other hand, drawn-out discussion of each topic wastes valuable time. The sum-up technique helps determine when a topic has been adequately covered and facilitates the transition from topic to topic.

With this technique, you first summarize the candidate's main points and then say, "Is there anything else?" For example, "You've decided to leave your current job because you've advanced to the highest level you can and you are frustrated with the frequent changes in policies and procedures. Is there anything else?" If all the important points have been covered, the candidate will say something like, "Yes, that's about it." This is the signal that the topic has been covered completely and that it is time to introduce the next area of inquiry. At that point, a candidate who has more to add will do so ("Yes. And I can't make ends meet on my current salary").

The sum-up technique is an effective way to terminate the interview. To use the technique for this purpose, summarize the main issues that were discussed during the interview and then follow with, "Is there anything else?" For example: "You've had considerable sales experience in a variety of settings. You want to move into a managerial position because it poses a challenge and will give you an opportunity to grow. You feel you can excel as a sales manager because you work well with people and can stimulate enthusiasm in others. Finally, you are frustrated in your current position and feel the need for a change. Is there anything else?" When the candidate agrees and there are no additions or changes, you can terminate the interview feeling confident that the candidate has said all that has to be said.

An advantage of the sum-up technique is that it reduces pressure on you, the interviewer. Sometimes you might be distracted or preoccupied and actually not hear portions of the candidate's responses. At other times you might have forgotten part of what was said. When the forgotten or missed information is important to the candidate, the person will repeat it. If the candidate does not repeat the information, then it was probably not particularly important. If you have misunderstood the candidate, this will become apparent during the sum-up, and the candidate will correct your summary. Thus, the sum-up technique is self-correcting in that it catches and corrects points that you have missed, forgotten, or misunderstood. Another advantage is enhanced rapport: Summing up what the candidate has said and asking for additional information communicates your sincere interest.

The sum-up can also be used as a control technique. If the interview drifts into irrelevancies, the sum-up can be used to get the interview back on target. You can redirect by summarizing the relevant points and following up with an on-target probe (rather than saying, "Is there anything else?"). Consider this interview with the man who had been an agent with Bold Travel:

Interviewer:	What were your duties in your last position? (*Probe*)
Candidate:	I set up tours for special groups.
Interviewer:	Set up? (*Repeat*)
Candidate:	Yes, I contacted people in different professions, like dentists or nurses, and arranged tours.
Interviewer:	Do you mean you sold tours? (*Specific checkout*)
Candidate:	Yes, in a sense, though we didn't call it "selling." I'd contact the professional organizations and describe our services. I'd arrange tours on the basis of their interests rather than fitting them into existing packages.
Interviewer:	How did you find out their interests? (*Probe*)
Candidate:	I'd talk to clients on the phone and ask them what they wanted to see and do. All our tours were unique. It took a lot of time, but they were exclusive tours.

Interviewer:	Uh huh. (*Active listening and silence*)
Candidate:	Then I'd do a lot of research and make a lot of calls. I'd draw up a proposal and meet with them as a group to present it.
Interviewer:	Uh huh. (*Active listening and silence*)
Candidate:	Sometimes it could take a couple of meetings. Getting them to agree was hard. There was always someone I couldn't satisfy. Like this one woman who just *had to* sleep on the crater's edge of a volcano on Maui to see the sunrise. The others weren't interested and we couldn't send her up alone. Well, I finally found a guide to accompany her. There was a man who—
Interviewer:	(Cutting off candidate) You surveyed their interests and tailored a tour for them. What else did you do? (*Redirected interview on target with sum-up plus probe*)
Candidate:	After that it was just busywork. I'd call hotels and make reservations, call restaurants and order special meals, arrange for tour guides in each area, order tickets for plays, make bookings on all the planes, and so forth.
Interviewer:	Do you mean you handled all the scheduling and booking yourself? (*General checkout*)
Candidate:	Pretty much. I had an assistant who did a lot of it. But I was responsible for making sure everything went off smoothly.
Interviewer:	So you were responsible for locating and selling clients. You found out their interests, presented them with a proposed tour, worked out the disagreements, and coordinated the scheduling and booking. Is there anything else? (*Sum-up*)
Candidate:	No, that's about it.
Interviewer:	What caused you to leave? (*Probe*)
Candidate:	Oh, there was a shake-up and several people were let go. And that brings me to an important question. What are the chances that this position will last longer than the year advertised? I'm interested in job security.
Interviewer:	Good question. We'll get to that next (*Maintained control by postponing question*). But first, what did you say made you leave? (*Probe*)
Candidate:	Ah, there was a shake-up and I was let go.
Interviewer:	Let go? (*Repeat*)
Candidate:	Ah, yes—1, uh, left.

Interviewer: Do you mean you resigned? (*Specific checkout*)
Candidate: Not exactly. I, uh, was asked to leave.
Interviewer: I get the feeling you're hesitant to talk about what happened. (*Feeling checkout*)
Candidate: Well, yes I am. There was a big misunderstanding and even though it wasn't my fault, it was best for me to go.
Interviewer: What happened? (*Probe*)

PRACTICING THE TECHNIQUES

At first these techniques may seem deceptively simple. As an experiment, the next time you need to get information from someone, notice how many times you violate the principles by asking closed or leading questions. When attempting to use the techniques without first practicing them, you're liable either to forget or to become so preoccupied with how to ask what that you miss much of what is said. As is true of any skill, with practice you'll learn to use the techniques effectively.

The best way to practice is with a "buddy." Ask a colleague, friend, or your spouse to be your buddy. With your buddy, read over and discuss the section about basic principles and techniques. Then select one technique to practice first and brainstorm a list of stimulus statements. The second column of Table 2 contains a description of the type of stimulus statements needed to practice each technique, followed by an example statement in the third column.* The practice exercise goes as follows: Your buddy reads one of the stimulus statements from your list and you respond with the technique you are practicing. Then you and your buddy discuss how you used the technique. Did you use it correctly? How could it have been improved?

When you feel comfortable with the technique, select another technique to practice, generate another list of stimulus statements, and repeat the exercise. The next step is to listen to a variety of different types of stimulus statements and to use an appropriate technique. To do this, repeat the exercise above and have your buddy make statements picked randomly from any of your lists. The point of this exercise is to learn to identify the problem presented by the statement and to determine the technique that will elicit the information you need. For example, if the stimulus statement is vague, you should use a repeat, probe, or specific checkout, but not a sum-up.

Once you have mastered this step you will be ready to practice mini-interviews. This time make a list of general but restricted ques-

*Active listening and silence should be practiced in conjunction with the other techniques.

TABLE 2. Examples of statements for interview technique practice.

Technique	Type of Interviewee Stimulus Statement	Example of Interviewee Stimulus Statement	Example of Interviewer Response
Repeat	Vague, general, or ambiguous	"I want a job with potential."	"Potential?"
		"The conditions were terrible."	"Terrible?"
		"It was a valuable experience."	"Valuable?"
Probe	Vague, general, or ambiguous	"I want a job with potential."	"What type of potential?"
		"The conditions were terrible."	"In what way were they terrible?"
		"It was a valuable experience."	"What aspect was valuable?"
Specific Checkout	Vague, general, or ambiguous	"I want a job with potential."	"Do you mean you're looking for possible promotion?"
		"The conditions were terrible."	"Do you mean the conditions made it difficult for you to work?"
		"It was a valuable experience."	"Do you mean you learned to remain calm in a crisis?"
General Checkout	Numerous details related to one specific point	"During one week there were three angry calls from the home office, then they visited for review. Later another big shot visited to give advice. After that we found the bookkeeper had left everything in confusion when he quit. And as a last straw, my best man announced he'd gotten a new job."	"Do you mean there was a continual crisis?" or "Do you mean there was too much pressure?" or "Do you mean that is why you left?"

(Continued on following page)

TABLE 2. (Continued)

Technique	Type of Interviewee Stimulus Statement	Example of Interviewee Stimulus Statement	Example of Interviewer Response
Feeling Checkout	Any statement said while communicating an emotion nonverbally	"Well, we had to sell our house and move from the East Coast. My wife had to quit her job. The kids had to change schools. Then I discovered my salary was actually less and our new house payments were much more." While frowning: "I liked a lot of things about my job." While smiling: "I worked very hard."	"Do you mean you wish you'd stayed in your former job?" or "Do you mean you're under a lot of pressure from home?" "I get the feeling there were some things you didn't like." "I get the feeling you like demanding work."
Sum-Up	Three or four major points related to one overall issue	"Yeah, there are a number of things that I'm looking for in a job. The people I work with are very important. I like to be around people who are friendly and energetic. And I like to socialize with the people I work with, at least at lunch. But the conditions are also important. I like to have a good work space with proper lighting. And a	"So you're looking for a job that has good working conditions and friendly people. You also want a good salary and some degree of respect and status. Is there anything else?"

TABLE 2. (Continued)

Technique	Type of Interviewee Stimulus Statement	Example of Interviewee Stimulus Statement	Example of Interviewer Response
		little music—it soothes me. If I can have a window, that's great. And naturally money is essential. The higher the salary, the better. Then I can save more and play more. Also, with higher salary comes more respect. I like a job where I have status and others look up to me."	
Sum-Up *(continued)*		"I found the classes in school to be pretty useless. They just didn't relate to anything real— they were much too academic. There was so much homework that I didn't have time for anything. I just worked from nine to five, grabbed dinner, ran to class, and then tried to study. It was terrible. When I was promoted, I realized that it was how well I did on the job— not the degree— that mattered."	"So you dropped out of college because you felt that what you were learning in classes wasn't helping you and there was so much homework that you had no time, and then you discovered you didn't need the degree to get ahead. Is there anything else?"

tions such as "What are you looking for in a job?" or "What type of setting do you like to work in?" or "What did you like about your last job?" Ask your buddy the question and then use the techniques to gather information. The mini-interview should be short—about two to three minutes. You'll know it's complete when you can sum up and your buddy has nothing more to add. Talk over each interview with your buddy before going on to the next one.

If you can't find a buddy, you can do the first two exercises with file cards and a tape recorder. Instead of making a list of statements, write each one on a separate card (like flash cards). Then, while recording, draw one card, read the stimulus statement, and use the technique you are practicing. After each stimulus-response sequence, listen to the recording and do a critique of yourself. You can practice mini-interviews almost any time you need information from someone —on the phone, at parties, or at work.

Preparing for the Interview

Not preparing for the interview in advance is a serious error. Being able to gather information efficiently is not enough; you need to know *what* information to gather. Remember that the information you gather during the interview tells you how candidates behave in an interview and how they talk about their experience, skills, goals, and so forth, but it is not necessarily a reliable method for determining how they will actually perform on the job.

The only way you can know for certain how the candidate performs on the job is through observation. Obviously, in most cases this is unfeasible. Recommendations from previous employers have traditionally been an attempt to gather information about job performance, but to rely solely on this source is inefficient: People perform differently in different settings, different supervisors have different expectations and standards, and different jobs require different skills. The more you know how the candidate would actually perform in the position under consideration, the more likely you will be to select the person most suitable. The problem is how to gather information about actual job performance.

The Behavioral Sample

You'd probably never consider hiring a typist without first asking that person to demonstrate typing ability. Yet few companies require prospective executives to demonstrate decision-making ability, few ask prospective accountants to review company books or prospective managers to direct subordinates. What could be a better way to evaluate candidates than to observe them performing the very tasks required by the position? It is easy to obtain a sample of typing behavior; it is more difficult to obtain a sample of decision-making behavior, accounting behavior, or directing behavior, although it is possible.

There is no one method for collecting a sample of behavior. In general, the best way is to observe the candidate performing the actual tasks required for the position. Because this is rarely feasible, an alternative is to create a simulated experience that will require the candidate to engage in the behavior you are seeking. The most common method is the demonstration. Ask the candidate to demonstrate each of the important skills required to perform adequately in the position. For example, at the end of an interview with a candidate for a secretarial position, you might dictate a brief letter and ask the candidate to type it in completed form. In this way you can check shorthand, typing, and setting up a letter in correct form. If the position is copywriter for a radio station, you might give candidates information about a selected sponsor and ask them to write 10-second, 30-second, and 60-second "spots." When editing skills are required, you can request the candidates to edit a sample of the kind of material they would actually be working with. If the position is sales, you might ask each candidate to prepare and deliver a 10-minute "sales pitch" for a selected product. When public speaking is required, you might ask candidates to prepare and deliver a brief talk on an assigned topic.

Demonstrating skills is a common practice in academic settings. Candidates for assistant professorships are invited to the college and asked to deliver a colloquium to the faculty and students in their area of research followed by a "coffee hour." In this way, the search committee can evaluate candidates' demeanor in front of a group, as well as in a social situation; their ability to communicate complex material; the way in which they handle questions; and the nature and depth of their research. If you opt to use the demonstration method, it is important that you not surprise candidates with the request to demonstrate; rather, when the interview is scheduled, inform them that they will be asked to demonstrate specific skills. At that time you might also ask them to bring to the interview pertinent samples of their work, such as articles they have written, graphics, class lesson plans, and so forth.

Another approach is the "in-basket." This is particularly useful when evaluating complex skills such as administrative ability. All you do is ask the incumbent to prepare a packet of actual letters, memos, phone calls, and complaints that he or she has had to deal with. To this add a brief scenario of the situation and responsibilities. The candidate's task is to read over each item and decide upon an appropriate action. Instruct candidates to respond to each item in writing as if they were already in the position and to write out the rationale for each of their decisions or actions. Because this exercise requires considerable time, have candidates take it home and return it later. In this manner you can evaluate how candidates handle specific problems inherent in the position, and how they make decisions and why. You can also learn a lot of information about candidates' work styles. Did the candidate scribble out in longhand or carefully type the responses? Were the responses concise, and to the point, or were they overly detailed and drawn out?

When the position requires complex interaction skills, you might utilize role playing. Develop several scenarios of typical problem situations. Then present a scenario to the candidates and ask them to act out what they would actually do in that situation. You assume the role of the other person involved in the scene. Role playing is a way to evaluate a candidate's supervisory skills. For example, you might present candidates with a situation in which an employee's performance has deteriorated, with the purpose of observing how candidates go about determining the cause of the drop in performance and what actions they will take to correct it. Or you can give candidates a situation in which an employee must be terminated and see how they react.

After role playing such situations, you will have considerable information about how candidates actually relate to employees: Are they overly apologetic? Too curt and abrasive? Did they give constructive feedback? After each situation, discuss what the candidates did and why they chose that particular action. When time and facilities permit, the role-playing sessions can be tape recorded or videotaped for later evaluation. If actual role playing is not feasible due to time constraints or discomfort with role playing, you can present candidates with the problem scenarios and ask them to describe what actions they would take and why. This is less effective, of course, because once again you are evaluating how the candidates talk about the situation and not how they actually perform.

Another approach is the performance exercise. You might use this when it is not possible to present candidates with an actual situation they will encounter on the job. Suppose that you are screening people for a position for which they will have to be trained, and your objective is to discover whether or not they have the potential to learn the skills. For example, take an electronic assembler. Here you would be seeking a person with excellent eye-hand coordination and manual dexterity. You might have the R & D department develop a performance task that requires all the necessary movements. When you present the task to the candidates explain the procedure and ask them to complete the task. Now you have an opportunity to evaluate how rapidly each candidate learns, follows instructions, and completes the task. If the position involves debugging electronic equipment, present the candidates with a component that has a specific problem and ask them to locate and correct the problem. Here again you can observe how candidates approach a problem situation. Do they proceed systematically? Do they become frustrated easily?

Performance exercises can be developed for more complex skills as well. Suppose you wanted to evaluate executive leadership skills. One exercise you might try is the "leaderless" group. Here you place six or eight candidates in a group and present them with a written list of 10 or 12 qualities of a group leader. The candidates' first task is to rate the skills in order of importance. Then ask candidates to arrive at a group consensus as to the priority of skills. During the discussion, an observer can rate each candidate on the leadership skills you are seeking. You can quickly observe how assertive each candidate is in getting an opinion across; whether or not the candidate quickly drops his or her position or clings to it tenaciously; how carefully each listens to another's view, and so forth.

The final method is the "two-week consultancy." This approach is used when hiring for upper-level, highly paid positions. Hiring the wrong candidate for such key positions can damage morale and jeopardize productivity. Once you have settled upon a candidate who appears most suitable for the position, hire that individual for two weeks or for a short-term project. At the end of this period, you can decide whether to retain the person permanently. With this approach you can observe the candidate in action, and at the same time the candidate will be able to evaluate the company. If you discover that the candidate does not perform well or does not fit into the company, you will have lost only two weeks rather than months or years. Likewise, if the candidate is not comfortable in the position, he or she will leave immediately rather than in six months.

Behavioral sampling has been used in corporate assessment centers since the early 1950s. The difference between the method described here and the assessment center method is one of degree. Conducted in a retreat setting over a two- to three-day period, the assessment center approach involves extensive evaluation of several candidates. Trained raters observe candidates perform in exercises that simulate the demands of the job. The data collected forms the basis of reports on each candidate. The fact that in the 1970s nearly 2,000 leading companies used the assessment center method attests to its usefulness.[3] A major drawback is cost: Preparation of materials and evaluation of candidates require a large, specially trained staff. Consequently, assessment centers are used primarily in large companies to select senior executives or when there are several openings in one job category. Therefore, it is difficult to tailor the exercises to a specific job in a specific work unit. By following the guidelines described here, any manager can develop with minimal expense a mini-assessment center tailored to measure candidates' potential to perform in a specific position.

Clearly, behavioral sampling requires greater preparation than the personal interview alone, but the advantages are great: Not only is a wider variety and greater depth of information about each candidate obtained, but by presenting each candidate with the same task it is much easier to compare candidates with one another, thereby maximizing the chances of hiring personnel who will perform well and offering such people a better opportunity to know more about the work they will be doing. All too often, candidates are unclear about the actual duties of a job and, once they are in the position, are dissatisfied. This leads to lowered performance and high turnover. Time and money can be saved in other ways as well. A personnel officer can collect the behavioral samples, and at a later date the supervisor of the position in question can review the material from all the candidates. This can save the supervisor the time of interviewing each person and solve some of the problems inherent in personnel officers interviewing people for positions about which they know little. Based on this initial screening of work samples, the supervisor can select the two or three most qualified candidates for intensive interviewing. The supervisor can use the work sample as a springboard during the interview.

Determining Necessary Behaviors

Of course you can't obtain a sample of work behavior unless you have first identified the behaviors essential for performing the tasks required by the position in question. To be successful in a particular job, every candidate must be able to perform certain skills or behaviors (*essential behaviors*). At the same time there are behaviors that are not essential but are highly preferred (*preferred behaviors*). For example, a court reporter must be able to take a deposition accurately using a stenograph and must be able to type and spell without errors. These would be three of the essential behaviors required of a reporter. Yet one law firm might prefer that reporters on the staff be personable, cheerful, friendly, and well-groomed, whereas these behaviors might be less important for the reporter who takes depositions for disputed unemployment claims.

Generally, the essential behaviors remain the same for the same position, no matter what the setting, whereas the preferred behaviors may vary dramatically from company to company. For example, one radio station will prefer that its sales manager know most of the blues and jazz artists, whereas another station will not. Yet in both settings the sales manager must be able to motivate the sales staff to sell. Before being able to select an appropriate method of sampling essential and preferred behaviors, an interviewer must be able to identify them. Although this may sound obvious, when you haven't clearly delineated what is essential and what is preferred, you can easily put too much emphasis on preferred behaviors and overlook essentials during the interview and behavioral sampling. Or you may explore one area with one candidate and another with the next candidate, making it impossible to compare them.

It is all too common to assume that you do in fact know what skills are essential or preferred in a position. Many interviewers rely on company job descriptions. Yet these are frequently not only inadequate and outdated, but are sometimes actually inaccurate. Thus, before interviewing candidates, it is important to pinpoint what behaviors or skills you are seeking. Basically there are three ways to do this. One is to ask the position supervisor to provide a list of essential and preferred behaviors. (Keep in mind, however, that supervisors' descriptions of job behaviors reflect their whims, prejudices, and personal feelings. So while supervisors are valuable sources of information, they will undoubtedly be biased.)

Another source of information is the incumbent. But as with the supervisor, the incumbent is likely to overemphasize the importance of his or her own personal assets and work style. In fact, it is a good idea to reappraise the position after there has been a long-time incumbent. The position might no longer be necessary, or it might be preferable to divide it into two positions. But the third—and most reliable—source of information is observation: What does the individual actually do, and what is the relationship between what this person does and what others in the company do? Extensive observation is best, but any observation is better than none. Observation of the incumbent for five- to ten-minute periods at various times in the day should be a minimum. Additional information is gained by observing persons who perform well and those who perform poorly in similar jobs.

List the essential and preferred behaviors you have identified. For each one, ask: Is this an action that can be observed by at least one person? Whenever you can't answer in the affirmative, question whether or not it is really a behavior. (Review the discussion of behaviors in Chapter 1.) Perhaps you have listed an attitude or value such as "conservative" or "nonsexist." Attitudes and values are extremely difficult to observe or to measure. Of two candidates, you can measure which one is the more competent typist, computer programmer, or writer—but how do you measure sexism? The same problem exists with generalized descriptions, such as "relaxed," "confident," "aware," "hard-working," "reliable," or "committed." You can't be sure that two observers will have the same notion of such descriptions. What one person calls confidence, another might see as arrogance; what one calls relaxed, another might see as lethargy or lack of interest.

The major reason most interviewers include such attitudes, values, or generalized descriptions ("abstractions") is that they tend to use them as the basis for predictions about the candidate's future performance. Yet when you attempt to define any of these abstractions, you find that you eventually come up with a list of observable behaviors. Reliable, for example, might be defined as "completing all tasks started," or "carrying out promised actions." Thus, it is important that you identify the component behaviors for each abstraction and add these to your list. This step is very important in cases where you are instructing someone else to conduct the interview. One reason the interviewer may be sending you candidates who you feel are inappropriate may have to do with abstractions. Suppose you state that you want someone who is cooperative—by which you mean he or she should make efforts to be tactful, friendly, and work with others for a common goal. But the interviewer may think cooperative means to do what others want. You can see the kind of problem this might create and how it contributes to selecting the wrong candidate.

When you have rewritten your list, you will be ready to devise methods for behavioral sampling. For each behavior on your list, write next to it what action you might ask of the candidates in order to observe them at that particular behavior. As you review possible sampling methods, you'll probably discover considerable overlap. Suppose that for the position of editorial assistant, the essential behaviors identified were the ability to write clearly and concisely, to condense long reports, to understand technical language, to convert technical language to popular language, to use good grammar, to spell correctly, and to type well. All of these can be evaluated by asking each candidate to write a hundred-word review of an assigned technical report. By having identified the essential behaviors, you will have a guide for evaluation of the review. Of course, time, financial, and facility constraints make it impossible to sample all the behaviors required to perform adequately in the position, but this analysis procedure will help in a number of ways: You will have clarified what you are looking for and how best to evaluate candidates. You have a checklist to use during the interview so that you can explore *each* important issue with *each* candidate. This alone will help you compare candidates. Finally, you will know what specific information you need to get during the oral part of the interview—that is, you will be less likely to ask vague questions or to accept vague answers.

The Behavioral Balance Sheet

Thus far we have discussed methods of gathering information about the competence of individual candidates. But there remains the problem of comparing one candidate with another. How do you compare the candidate who excels in one or two of the essential areas, yet is deficient in several preferred behaviors, with the candidate who is average in all the behaviors you are seeking? Suppose you are seeking an editorial assistant who will be primarily responsible for putting together a monthly pamphlet containing pictures and descriptions of single-family dwellings listed in your real estate firm. And suppose one candidate has an unusual ability to translate technical language into popular language, to letter and to draw, and to lay out material for printing, but has limited knowledge of real estate; whereas another candidate's writing and editing skills and knowledge of real estate are adequate, but that person has no experience with lettering, drawing, or layout. Which one should you choose? You can increase your objectivity with the behavioral balance sheet. Basically, the behavioral balance sheet is a conceptual tool that can assist in quantifying evaluation and comparison of the assets and liabilities of one candidate with those of another.

Table 3 is an illustration of the balance sheet for each of our candidates. Rate the candidates on the degree to which they possess or do not possess each skill you are seeking. The essential skills are weighted more heavily than are the preferreds or extras (those skills unique to each candidate), and the resultant indexes can be compared. Obviously the rating of each skill or behavior is still highly

TABLE 3. Using the behavioral balance sheet to compare two candidates.

	Rose			Tom		
	Weight	*Rating**	*Score*	*Weight*	*Rating**	*Score*
ASSETS						
Essentials:						
Concise, clear writing	3 ×	3 =	9	3 ×	2 =	6
Grammar	3 ×	3 =	9	3 ×	3 =	9
Punctuation	3 ×	3 =	9	3 ×	3 =	9
Can condense reports	3 ×	3 =	9	3 ×	2 =	6
Spelling	3 ×	3 =	9	3 ×	3 =	9
Use of proofreading marks	3 ×	2 =	6	3 ×	3 =	9
Score			51			48
Preferreds:						
Typing	2 ×	2 =	4	2 ×	3 =	6
Knowledge of real estate	2 ×	0 =	0	2 ×	3 =	6
Friendly	2 ×	3 =	6	2 ×	2 =	4
Well-groomed	2 ×	3 =	6	2 ×	2 =	4
Enthusiastic about work	2 ×	3 =	6	2 ×	2 =	4
Score			22			24
Extras:						
Layout skills	1 ×	3 =	3			
Lettering and drawing skills	1 ×	3 =	3			
Can write in popular language	1 ×	3 =	3			
Is getting sales license				1 ×	3 =	3
Assets score			82			75
LIABILITIES						
First paying job	2 ×	1 =	2			
Medical problems: back pains				2 ×	3 =	6
Liability score			2			6
Candidate index:						
Assets score − Liability score	82 −	2 =	80	75 −	6 =	69

*Rating code: 3 - High; 2 - Medium; 1 - Low

subjective, but the behavioral balance sheet gives you a basis on which to begin your comparison. When the two candidates for the editorial assistant position are compared, we can see that despite Rose's limited knowledge of real estate and her general inexperience in the work world, she rated higher than Tom did. Of course, you wouldn't base your decision solely upon this rating, but it could be an additional aid in your selection. You may decide that despite her superior rating, Rose still presents considerable risk and that Tom will fit in better with the other staff. The form of the balance sheet and the arbitrary weighting should be altered to serve your unique purposes. Under extras, you might also include potential assets such as degrees in progress; under liabilities, you might consider potential future problems such as knowledge of a computer language that appears to be becoming obsolete.

Subjectivity can never be eliminated, but it can be reduced. The procedures outlined can help make evaluation more objective and help interviewers become more aware and critical of their own assumptions. The more skilled you become with the information-gathering techniques, the more precise you will be in determining what you are seeking. The more you employ behavioral sampling methods, the more likely you will be to hire employees who perform well and remain with the company. You are always seeking the best "degree of fit" between candidate and position, and it will always be to some extent a guessing game. One source of high turnover is overselling the attractiveness of the job and company. Once on the job, the new employee may be disappointed and become dissatisfied because initial expectations have not been realized. At this point the employee probably will conclude that the job does not suit his or her needs and will either leave or remain on the staff as a dissatisfied worker. On the other hand, candidates who have participated in a behavioral sampling assessment process can get a realistic preview of the job. In this way the candidates are better able to determine whether or not the job will meet their needs.[4]

Although the preparation and time required to do the type of evaluation suggested herein may at first appear to be extensive, the expense incurred over time will be recouped tenfold. In-depth evaluation becomes essential when the position to be filled is a key one such as manager or department head. Yet, even for assembler or receptionist jobs, selection can be made more efficient by determining prior to the interview what you are seeking and how to evaluate candidates. You need only go through the preplanning procedures once, and you can utilize them over and over again.

NOTES

1. The information-gathering principles and techniques were adapted from the crisis intervention procedures developed by Jeffrey A. Schwartz and

Donald A. Liebman, Law Enforcement Training and Research Associates (LETRA), 618 National Avenue, Mountain View, California 94043.

2. Mark Snyder, Elizabeth Decker Tanke, and Ellen Berscheid, "Social Perception and Interpersonal Behavior: On the Self-Fulfilling Nature of Social Stereotypes," *Journal of Personality and Social Psychology*, Vol. 35 (1977), pp. 656–666.

3. Berkeley Rice, "Measuring Executive Muscle," *Psychology Today*, Vol. 12, No. 7 (December 1978), pp. 94–111.

4. John P. Wanous, "Tell It Like It Is at Realistic Job Previews," *Personnel*, Vol. 52, No. 4 (July–August 1975), pp. 50–60.

SUGGESTED READINGS

Anundsen, Kristin, "An Assessment Center at Work," *Personnel*, Vol. 52, No. 2 (March–April 1976), pp. 29–36.

Bray, Douglas W., and Campbell, Richard J., "Selection of Salesmen by Means of an Assessment Center," *Journal of Applied Psychology*, Vol. 52, No. 1 (1968), pp. 36–41.

Bucalo, John P., "The Assessment Center—A More Specific Approach," *Human Resource Management* (Fall 1974), pp. 2–13.

Kraut, Allen I., "New Frontiers for Assessment Centers," *Personnel*, Vol. 53, No. 4 (July–August 1976), pp. 30–38.

5

Managing Authority: How to Give Directions

MUCH of our waking life is perceived through the medium of words. Radio and television entertain with words; books transmit messages with words; teachers guide with words; interactions with family, friends, and colleagues are dominated by words—even solitude is invaded by an endless stream of thoughts. Perhaps it is only in dreams (and in the movies) that words assume a secondary place to images.

Yet, despite the importance of words, it is likely that you seldom think about language and its impact on virtually every aspect of life. When things go wrong—when you are confused, worried, or depressed; when social or business affairs don't work out; when you see yourself making blunders in personal or work matters—you blame many things for the difficulties. Sometimes you may blame your physical health or nerves, other times you may blame the establishment or world events. If the problem involves an interaction with other people, you may blame their attitudes or lack of ability. Even when you suspect that there is a problem in communications, you will probably neglect to investigate your specific words as a possible source of trouble.

It is hard to believe that thinking about language is so limited when its uses and effects are so extensive. Few understand the relationship between the specific words used and their effectiveness in supervising others. It is easy to believe that the basic message to be communicated is more important than the words themselves. It is assumed that once the idea is straight, the words will just fall into place. But the words you use are as important as the ideas they express.[1] Your words influence the way subordinates feel about you as well as the way you feel about yourself.

When people meet you for the first time, they use many clues— such as title, clothes, grooming, hair style, general demeanor, and speech—to assess your affiliations, status, and authority. Some of these indicators can be more easily manipulated than others. Consider George, the undercover "nark" (narcotics agent) who wants to infiltrate the drug subculture. He will most likely grow his hair, cultivate a beard, and wear jeans and casual shirts. It is important that George look like a dealer in order to be accepted and to do his job, but his speech can give away his disguise. His attempts to assimilate will fail unless he correctly uses the subtle nuances of drug culture argot. One serious error in wording can generate suspicion and make him ineffective or even put him in danger.

The language you use is one of the best indicators of your position in an organization. Not only can the use of a less prestigious form of speech cost you status and authority, but it can limit your advancement as well. That speech can be a social barrier is well illustrated in George Bernard Shaw's *Pygmalion,* the play on which the musical comedy *My Fair Lady* was based. The Cockney flower girl, Eliza, can be installed in a West London apartment, clothed fashionably, and taught socially sophisticated behaviors, but she will still be a Cockney as long as she speaks like one. Her social status will change only when her speech changes. Likewise, a person making a vertical move in the corporation is confronted with subtle but real speech barriers.[2] This is particularly evident in the case of the person entering management for the first time: The new manager must drop deferential speech and adopt authoritative speech with subordinates. Failure to do this can cause serious problems.

Social class, status, and authority are only a few of the unconscious indicators about yourself that you reveal in your speech. In a linguistics study, English and French Canadians made personality judgments from tape recordings of identical sentences spoken in Canadian French and in English.[3] Both French and English listeners judged the unseen French speaker to be less intelligent, dependable, kind, ambitious, and attractive—even shorter—than the unseen English speaker. The experiment suggests how quickly you are likely to be stereotyped according to your speech. It also illustrates that the group holding power sets the standards for speech. In Canada, the English have social and economic power over the French, and the English set the speech standards. In the business world, management holds power and sets speech standards. Thus, the more you use authoritative speech—the language of management—the more positively you will be viewed. You will be seen as more competent and more in control of yourself and of the situation. In short, you will be allotted greater respect and authority.

The impact of your speech is not limited to others' perceptions of you; it influences your perceptions of yourself as well. Stanford psychologist Daryl Bem developed a theory of self-perception which states that people make judgments about themselves in the same way that they make judgments about others.[4] For example, if at a staff party you observe a person standing alone, speaking only when spoken to (and then very hesitantly), refusing to look directly into other people's eyes, you might conclude that the person is self-conscious. Likewise, if you notice yourself engaging in this kind of behavior, you might conclude that you feel self-conscious.

Such judgments about yourself need not only follow from your overt behavior; you might also note internal behaviors, such as pounding heart, fluttering stomach, and sweating palms. According to Bem's theory you look to your behavior—internal and external—to make judgments about yourself. If you see yourself doing a favor for Jones, a co-worker, you might conclude that you like Jones; if you see yourself doing the same favor for Smith, an upper-management type who is considering you for an important assignment, you might conclude that you're "playing the game."

One of the many behaviors people use to make judgments about themselves is their speech. When you hear yourself speaking with hesitation and confusion to an employee, you might conclude that you lack confidence and are incompetent as a supervisor. On the other hand, when you hear yourself speaking authoritatively you will probably draw the opposite conclusion. The words people use with others are only part of the speech behavior that they use to make judgments themselves. People can also observe their covert or silent speech, or thoughts, which behavioral psychologists refer to as self-statements. Thus, if you hear yourself speaking to employees in a wishy-washy, hesitant way, you might then say to yourself: "I just can't give directives. I can't manage people and get them to do the things that need to be done." You probably use these self-statements as further evidence to support your negative perceptions of your competence as a manager.

It's easy to see how this can lead to a vicious cycle. Negative self-statements erode self-confidence; lowered self-confidence makes it difficult to perform; inhibited performance leads to more negative self-perceptions, resulting in still lower self-confidence. Intervention into such a vicious cycle can be made at two points—changing overt speech and changing self-statements. (Methods of altering self-statements were reviewed in Chapter 3.) It is important to recognize that speech, both external and internal, can have an enormous impact on your perceptions of yourself: who you are, how you feel, and how you function.

You're making a serious error if you always attempt to use the same kind of speech. If you want to function effectively and be taken seriously, you must be responsive to the situation. Neil Postman points out that the situation, which he calls the semantic environment, includes the setting, your purpose, and your relationship with the listener.[5] As you move from one setting to another, you must alter your speech or suffer serious consequences to your credibility. For example, if you use the same words in the boardroom as you use in the bedroom, your sanity will be immediately suspect. You alter your speech to achieve different purposes. You would use very different words if you wanted to complain about poor service than you would if you were trying to obtain a $30,000 personal loan. Finally, your relationship with the listener influences your speech. You'll be job hunting if you speak to the president of the firm in the same way you speak to your troublesome teenaged son.

Generally, in the world of commerce, people who express their opinions strongly and forcefully will be taken more seriously than those who state their views tentatively. A stronger means of expression suggests confidence in one's assertion. Consider the following examples:

> Gosh, John, you've lost two good people in the last month! And both left in a huff, didn't they? Maybe I'm an alarmist, but this could lead to serious morale problems, couldn't it? Perhaps I'm wrong, but it could be indicative of some kind of communication problem. Next week the company is sponsoring a seminar in communications. It may surprise you, but I've gone to a couple of these in-house seminars and they gave me a lot of ideas. Won't you please attend this one?

> Hell, John, you've lost two good people in the last month! And both of them left in a huff. This kind of thing could lead to serious morale problems. And it could be indicative of some kind of communication problem. Next week the company is sponsoring a seminar in communications. I've gone to a couple of these in-house seminars myself and they gave me a lot of ideas. I want you to attend this one.

There is a marked difference in the feeling of confidence conveyed by the two managers in the example. Manager A sounds apologetic and almost embarrassed by the discussion, comes across as being uncertain, and makes attending the seminar sound optional. John could easily challenge manager A and refuse to attend the seminar, saying, "There's no communication problem here. Both of those guys were freeloaders. I told them to shape up or get out. They got out."

Manager A has placed himself in a position where he might have to defend his opinion and eventually resort to threats and ultimatums. He has created a potential problem for himself with his own words. Manager B, on the other hand, sounds confident in his analysis of John's problem and there is no doubt as to what action he expects of John. The difference lies in small but important changes in speech patterns.

Many managers, especially neophytes to the management hierarchy, have difficulty telling a subordinate to do something. Linguist Robin Lakoff identified several speech patterns that decrease a manager's credibility when giving directives: weak expletives, tag-questions, and directives stated as requests.[6] In the following sections I will review these problem areas, along with disqualifying prefaces; then I will show you a step-by-step process for giving directives.

Weak Expletives

Consider the following statements:

> Good grief, sales have dropped ten percent.
> Hell, sales have dropped ten percent.

> Dear me, I'll never find a replacement.
> Christ, I'll never find a replacement.

> Oh fudge, I've lost the quarterly report.
> Damn, I've lost the quarterly report.

Although the specific information transmitted in each pair is identical, the implied importance varies dramatically. The expletive is meaningful only insofar as it conveys that the speaker has an emotional reaction to the information contained in the remainder of the statement. The force of the speaker's feeling is implied by the strength of the expletive: "Hell" is more forceful than "good grief," for example. Of course, the speaker who says, "Good grief, sales have dropped ten percent," might in fact feel more strongly than the one who says, "Hell," but "good grief" is a weak expletive.

According to Lakoff, weaker expletives tend to trivialize the statement that follows. Because words influence the listener's perceptions, it is easy for the listener to conclude that the topic is trivial. Speakers who use weak expletives frequently find that their credibility drops. On the other hand, a person in authority tends to be excused for a show of temper (within limits), whereas the person with little authority is not. Because swear words are often used to express anger, it is not surprising that they make stronger expletives.

Some weak expletives: Oh fudge, dear me, golly, gosh, gosh darn, drat, goodness, gracious me.

Some strong expletives: Damn, hell, goddamn, Christ, Jesus, and some stronger expressions.

I don't want to suggest that you take up swearing to increase your credibility and authority, but if you catch yourself frequently using weak expletives, it would be wise to practice making such statements without any expletive at all. Or use one of the more acceptable strong expletives—such as "damn"—to express strong feeling.

Tag-Questions

An authority person projects an air of confidence and conversely the person who conveys confidence is perceived as having more authority. That is, confident-sounding people are listened to more carefully, and what they say is more likely to be heeded. On the other hand, people who express their opinions in a tentative way project an air of uncertainty and are not listened to as carefully, nor are their statements taken as seriously.

Suppose a supervisor said to a typist: "This report has to be re-typed, doesn't it?" The fact that the statement is phrased as a question suggests that the supervisor is unsure whether the report needs retyping. Or you might think the supervisor believes the report needs retyping but is asking for the typist's confirmation. In either case, asking for confirmation still implies uncertainty. Thus, the supervisor has diluted his or her authority with the tag-question. On the other hand, had the supervisor said, "This report needs to be retyped," that would have conveyed confidence in the assertion.

There are times, of course, when a tag-question is useful and appropriate. If, for example, you want to initiate small talk on the elevator you might say, "Elevator's slow, isn't it?" Here the tag-question conveys friendliness and elicits talking on a subject common to both people. At other times you might actively seek confirmation to check out your understanding of what the other person has said. A manager might confirm an assistant's opinion by saying, "You think this is a good idea, don't you?" Finally, asking for confirmation can be used as a way of getting a commitment for some action: "You'll complete the sales report before you leave today, won't you?" Here the request for confirmation actually reaffirms the manager's authority because the manager is confirming another person's promised actions.

But in general, the tag-question is inappropriate in a supervisory situation when you as the manager are stating your opinion or making an assertion to your subordinate. In such a situation you lose credibility if you ask the subordinate to confirm your opinions. Fortunately, the tag-question is easy to correct. If you become aware that you are using tag-questions frequently, simply drop the tag and use a simple declarative statement.

Disqualifying Prefaces

In a staff meeting I observed a novice manager pose a suggestion with the preface: "This may sound like a silly idea, but. . . ." Not unexpectedly, no one in the meeting looked at the speaker or made any response to the suggestion. Undaunted, the novice persisted with several other suggestions prefaced with disqualifiers such as, "Perhaps you have already tried this, but I think. . . ." Each suggestion was either rejected abruptly or simply ignored. The suggestions themselves, while not earth-shattering, were as reasonable as any of those presented by others, but the implicit message was, "Don't listen to my ideas—they aren't any good." The group heard and accepted the implicit message, and nobody listened.

Attaching a disqualifying preface to a statement not only instructs listeners to dismiss the statement in question as unimportant; it also influences their general impression of the speaker and of his or her future statements. The person who uses disqualifying prefaces sounds unsure and even incompetent; in fact, the speaker is explicitly stating his or her doubt about that particular statement. Certainly, if you are going to go to the trouble of thinking of an idea and stating it, you want the idea to be considered. Disqualifying prefaces defeat your purpose. People generally believe what you say about yourself.

If you tell people that what you are about to say is without value, then those listening will probably believe you and will not continue to listen. Once you have set this cycle into motion it becomes difficult to get an audience, and many of your good ideas fall on deaf ears.

Certainly a disqualifying preface might be politic in a social situation in which the listener is resistant to a certain suggestion. For example, you might say to a distraught friend: "You probably really don't need to do this, but perhaps you should see a shrink." Here the listener can save face by agreeing that he or she doesn't need a psychiatrist, and at the same time you offered what you felt was good advice. The business world doesn't have time for such tentative communications; it simply doesn't have time to listen to statements labeled as valueless.

Obviously, if you want what you say to be taken seriously, then it is wise to listen carefully to your own speech patterns and drop the disqualifiers. Some people use the preface as a way of gaining the listener's attention. Unfortunately, the disqualifier often has the opposite result. If you feel you must preface your suggestions in order to get an attending audience or simply to build up momentum, then you should practice more assertive prefaces. For example, you can gain the attention of a listener with assertive prefaces such as: "I have a suggestion. Perhaps we could. . . ." or "I want to make a suggestion. If you. . . ." or "Have you considered . . . ?" Of course, the preface is not necessary; you can simply state your suggestion or directive. In a group situation, if the others continue to speak, then begin again and speak louder.

Directives Stated as Requests

A manager is responsible for seeing that specific company objectives are met, and those being supervised are by and large employed to perform tasks that ultimately result in achieving these objectives. In most cases the manager does not hand over to the subordinates the authority to decide who should perform these tasks, yet many managers feel uncomfortable giving directives—they feel it is impolite.

When you want someone to do something and at the same time wish to be polite, you should probably make a request or suggestion. Both requests and suggestions allow the addressee to decide whether to comply. The implication is that the action you are requesting is a favor. This is appropriate in a social situation or a work situation with a peer, but framing a subordinate's required tasks as a favor is inappropriate and can cause you problems. On the other hand, an overt directive implies that the speaker is in a superior position and can enforce compliance if necessary. Although by definition a manager is in a superior position to that of his or her subordinates, many managers find it extremely difficult to give simple directives. Even in my workshops a large percentage of managers have difficulty giving directives in behavioral rehearsal exercises where the stated goal is to practice giving directives. Consider the following directives stated as requests:

1. Please retype this report.
2. Will you retype this report?
3. Will you please retype this report?
4. Won't you retype this report?
5. Won't you please retype this report?

Examples 2, 3, 4, and 5 can be translated into "Are you willing to retype this report?" If in fact the typist has an option (if another typist can do the typing, for example), then such a request would be appropriate. But if there is no option involved, the speaker is undercutting his or her authority by stating the directive as a request, and anybody who makes such requests too frequently will lose credibility in the eyes of subordinates by being put in the awkward position of repeatedly having to ask them to do tasks that are part of their required work. In extreme cases the supervisor might even end up doing the work!

Although the use of "please" in example 1 also converts the directive to a request, it is an effective form to use when you want to soften the directive. But if you feel compelled to preface all directives by "please," then you are probably having trouble exerting your authority. Of course, you do not want to be seen as an insensitive autocrat who does nothing but give orders; it is a matter of degree and timing. An occasional directive stated as a request can be effective in establishing rapport with a subordinate. In short, as a manager you ought to be able to give a directive comfortably and to rely on the request form only when you feel it is particularly politic to do so.

Sometimes a directive stated as a request can actually be antagonizing. For example, if you place special emphasis on the "please," as in "Will you *please* . . ." or "Won't you *please* . . . ," it can come across to the listener as sarcastic. This is especially true if you are somewhat irritated—it sounds as if you're saying, "Won't you *please* do the work you're paid to do." Certainly it would be better to make the overt directive expected from a manager than to risk alienation through sarcastic politeness.

If you feel compelled to be polite at all times with subordinates and if you hear yourself giving many of your directives as requests, practice the "please" formation in example 1 until you can do so comfortably. Then practice giving directives with no preface. As a manager you should be able to give an overt directive comfortably and confidently. Use the request formation when you have a specific purpose for softening the directive.

Putting It All Together

In my workshops on authoritative directives, many students object to the idea of telling an employee directly to do something. On the one hand, they know that they must give directives, yet they want to be liked and not be seen as aggressive, pushy, or authoritarian. Some students make the point that few people like to be told what to do, even though they are in a system in which they are being paid to perform tasks under the direction of someone else. They say people like to "feel" that they have an option. Others point out that softening a directive with qualifiers or framing it as a request gives employees the feeling that they are being considered as people. Certainly these objectives are valid—it is important that managers be sensitive and considerate of employees. Nevertheless, the goal of business is to get the job done. Managers who set up a false dichotomy between treating employees humanely and getting work done have a problem on their hands.

Some managers go to the opposite extreme—giving directives with no consideration for the employees. Many employees have excellent ideas; in fact, they may have more expertise about their particular job than the supervisor does. It is a foolish manager who doesn't seek out such ideas or who overrides suggestions without consideration. Such a person can be seen as a despot. Certainly this is not conducive to cooperation, rapport, and productivity. And although at first glance such people may seem confident, upon closer observation they are often revealed to have an abrasive facade covering a lack of confidence. Such a person is not respected but feared. Managers who have genuine confidence reserve decisions until they have carefully evaluated the situation. Part of a careful evaluation includes eliciting the opinions and suggestions of the employees involved. The confident manager will give a directive only when there is a high probability that it is the most appropriate one. Nothing is more damaging than leaping into a situation without adequate information and giving orders that will have to be retracted later.

There is a step-by-step process that can resolve most of the problems in giving directives. The acronym DAD stands for three important steps: Describe, Ask for clarification, and Direct. Describe the problem situation objectively to your subordinate, ask how that person feels about the situation and what suggestions he or she might have, then give the directive. The DAD components provide a guideline for giving a directive with authority.

You begin the directive process by describing to your subordinate the situation or the problem in question. Be objective and specific and, whenever possible, describe observable behaviors. Suppose there have been complaints that a male employee has been making flirtatious advances toward several of the married women in the office, creating tension. If you say, "You know, Bob, you've been letching after the ladies around here," chances are that Bob will react negatively to this description. Avoid inferring motives; simply describe overt behavior: "You know, Bob, I've noticed that you frequently talk with the women during work hours and you've asked a couple of them out on dates." Likewise, avoid judgmental or emotional labels: "Betty, that feasibility report was the most half-assed thing I've seen in years." A better description would be: "Betty, that feasibility report was vague and confusing in several places. It left me with a lot of questions." Finally, avoid vague terms such as, "You have a bad attitude." Use simple, concrete terms: "You have made a number of negative remarks about the company." Don't make accusations—this only puts the employee on the defensive and reduces the possibility that your directive will be followed cooperatively.

Next, ask employees how they feel about the situation and find out what suggestions they might have. If an employee is new to your unit or if asking for clarification is new to you, then you'll need to work a little at this step. Employees may not believe you are sincerely interested in their ideas and feelings, and may dismiss the question as patronizing. Remember, you want to find out the employee's position; otherwise there is no point in asking it at all. If that individual is reluctant to state an opinion or communicate feelings, or if what he or she says is vague, incomplete, or confusing, use the techniques for gathering information described in Chapter 4. By asking for clarification you communicate to the employee concern and interest in his or her ideas. Once you have set a precedent of asking for clarification, you will be amazed at how differently you see situations from those who work under you. And the quality of suggestions you'll receive will probably surprise you.

Once you have clarified the employee's position, you are ready to direct. You now know how the employee feels and what that person thinks ought to be done. Frequently, an employee's suggestions will be exactly the same as the directive you would have given had you not used the DAD method. Great! All you have to do, then, is to agree that this suggestion is the best course of action! At other times, the employee's feelings or suggestions will differ from what you have anticipated. Sometimes the suggestion will be one you hadn't previously considered; sometimes the suggestion will be one you must reject. Here, of course, you hold the final authority, but whatever directive you give, the employee will be much more likely to be cooperative in following it.

Remember to state the directive as a simple declarative sentence. Avoid the disqualifying prefaces, the weak expletives, the tag-questions, and the request formation. You'll get the best results if you use simple, concrete terms and avoid vague generalities: The clearer the directive, the less opportunity for confusion and error. Whenever there is any possibility of confusion, ask for clarification a second time to determine whether or not the directive was understood.

When you use DAD, the employee feels included in the decision and consequently will be much more likely to cooperate in following the action you have decided upon. And you will be less likely to find yourself in the awkward position of having misread the situation and thereby demanded an inappropriate or ineffective action.

Let's return to the example of John, who had two good employees quit on him in the last month, and see how the DAD process would work.

Describe:	Two good people left your unit in the last month and both of them made negative remarks about you in the process.
Ask for clarification:	What happened?
John:	You know, both of those guys were pretty educated, though neither one had any real experience. Well, it got to be a problem because they didn't like the way we do things around here, and they got to resenting me.
Ask for clarification:	How can we prevent this from happening again?
John:	Well, I don't know. I just can't talk to these schoolboys. They think they have all the answers, and they just don't listen.
Direct:	Next week the company is sponsoring a seminar in communication. I've gone to a couple of these

> in-house seminars myself and have gotten a lot
> of good ideas. I want you to attend this one.
> How does that sound to you?
>
> **John:**   Well, I don't know what good it'll do, but I'll
> sure give it a try. How do I sign up?

Clearly, the situation with John was loaded. He had just lost two "good people" and it was at least partially because of his own behavior. John was probably feeling more than a little defensive at the beginning of the conference with his supervisor. However, the situation was defused by using DAD, because possible morale problems were not mentioned. Speculating about future dire consequences would have only aggravated John's insecurity. And since John actually brought out the communication problem himself, he was more receptive to the directive to attend the seminar than if the supervisor had jumped to the conclusion that there was a communication problem.

Let's look at another example of a poor directive.

Manager: This grant application has got to be typed immediately. You've got to get on it right away.

Typist: But I can't, I just can't. You're not the only person I work for, you know. Everyone around here thinks their stuff is so important. Well, I've had it—I just can't do it!

Manager: Look, this grant means a quarter of a million bucks. Part of that money pays your salary! Get on this report now!

It's pretty easy to guess what will happen here. If the typist doesn't quit or get fired, the manager will probably find all kinds of typos, incorrect spellings, and deletions in the final copy. Furthermore, neither the typist nor the manager will forget the argument. By giving a directive too soon, this manager has created a problem. Let's see how it would sound with the use of DAD principles.

Describe: I'm really in a bind. This grant application must be postmarked by midnight tomorrow. It means a quarter of a million bucks to the company.

Ask for clarification: What's your workload like today and tomorrow?

Typist: Gee, I have several reports for Williams due and then that marketing prospective for you. Oh yes, transcripts for Montgomery. He said it's urgent.

Ask for clarification: Do you think you can squeeze this grant in?
      Typist: I can delay on everything but Montgomery's transcripts. You know how he is!
      Direct: Look, I can handle Montgomery—don't worry about that. Just get on this grant right away. Can you do that?
      Typist: Well, as long as you talk to Montgomery I think I can get it done. If not, I'll stay late tomorrow.

The typist was overloaded with work and probably not too receptive to an additional job. The DAD process, however, helped to obtain willing cooperation. The *Describe* step enabled the typist to understand the manager's predicament and the importance of getting the grant application completed as soon as possible. The *Ask for clarification* step conveyed the manager's concern and elicited the problem with Montgomery's transcripts. Thus, it was easy for the manager to give the directive. The typist was cooperative and even volunteered to work late to complete the grant.

Body Language and Voice Quality

Up to this point I have emphasized the importance of selecting words that enhance your authority, but listeners are influenced by nonverbal communication as well. Such things as eye contact, posture, gestures, and tone of voice will influence your subordinates' perceptions of you. Because there are a number of very detailed books on the market that discuss nonverbal communication, I will not go into this area in depth.

In general, however, it is important to maintain good eye contact with your subordinate when you are using the DAD technique. Staring fixedly into a person's eyes will make you seem aggressive and will make the other person uncomfortable. On the other hand, not looking at that individual at all, blinking rapidly, or squinting suggests that you are uncomfortable and unsure of yourself. Strive for a "soft" gaze about the inner core of the subordinate's face as you speak and listen —facial expressions that suggest relaxation and receptivity are the most helpful. Wrinkling your forehead, pursing your mouth, swallowing, clearing your throat, wetting your lips—all suggest tension. If you engage in these behaviors excessively, do use the systematic relaxation exercise described in Chapter 3 twice a day and practice relaxing your face and neck muscles.

If you feel tense while using the DAD process with an employee, concentrate momentarily on a relaxing scene. Tension can also be communicated through your posture and gestures. If you cover your mouth when you speak, scratch your head, rub your eyes or the back of your neck, preen, play with jewelry or papers, or adjust your clothing, you need to learn to keep your hands under control. An easy approach is either to fold your hands or to keep them in your pockets. Sharon and Gordon Bower suggest that you can break these annoying habits by speaking while holding two objects, one in each hand.[7] Finally, shifting your weight from foot to foot and pacing about can also communicate nervousness. The easiest way to control these nervous habits is to seat yourself in a chair or on the corner of a desk while delivering your directive.

According to the Bowers, the quality of your voice can enhance the authority of your directive or detract from it. If you speak rapidly, it will convey impatience or anger, whereas speaking slowly connotes hesitancy or fear. A flat, monotonous voice is difficult to listen to for any length of time because it is dull and uninteresting. Friendliness, on the other hand, is conveyed through warmth and modulation. If you're too loud, you may seem aggressive; if you're too soft, you may sound timid. It is actually quite difficult for you to evaluate the quality of your voice while you're speaking: It sounds perfectly natural and comfortable. Ask a friend for feedback, or make a tape recording of yourself speaking and listen to it a day or so later. If you find some of these problems in your voice, consider taking a speech or drama class. You'll find the gains in voice control will easily repay the investment of time and money.

Short of a formal class, however, you can begin working on your breathing and voice strength. Breathing, of course, is important to the quality of your speech. Problems with breathing can occur because you are tense, in which case you will tend to breathe in shallow, rapid spurts. You can reduce the tension by practicing the relaxation exercise in Chapter 3. Once you have mastered the relaxation technique, you can think to yourself, "Relax," and momentarily visualize your relaxing scene while you are in the tension-producing situation. One popular exercise that will help you breathe correctly is to deliberately push out the area below your ribs (your diaphragm) as you *inhale*. If you do this just as you inhale, placing your hand over the area, it will be forced out a little. Practice pushing your hand out as you inhale. Do this several times a day.

You can improve your vocal strength by learning to control your use of air as you produce sounds. Sharon Bower recommends practicing the following exercise for several short sessions each day:

Standing erect, put one hand flat on your diaphragm; use a finger of the other hand to close one ear (with one ear closed you can hear the quality of your voice better). Take a deep breath (push the diaphragm *down*), and then say "Ah" for as long as your breath lasts. Note the number of seconds you can say "Ah." Count off seconds by thinking "Mississippi 1, Mississippi 2," etc. Record your time during each session. Your goal is to produce the sound steadily for at least 45 seconds. Once you have achieved your goal using the "Ah" sound, repeat the procedure for the other vowels—E, I, O, and U.[8]

Conclusion

When used excessively, weak expletives, tag-questions, disqualifying prefaces, and directives stated as requests can undermine your authority in the eyes of subordinates. The basic rule of thumb is to avoid using these speech patterns except when you have a specific purpose for doing so. The DAD process is a useful guideline for giving a directive. It enables you to convey to employees the problem situation, to elicit their reaction and suggestions, and to give a directive in such a way that it maximizes the possibility that the employees will follow the directive cooperatively.

NOTES

1. For an in-depth discussion, see S.I. Hayakawa, *Language in Thought and Action* (New York: Harcourt Brace, 1939).
2. Sports and military language present unique problems to women managers. For a detailed discussion see Betty Lehan Harragan, *Games Mother Never Taught You: Corporate Gamesmanship for Women* (New York: Warner Books, 1977), pp. 37–95.
3. W.E. Lambert, R.C. Hodgson, R.C. Gardner, and S. Fillenbaum, "Evaluation Reactions to Spoken Languages," *Journal of Abnormal and Social Psychology*, Vol. 60 (1960), pp. 44–51.
4. Daryl J. Bem, "Self-Perception Theory," in L. Berkowitz, ed., *Advances in Experimental Social Psychology*, Vol. 6 (New York: Academic Press, 1972), pp. 1–62.
5. Neil Postman, *Crazy Talk, Stupid Talk: How We Defeat Ourselves by the Way We Talk—And What to Do About It* (New York: Delacorte Press, 1976).
6. Robin Lakoff, *Language and Woman's Place* (New York: Harper Colophon Books, 1975).
7. Sharon A. Bower and Gordon H. Bower, *Asserting Yourself: A Practical Guide for Positive Change* (Reading Mass.: Addison-Wesley, 1976).
8. Ibid., p. 179, reprinted with permission.

SUGGESTED READINGS

Bower, Sharon A., and Bower, Gordon, *Asserting Yourself: A Practical Guide for Positive Change*. Reading, Mass.: Addison-Wesley, 1976.

Farb, Peter, *Word Play: What Happens When People Talk*. New York: Alfred A. Knopf, 1974.

Harragan, Betty Lehan, *Games Mother Never Taught You: Corporate Gamesmanship for Women* (New York: Warner Books, 1977), pp. 37–95.

Lakoff, Robin, *Language and Woman's Place*. New York: Harper Colophon Books, 1975.

Postman, Neil, *Crazy Talk, Stupid Talk: How We Defeat Ourselves by the Way We Talk—And What to Do About It*. New York: Delacorte Press, 1976.

6

Managing
Meetings

A GROUP is more than a collection of individuals assembled in the same place. Five people sitting in the lunchroom do not constitute a group. But suppose these five people discover that they are trapped by a fire that blocks all exits. They will become a group when they start working cooperatively to plan an escape. In planning an escape the five individuals become interdependent, so that all of them accept the group's common goal—to escape—as their own. By so doing, the accomplishment of the group's goal satisfies a need of each individual: self-preservation. However, interdependence can develop only if the individuals interact or communicate. The interaction that develops and maintains the interdependence of the individuals is called the *group process.*

Government, business, and volunteer organizations rely heavily on committee meetings as a mode of problem solving and decision making. Unfortunately, in such task-oriented groups, the leader's attempts to mobilize the group resources are frequently frustrated by an unproductive group process. There are incidents in which the process is deliberately sabotaged by its members, although this is generally the exception. The more frequent cause of counterproductive interaction is that the members do not feel "safe" enough to voice suggestions and concerns, because they may fear ridicule, negative

160

judgments, or even retaliation. Sometimes the problem process is a consequence of a covert or unstated norm. For example, socializing in meetings is difficult to stop because socializing has become the expected norm. Most frequently, however, the members and leader simply do not know how to foster group processes that promote task accomplishment. Thus, the development of this important dynamic is left to chance and, as often as not, counterproductive processes become entrenched. It goes without saying that it is the leader's responsibility to orchestrate the transition from a collection of individuals to an effective problem-solving group. Thus, facilitating productive group processes is a major concern for all committee leaders.

A wealth of data from the group dynamics social-psychological literature attests to the powerful impact of a group environment on its members. An environment that fosters trust is an important precondition to effective group functioning. If members feel mistrustful of each other or of the leader, they will not be inclined to share their opinions and ideas openly or to offer feedback to others. Trust and openness are an essential ingredient for the development of cohesiveness.

Studies of group dynamics have demonstrated that the members of highly cohesive groups can be more influenced by each other.[1] Cooperation among members is one manifestation of cohesiveness. Researchers have found that groups ranked high in cooperative actions demonstrated more solutions to problems, acted in more positive ways with each other, and reported fewer communication problems than did members of less cooperative groups.[2] Although cohesiveness is a tremendous facilitator, it alone does not guarantee a problem-solving focus. In fact, the cohesiveness might inhibit problem solving if the group develops a subtle antitask bond.

Since trust, openness, and cohesiveness are necessary conditions for the productive functioning of task-oriented groups, the difficult question becomes what actions you as a leader take to facilitate the development of these elusive processes. Recent developments in the behavioral approach to groups offer specific techniques.[3]

Laying the Foundation: The Leader's Preparatory Actions

To be an effective leader you must take action to facilitate the committee's productivity *before* the first session and during each subsequent session. However, before discussing these preparatory actions, it is important to specify several basic assumptions:

1. The current environment influences what people do in the group.
2. Each member and the leader are part of the environment of the other members.
3. The current environment can be changed by the actions of the members and of the leader.
4. All member and leader behavior is potentially measurable— that is, data can be gathered on the behavior of members and of the leader, as well as on the group process.
5. Member and leader actions and interactions are susceptible to change by behavioral methods.
6. A committee meeting can be viewed as an educational process where teaching and learning take place, as well as a work process where problems are solved and decisions are made.
7. Committees should set clear goals and clear objectives for reaching the goals.

Setting the "Metagoal"

A basic question confronting all potential committee leaders is, "Is a group effort necessary for solving the problem of concern, or might it be more effectively handled by a single individual?" A problem such as identifying what factors caused a drop in sales last year can only be answered by investigation, and is probably most efficiently pursued by an individual. By contrast, the problem of determining which marketing strategy to adopt for the next fiscal year requires a creative solution based on a blending of expert opinion and prediction. Here a group approach would probably be most efficient.

A second basic question concerns the committee's power to act on the decisions it makes. When decisions and solutions have little possiblity of being implemented, then the committee's efforts become academic. Few companies have the resources to explore interesting but basically unfeasible solutions. In short, your first task is to identify a real problem that is potentially solvable and to determine whether it is best pursued individually or with a group.

Translate the purpose of the committee into a "metagoal." A metagoal is a statement of the overall goal or purpose for the existence of the committee. When the metagoal is reached, there is no further reason for the committee to continue meeting. The metagoal defines the focus of the committee—the performance area to which each member contributes. A specific and explicit statement of the metagoal is crucial; confusion and ambiguity about general goals of a committee often cause frustration and failure.

Group process research has demonstrated that members who have a clear picture of the group goal and the path to accomplishing it—typically like their own task and the group task more, experience less hostile feelings toward the group, and are more responsive to group influence than persons in groups in which goals and means are unclear.[4] A metagoal such as "to open communication channels among departments" is too vague to suggest a concrete direction for the committee, because members are likely to have divergent ideas of what is meant. The committee can become frustrated just in the attempt to come to an agreement as to its actual purpose. A more productive metagoal might be "to develop and implement a procedure for coordinating the goals and functioning of research and development, accounting, marketing, and production." Determining the metagoal must be accomplished before you can determine who should participate in the committee.

Selecting Members

The degree of control allotted to leaders in selecting members of task groups varies greatly. When membership is predetermined by job position, as in an executive staff meeting, leaders of course have virtually no determining power. In fact, leaders may hold a position simply because assuming the leadership role is part of their job responsibilities.

In committees formed to handle a specific problem, leaders generally have more latitude in selecting members. A major reason for employing a group approach is the wider range of skills and areas of expertise available to the problem-solving process. Much in the same way as selecting a new employee, you should strive to find the best match between the skills required to solve the problem (reach the metagoal) and the skills of the prospective members. Attempt to select a group that collectively has the skills needed to solve the specific problem.

A requirement that seems obvious—but that is often not considered—is that members must be able to participate fully in the group. Other responsibilities should not make it difficult to attend meetings and to carry out between-session tasks. Equally important is that members should *want* to join the committee. When you select members who find the committee a burden, or who do not want to participate for other reasons, then you have a problem. The relative status and power among members is another important consideration. When there is a power disparity, there exists the potential for the development of second-class citizenship. The more powerful members generally tend to dominate, whereas the less powerful tend to agree or simply to not participate at all. Therefore, whenever possible, select members who have equal status.

Arranging the Environment

A task group does not exist in a vacuum; it is conducted within the context of several physical, social, and functional environments. These environments include the physical meeting place, peers in the work unit, employees supervised by group members as well as their own supervisors, persons who might be competing with members, and those in other departments with whom members interact regularly in either a social or a work capacity. Meetings that require going to a different location such as a retreat might also include families and friends in the environmental context. Such social relationships may affect and be influenced by members' involvement in the committee.

To be successful, you must gain some support from the environment. This is especially true when a group approach to solving problems is first introduced. Misunderstanding and confusion about the purpose of groups can lead to many problems. In some situations, people believe that their authority is being challenged when they learn indirectly about a committee. Others who have adequate information about the purpose or procedures may believe it to be a waste of time. Significant others in the environment who have a negative view of the committee can subtly create problems for members. A resentful supervisor can make demands upon a member that result in his or her missing meetings. A peer who feels left out may cause problems by displaying hostility and being uncooperative. Subordinates who feel that they are being overly burdened with a member's responsibilities while the member is in committee sessions might sabotage that member's productivity by delaying tasks or losing important documents.

Such problems can be reduced if actions are taken to arrange the environment for success prior to the first meeting. For example, police officers who were participants in an intensive seven-week instructor's training program were the recipients of considerable hostility from other officers in the department as well as from their spouses. The other officers thought the trainees were "just off having a good time"; the spouses resented the homework demands on evening and weekend time. The training consultants solved the problem by providing written and oral communications about the training program and by inviting the Chief of Police and other officers to visit the training site. Spouses were encouraged to participate as role players in video training tapes, and a number of social activities involving

families were arranged. The demoralization experienced by the trainees could have been avoided had the consultants taken these steps
prior to the beginning of training. These steps were repeated in subsequent training projects in other departments, and resulted in cooperation from significant others from the first day of training on.

Begin by analyzing who constitutes the environment. Who is likely
to be concerned with members' participation, or to be affected by it?
This will invariably include at least the members' direct supervisors.
Meet with those you've identified to discuss the problem and to explain why the group approach is appropriate, and why the supervisee
has been selected to participate. Explain the metagoal, the nature of
participation, and the duration of sessions. In this way significant
others in the environment have an opportunity to make suggestions,
voice concerns, and provide support. Being given the opportunity to
feel involved and to offer support helps to reduce potential resistance
and resentment.

In addition to talking to significant others, meet with each member
prior to the first meeting. Present the committee in a positive manner
and stress its importance. Carefully explain the metagoal and the
outlines of the meetings. Each member should understand what will
be expected during the meetings. Do not overlook explaining your
responsibilities as leader.

Whenever possible, membership should be voluntary. When
members feel they are being invited to participate and that they have
the option to decline, they will enter the first meeting with a higher
level of commitment. When membership cannot be optional, encourage members to voice any concerns or reservations. This will help
reduce possible resistance from unenthusiastic members. At the very
least, the members will feel that their positions were heard and
considered.

In these preliminary talks you are laying the foundation for the
development of a productive group process. Such pregroup talks
assist in facilitating trust ("I have been told what to expect"), openness
("I have been asked how I feel"), cohesiveness ("I want to participate"
or "the group serves an important function"), and task orientation ("I
know the goal of the group").

Leader Goals

The leader's preparatory activities lay a foundation for a productive meeting, but they do not ensure that problem-solving processes
will occur and continue. Prior to the first meeting and to each subse-

quent meeting, it is vital to develop specific goals to guide your actions during the meetings. Although the two are intertwined and are pursued simultaneously, it is convenient to conceptualize the leader's goals in two categories: (1) process goals to control or *regulate* the group process, and (2) task goals to *guide* the group to accomplishing the metagoal.[5] The process goals are aimed at developing an interdependent dynamic which includes trust, openness, cohesiveness, and task orientation. The task goals address themselves to the specific tasks or objectives that must be accomplished by the committee in order to reach the metagoal.

Regulating the Group

Before you can establish regulating goals, you need to determine which member behaviors indicate that trust, openness, cohesiveness, and task orientation are present. The first step is to operationally define communication behaviors that make up these processes. When a specific category of behaviors has been defined, you know precisely what behaviors to increase or decrease. Table 4 presents the beginnings of such a behavioral definition. Of course, you need to adapt the suggested list of behaviors to the unique characteristics of your particular group.

After defining the process in terms of observable behaviors, the second step is to assess the amount of trust, openness, and task-oriented activity occurring during meetings. If the committee has not yet met for the first time, you can assume that few of these activities will occur. If you have an ongoing group, assessment is necessary to determine the current frequency of these process behaviors. One method is to have an observer tally the occurrence of each target behavior selected from Table 4—a secretary who takes minutes could be instructed to perform this function.

This approach has potential drawbacks, however. A live observer may inhibit openness, but a recorder who is usually present at meetings will be rapidly forgotten (although a live recorder may be expensive), and you or committee members can request immediate feedback at any point. Another method to assess frequency of target behaviors is to tape record a meeting, select at random one or more 10- to 15-minute segments, and count the frequency of the target behaviors from Table 4. Although it is difficult to get immediate feedback on the frequency of various behaviors from a tape recording, it does offer you the tremendous advantage of being able to listen at a later time to the entire session. It can be beneficial simply to hear how one phrases questions and comments and to see what makes one respond.

TABLE 4. Behaviors defining trust and openness, cohesiveness, and task accomplishment.[6]

TRUST AND OPENNESS

A high frequency of:
Making here-and-now statements
Making self-disclosing statements
   Members request and reinforce self-disclosing statements
   Members make self-disclosing statements
   Members ask for and give feedback to other members
   Members ask for help with problem
Spontaneous unprompted participation
Members reinforce each other

A low frequency of:
Anecdotes
Making non-self-disclosing statements
   Self-disclosing statements cut off, rejected, ignored
   Irrelevant talk about other people or things
   Members cut off or reject feedback
   Members minimize problem
Silence
Defensive statements

COHESIVENESS

A high frequency of:
"We" statements (referring to the whole group)
Statements expressing liking for group
Statements expressing desire to continue group
Attention directed to speaker
Talk directed to other group members
Equal participation of members
Talk relevant to previous member's statements
Cooperative statements ("Here's a way we could do this. . . .")

A low frequency of:
Negative statements about whole group with positive remarks about subgroup (clique)
Statements expressing dissatisfaction with group
Statements expressing desire to terminate group
Absenteeism
Tardiness
Distracting behavior (yawns, arranging papers)
Statements directed to leader only
Time monopolized by leader or one or two members
Statements cutting off others by referring prematurely to oneself ("I have the same problem in my department. . . .")
Statements changing the subject
Competitive statements ("That's nothing. . . .")

(Continued on following page)

TABLE 4. (Continued)

TASK ACCOMPLISHMENT

A high frequency of:	*A low frequency of:*
Statements to develop agenda	Social conversation
Statements to describe problem	Critical statements in reference to
Statements to develop goals	other members' task-oriented
Statements proposing course of action	statements
Statements to evaluate progress	
Reinforcement for others' task-oriented statements	
Statements that initiate and implement problem-solving actions	
Reports of relevant actions taken between meetings	

Before setting any goals or objectives or making any intervention to alter the process, it is necessary to gather baseline data on the current level of member performance (see Chapter 2). For example, suppose that Doris, chairwoman of a policy review committee, randomly selected for assessment two 10-minute segments from the third session. By counting she finds that only three of the eight members made any statements indicating their personal opinions (self-disclosing statements), and there was a total of ten such statements; that four members were late for the meeting and that this had been a typical occurrence; and that there were 17 incidents of statements irrelevant to the committee goals (social conversation). Merely having gathered this information gives Doris a clear idea of what she needs to change —that is, what behaviors she wants to increase or decrease.

From careful analysis of baseline data you can set clear regulating objectives for subsequent group meetings. Just as precise objectives are important in coaching a single employee, a very specific objective is necessary when working with a group. The objective should specify (1) an observable behavior, (2) whose behavior is the target, (3) how much of an increase or decrease in the frequency of the behavior is desired, and (4) under what conditions (when and where) the behavior is to occur. By stating objectives in such precise terms, you can determine when the objective has been achieved. And by continuing to monitor the process with a tape recorder, you can determine if your intervention has been effective. When the data indicate a trend in the desired direction, feel confident in your strategy. On the other hand, when no such trend emerges, reanalyze the problem and develop a more effective strategy. Although data collection on the face of it may appear to be extra work, in the long run it is cost-effective because it minimizes waste of time, energy, and money.

The following examples should assist in clarifying the difference between a poorly stated objective and a well-stated one. Here is a poor one: "Members will make more personal opinion statements." This objective has several weak points. Although the behavior is observable (statements of personal opinion), it does not specify how many personal statements. The objective does specify *who* (the members) but under what conditions is only implied. Presumably Doris wants more personal opinion statements about task issues during the meetings. A well-stated objective would read: "By the sixth meeting all members will make at least one personal opinion statement about each task issue." Stating objectives in a precise manner makes evaluation of success quite obvious.

Another poor objective is: "Members will demonstrate more commitment by the fifth meeting." Here again the objective is vague. The most serious problem is the word "commitment." This is an abstract concept and not a specific, observable behavior. Once again the conditions and frequency are not stated. A better objective would be: "By the fifth meeting of the policy review committee, all members will arrive by 9:00 A.M. and will continue to do so at all future meetings." Another objective that Doris might set is: "By the sixth meeting Bill, Susan, and Murray will not engage in any social conversation during the policy review committee meeting." This objective meets all the criteria, but it specifies what *won't* occur (the behavior to be decreased) instead of what *will* occur (the behavior to be increased). Remember that reducing an undesirable behavior does not ensure that the desired behavior will increase. Thus, Doris should set a complementary objective: "By the sixth policy review committee meeting Bill, Susan, and Murray will each make at least one task-oriented statement on each issue."

A side benefit of precisely stated objectives is that they help clarify exactly what you want and make it easier for you to act in the group in a consistent and unambiguous manner. Once accustomed to such specificity, you will gain confidence in your ability to lead committee meetings.

After setting regulating objectives the next step is to determine a strategy and then intervene. Table 5 lists some possible intervention techniques. A brief discussion of each leader technique should assist in clarity and understanding.

TABLE 5. Illustrations of leader's intervention behaviors which facilitate trust and openness, cohesiveness, and task accomplishment.[7]

Leader Behaviors Which Facilitate	Trust and Openness	Cohesiveness	Task Accomplishment
Model the desired behavior by example	"I am disturbed by your blase attitude."	"You know, I've come to look forward to our weekly meetings."	"We can start by deciding exactly what our goals are. I have a suggestion."
Reinforce desired behavior with positive attention	"Henry, I am pleased that you voiced your reservations."	"Bill, you are right. We really are becoming a team."	"Rachel, that is an excellent idea."
Reinforce the reinforcer: Reinforce members for reinforcing (following up, supporting, making suggestions to) each other	"Jeff, you were very sensitive to pick up on how hard it is for Claire to express her doubts about this project."	"Jose, I'm glad you noticed that everyone is on time today."	"Jody, I imagine Jack appreciates the backing you just gave his idea."
Extinguish by ignoring or cutting off inappropriate talk and behavior	"Excuse me, Sally, but that is not relevant yet. Mary, what are your reservations about the proposed policy?"	After completely ignoring another member's inappropriate comments, focus on a member who is behaving appropriately: "I agree, Steve, becoming a team is our first priority."	"Excuse me, Ralph. Tom, what do you think is the best approach?"
Set norms by defining desired behavior Explicitly:	"It is important that we all express our frank viewpoints on this touchy matter."	"The reason we are here is to work as a team."	"The purpose of our meeting today is to analyze this crisis and arrive at a consensus as to the best course of action."

TABLE 5. (Continued)

Leader Behaviors Which Facilitate	Trust and Openness	Cohesiveness	Task Accomplishment
Implicitly:	"It is a lot easier to talk about numbers and facts than it is to say what we really feel about this report."	"I wonder if we can overcome our differences and work as a team?"	"We are having a lot of trouble deciding on what goals we want to achieve."
Confront by calling attention to inappropriate behavior	"Jenny, the last three times anyone suggested an idea to you, you defended your previous approach."	"Mark, I notice you always endorse what your colleagues Hal and Sharon say, but you ignore the comments of others."	"Mike, you have found a reason to reject every suggestion so far."
Restate harsh and negative statements to point out positive implications	"What Mildred said may have seemed abrasive, but sometimes saying something negative is a sign of concern."	"Perhaps what you mean when you say you are frustrated with this meeting is that you want to get through the barrier that is keeping us from becoming a team."	"I'm glad you mentioned how Jim rambles. It helps all of us to remember to keep on the agenda."
Redirect statements from leader to other members	"Ann, would you tell Herb directly how you feel about his negative attitude?"	"Grant, tell Carol directly that you wish she'd be more attentive."	"I think Jim would like to hear that proposal from you."

TABLE 5. (Continued)

Leader Behaviors Which Facilitate	Trust and Openness	Cohesiveness	Task Accomplishment
Make optimistic expectation statements	"Being frank about our feelings would help a lot."	"As we get to know each other better, we will learn how to work together as a team."	"Some of these problems may seem insurmountable, but if we keep working on small steps as we have been doing, we will be able to solve them."
Redirect attention to important content that was avoided or unnoticed	"Do you really think that Susan was saying she dislikes the procedure or was she saying she was afraid she might not remember to follow it?"	"I don't think Richard was saying he dislikes this committee. I think he was saying he feels he's being squeezed out."	"Eric made an important suggestion which no one noticed. Eric, would you repeat it, please?"
Set definite agenda and redirect members when they deviate	"Today let's each of us give our frank feelings about our progress."	"Today let's see how many priorities we have in common. This will help us to feel like a team."	"We are getting off our agenda for today. We decided to explore alternative procedures. What ideas do you have, Betty?"
Remain silent	In groups directed toward sharing interpersonal feelings as a goal, silence may be used to help members learn that they can enjoy being with each other without pressure to talk.	Silence after a moment of sharing in a group with interpersonal goals may enable members to appreciate their feelings of belonging.	Silence may be used to force members to take the initiative for problem solving and reduce dependence on the leader.

Model the desired behavior. Engage in the desired behavior yourself and the members will learn by example. They can observe what behavior is expected of them during meetings. Simultaneously, by modeling the desired behavior, you *implicitly* set a norm for expected appropriate behavior. It is not necessary to verbalize this by saying, "Do as I do." Members look to the leader for indications of appropriate behavior, particularly during the initial meetings.

Reinforce the desired behavior. Attention is usually reinforcing to most people. Give a member positive attention immediately following appropriate behavior. The attention can be overt with a direct statement, such as "Ken, that's an excellent idea," or covert by simply turning to Ken more frequently.

Reinforce the reinforcer. A major goal for leaders is to establish productive processes that are self-maintaining. One way this is accomplished is by having members assume the role of reinforcer. You can facilitate this by giving positive attention to members who reinforce other members.

Extinguish the undesired behavior. Just as you can use the technique of extinction with a single employee, you can use this technique to reduce inappropriate behavior in the group. Remember, the important principle is to make no reaction whatsoever to the behavior you want to decrease. Extinction is more powerful when it is combined with positive reinforcement. Respond positively to an appropriate behavior while simultaneously ignoring the inappropriate behavior.

Set norms. Setting norms is a way of establishing expectations that certain behaviors are appropriate and *should* occur and that other behaviors are inappropriate and should *not* occur. You can do this *explicitly* by directly stating the norm or expectation, or a norm can be set *implicitly* by making statements that indirectly imply desired behavior. Virtually every action or nonaction on your part implies appropriate or inappropriate behaviors. Your actions model expected behavior: What you reinforce implies what behavior you expect, and what you ignore implies what is inappropriate behavior. For this reason it is important that you constantly monitor your group performance in order to be aware of the implicit norms you may be establishing.

Confront inappropriate behavior. This technique has the potential for being punitive, because many people become uncomfortable when confronted, especially when the confrontation occurs in the presence of other people. Avoid this approach in the initial group meetings, because it does have the potential for inhibiting trust and openness. As a rule of thumb, reserve confrontation until after the more positively oriented techniques have failed. When you do confront, remember to immediately reinforce the desired behavior or approximations of the desired behavior as soon as they occur. Use a calm tone of voice and judgment-free language in order to reduce defensive responses.

Restate harsh and negative statements. By ignoring negative content or connotations and by commenting on a positive aspect of a statement, you can defuse hostile or negative comments. This can help prevent a negative vicious cycle of attack, criticism, and defensiveness from developing, and implicitly states what is expected. It also reinforces the positive aspects of the hostile person's comment and encourages that person to be more positive in the future.

Redirect comments from yourself to other members. This technique is useful in the initial group sessions. Neophyte members are typically unsure of what is expected of them in the meetings, and tend to fall back on behaviors they have learned to be appropriate in other group situations, such as classes and lectures, where all comments are directed toward the instructor. New members may be self-conscious, which further inhibits member-to-member talk. Despite the fact that you may have explicitly called for communication between members, this process is facilitated when you actively encourage member-to-member interactions. The technique is simple. First, request that the speaking member make comments directly to a specific member. ("Alice, would you tell Barbara your reaction to her proposal?") Second, watch for and reinforce spontaneous member-to-member comments. ("I know it is difficult at times to express our disagreements directly. Jeff, I'm glad that you could do that with Susan.")

Make optimistic expectation statements. A variation of setting implicit norms, this technique facilitates the development of positive feelings about the committee and its progress. In essence you are saying, "I'm positive we'll be successful." Optimistic expectation statements are particularly powerful when stated by a person in authority.

Redirect attention to important content. This technique has several uses. By focusing attention on an important point, you implicitly set a norm as well as reinforce the on-target portion of a statement. Ignore the irrelevant or less important content and focus the group's attention on the more important content.

Set definite agenda. This makes explicit what is expected in a particular session or portion of a session. In addition, it is educational. Once members learn that they can accomplish agenda items, they are more likely to set an agenda and stick to it.

Silence. At times silence can be a powerful tool. Generally people feel uncomfortable being silent in the presence of others. Of course, this is true of leaders as well. Consequently, be careful not to fall into the role of silence breaker. Once members learn that you will break the silence, they will simply wait. This can lead to your becoming the sole speaker. If you resist the tendency to break the silence, a member will usually speak up. In some instances, extended silence could generate inordinate anxiety. However, once a general atmosphere of trust, openness, and cohesiveness has emerged, silence can enhance positive feelings.

Doris, the policy review committee chairwoman, can use the techniques in Table 5 to guide her actions in the meeting to accomplish the committee objectives. To increase the frequency of personal opinion statements, she might frequently state her opinion (model), explicitly state that members should share their opinions (set a norm), and respond positively to members who state their opinions (reinforce). To increase on-time behavior, she might explicitly indicate that members are expected to be at the meeting on time (set a norm), make positive comments when they do arrive on time (reinforce), and remind those who are late that they are expected to arrive on time (confront). To reduce the frequency of social conversation, Doris might ignore irrelevant comments (extinguish), focus the attention on relevant discussion (redirect attention), and point out that social conversation is inappropriate when it occurs (confront). To increase the frequency of task-oriented comments, she could specifically request such comments (set a norm) and respond positively when they occur (reinforce).

To evaluate progress, continue to count the frequency of the target behaviors by one of the methods discussed previously, and then compare this data with the baseline. If the target behaviors increase or decrease in the desired direction, continue with your intervention. If the desired change is not in evidence, reevaluate the intervention strategy. Failure is most often a result of inconsistency on the part of the leader. For example, you may sometimes ignore social conversation and at other times become caught up in it and thereby reinforce social conversation. Carefully worded objectives and ongoing self-monitoring help to reduce such inconsistency. Sometimes member behavior will increase or decrease as desired, but will not reach the level stated in the objective. You may have expected too much too soon. It is better to follow the shaping procedures discussed in Chapter 2 and set a series of small-step objectives that are achievable. When a small-step objective is accomplished, set another objective and try to achieve it.

Guiding the Group

Many well-intentioned committees meander from one seemingly important tangent to another, making little progress toward accomplishing the metagoal. You can use the regulating techniques illustrated in Table 5 to facilitate task-oriented discussion by setting norms and reinforcing task-oriented discussion when it appears. This can be a slow process, especially with a committee that has not yet learned how to work together or that has strayed from the goal. Simultaneous regulation and guidance is a more efficient approach: The regulating techniques serve the control function by facilitating and maintaining task-oriented processes; the guiding techniques serve the leading function by carrying the group through the task-accomplishment maze.

Leading a committee will put a number of paradoxical demands on you—most noticeably, that you must move the committee toward a specific goal, and do so in a way that members are active in this movement. Leaders who attempt to lead by using directives usually find that they have assumed the lion's share of the decision making, and have squandered the collective problem-solving power of the committee, making such a committee in effect one problem solver with a staff of assistants who provide information and carry out delegated tasks. Obviously, this defeats the purpose of using a group to accomplish the metagoal. Productive processes usually deteriorate further as members become frustrated. Directive leaders are usually trying conscientiously to perform their leadership responsibilities. In fact, being conscientious might well be a contributing factor to their leaping in with a directive and cutting off the collective problem-solving process. A committee *can* be led by guiding. You guide by posing concisely stated problems, employing focused exercises, and using effective information-gathering techniques.

Guiding by posing a problem. A statement of the problem initiates discussion and sets the limits for its direction. To develop the proper statement, you need to carefully think through the metagoal that the committee was formed to accomplish, and then determine the most productive and appropriate problems for each session. Leaders who skip over preparatory analysis usually find themselves ad-libbing, and derail the committee. Much time can be lost in irrelevant discussion and getting back on the track.

In preparing a problem for discussion, you need to consider several issues. First, the problem must be related to the accomplishment of the metagoal. Suppose a company has had several burglaries in the past year. The board of directors may be curious about the factors that contribute to an increase in crime, but these issues are of indirect concern. Of more immediate concern is the question, "What steps should be taken to protect the plant at night?" Second, the problem should be one that the committee is competent to solve and for which it can make a workable decision. The board may be intellectually stimulated by discussing the personality profile of burglars, but an in-depth analysis of such problems should be left to psychologists. Similarly, for the board to make decisions about how society should be restructured to prevent crime would be equally unproductive.

Once you have identified a problem (or a series of problems), the wording of the presentation is important. Present the problem as a question. By definition, questions call for answers and elicit discussion. Limit the question to a single problem; a question that poses several problems at once creates confusion and diffuses the focus of the discussion. The question should be phrased so that it is open-ended. Discussions on closed questions that can be answered with "yes" or "no" die quickly, leaving you faced with generating another problem question. State the question clearly to avoid vagueness. What is meant by the question, "Should the firm adopt a policy of democratic management?" A vague question makes the discussion out of focus from the beginning.

The wording of a question should also be unambiguous. Ambiguous wording invites quibbling over definitions and deflects problem-solving discussion, whereas a concisely stated question focuses the group on the important issue. State the question succinctly. Members become discouraged and confused by such questions as, "Would an increase in benefits or vacation time and a restructuring of the salary scale be effective motivators, or are these proposals just impractical measures that sound good superficially?" Finally, questions should be impartially worded. They should not suggest your bias or the outcome that you desire. A biased or leading question such as, "Should we discontinue our union contract?" can be reworded to be impartial: "What are the pros and cons of having a union contract?" To summarize, begin the guiding process by posing a problem question that focuses on a specific issue and is worded clearly and impartially.

Guiding with focused exercises. Leaders of "growth" or "awareness" groups frequently use focused exercises. While participating in the exercise, members perform a behavior essential to the group process or to the accomplishment of the metagoal. Then the leader uses regulating techniques to encourage a continuation of the new behavior. The exercise prompts the desired behavior, and leader reinforcement encourages its continuation. For example, suppose an awareness leader wanted members to express positive and negative feelings toward others in the group as one step in accomplishing the metagoal of self-awareness. To simply instruct the group to express feelings probably would not work. Members may feel intimidated or not know how to talk openly about their feelings and reactions. With a series of focused exercises, the leader could guide them in small steps to learn to be comfortable when expressing feelings.[8]

For example, members might pair off and share one positive feeling about anything with the other. The next step in the exercise might be to share one positive feeling about their partner. By participating in the exercise, members are guided through the process of learning to give and receive positive feedback, a behavior that most awareness leaders believe is basic to the self-awareness experience. As the members become more comfortable with the new behavior of giving feedback, they are more likely to do so spontaneously, at which point the leader would use regulating techniques to encourage continued feedback.

The same approach can be used in problem-solving and decision-making groups. As leader, your responsibility is to guide the group toward accomplishing a specific task. You can start this process with a focused exercise: the development of group behavioral objectives. To do this, briefly explain behavioral objectives—what they are, how they are developed, and how they are used. You might use a prepared worksheet tailored to the committee's concerns such as the one illustrated in Figure 7.

After discussing the criteria for a behavioral objective, guide the committee (by means of questions) through the poorly stated objectives, and request that members identify and correct the weak points in each objective. Using the first objective in Figure 7 as an example, you might guide with the following questions: "Does the objective state who will perform the objective?" "Does it state what kind of recommendations should be made?" (Closed questions, such as those beginning "Does it . . . ?" can prompt members to speak up in a teaching situation.) "What would be an improved objective?" The structure makes it easy for members to participate appropriately. Encourage continued task-oriented discussion by using regulating techniques. Simultaneously watch for and reinforce behaviors indicative of trust, openness, and cohesiveness.

When you feel that members have a good understanding of behavioral objectives in the abstract, guide them with sequenced focused exercises into an examination of the committee's metagoal and develop two or more long-range objectives to accomplish that metagoal. Next, focus on one of the objectives just set and guide members in breaking it into agenda items to be accomplished in the next one or two meetings. You might also guide members in setting personal

Figure 7. A worksheet for teaching the criteria of behavioral objectives.

A *behavioral objective* specifies:

1. *Who:* the person(s) who will perform the behavior.
2. *What:* the behavior to be performed to an extent that it may be *reliably recorded* by an observer.
3. *How much* of the behavior is required to meet the objective.
4. *Under what conditions* the behavior is to occur.

Directions: Read each objective and determine if it meets all criteria. Correct those that are incomplete.

1. The steering committee will make recommendations to the executive director.
   Improved objective:

2. Each member will bring two new ideas to the next meeting.
   Improved objective:

3. The affirmative action program will be reviewed for compliance with federal guidelines.
   Improved objective:

4. The planning committee will gather statistics on last year's sales.
   Improved objective:

5. A program will be developed to reduce turnover.
   Improved objective:

6. The team will evaluate the success of the management training program.
   Improved objective:

7. The policy review committee will review and update all company policies.
   Improved objective:

8. Communication channels will be improved.
   Improved objective:

9. The committee will investigate the causes of absenteeism in the shipping room.
   Improved objective:

10. Members will evaluate the cost-effectiveness of employee benefits.
    Improved objective:

behavioral objectives for the task activities that they agree to carry out between meetings. It is a good practice to maintain a written record of objectives in the meeting minutes, for example, so that they may be used later to evaluate progress.

The beauty of this approach is that the group learns how to work toward the metagoal as it begins working on it. The sense of accomplishment gained enhances the group process and members' commitment and motivation to work on the task.

Selecting a focused exercise. Guiding with focused exercises is a technique that can challenge your creativity. There is no formula for developing focused exercises, and no one exercise is appropriate in all groups. There are, however, several principles or guidelines for the selection of a particular exercise. First, structure the exercise to elicit a *small number* of behaviors. Asking members to do too much too soon leads to anxiety, frustration, and failure. Second, use exercises that you feel confident all members can perform successfully. As members succeed, they usually become enthusiastic in attempting other new behaviors. A series of exercises that require smaller performance steps that build on one another is conducive to learning. Utilize the fact that success is self-reinforcing.

The third principle is that the exercise should elicit behaviors that are directly related to the development of the group process or to the accomplishment of the metagoal. Exercises that teach members to set objectives or that teach group decision-making steps elicit behaviors that facilitate the accomplishment of the metagoal. Exercises that guide members into sharing opinions or into giving feedback to other members facilitate the development of the group process.

Fourth, the rationale for participating in the exercise must have *credibility* for the members. For example, a relaxation exercise might enhance both the group process (because members are usually more trusting and open when they are relaxed) and the metagoal (because members are usually more productive when they are relaxed). But such an exercise would not have credibility in all groups. A relaxation exercise might have high credibility in a "think-tank" group whose members must let their imaginations run freely, whereas it might seem completely inappropriate to members of the policy review committee.

A related principle is that the specific actions asked of members during the exercise not be threatening or embarrassing. An exercise that makes members feel uncomfortable will only inhibit the group process you are attempting to facilitate. The final principle for selecting a focused exercise is that you should be comfortable with the exercise and be able to convey the belief that participation will assist in moving the committee toward the metagoal. If you do not convey confidence in the exercise, members will not participate fully and the behaviors you hope to elicit will not occur.

Developing a focused exercise. Carefully analyze the behaviors you want to elicit, then break them down into a graduated sequence. The analysis process is the same as that used in shaping. Begin by identifying several successive approximations of the desired group behavior. For example, the desired behavior might be for the committee to employ the behavioral objective model for mapping out its path to the metagoal and for evaluating progress. The successive approximations might be:

Step 1. To learn the importance and uses of behavioral objectives.
　　 2. To learn the criteria of a good behavioral objective.
　　 3. To discriminate between poor and better objectives.
　　 4. To convert a poor objective into a better objective.
　　 5. To identify an observable behavior.
　　 6. To analyze the sequence of behaviors necessary to reach a practice metagoal.
　　 7. To set a series of objectives necessary to reach a practice metagoal.
　　 8. To analyze the sequence of behaviors necessary to reach the group's metagoal.
Step 9. To set a series of objectives necessary to reach the group's metagoal.

The next step will challenge your imagination and creativity. For each step in the sequence, list the various activities that might elicit the desired behavior called for at that step. Ideas can be gleaned from a number of publications that contain directions for various focused exercises and tailored to the unique characteristics and goals of your committee. After generating a number of possibilities, make your selection by using the principles I've outlined. Finally, work out the exact directions and prepare any materials that are necessary.

Guiding with questions. The most versatile and frequently used guiding techniques are probes, checkouts, and summaries (see Chapter 4 for a discussion of these techniques). Probes draw out information, ideas, and opinions. A common error in using a probe is that it is addressing too broad an area. Such a probe can lead the committee to explore whatever aspect of the broad question that the first member answering happens to choose. The direction pursued may move away from problem-solving discussion, so that you must then interrupt and pull members back. This can be avoided by using focused probes.

If the problem to be discussed is complex, it will have many aspects. The danger is that the committee will become absorbed in a tangent that leads it away from the solution to the specific problem being discussed. Be alert to topics that, although related, do not contribute directly to progress toward the metagoal. When this occurs, cut off the tangent and follow with a probe that refocuses the group. Use the same approach to prevent derailment by irrelevant facts or opinions.

Guiding includes clarifying what is being discussed so that there is no confusion about where the discussion is and where it is going. When members' statements are unclear, use checkouts to help them make their comments more specific and to clarify words that might confuse, mislead, or deflect.

Summaries are an ideal technique to guide the transition from one phase of discussion to the next. Concisely review the discussion and follow this summary statement by, "Is there anything else?" to encourage members to present all their ideas. When no one adds any further comments, it is a signal that that phase of the discussion is complete. Use summaries to review decisions that the committee has made. For example: "We have discussed several ways to approach the problem and we have decided to begin by examining as many alternatives as we can. Each of us will bring to the next meeting at least two possible ideas for the marketing strategy. Is that agreed?" If all the members do not agree, then you know additional discussion is necessary. When members agree, you can feel confident that a decision has been reached. Record the agreed-upon actions to avoid confusion and misunderstanding later on and to have a guidepost for evaluation.

To illustrate how to use guiding techniques, consider the following:

Leader: What measures might we consider to reduce turnover in the shipping department? (*Guiding:* posing a question)

Member A: I think we need to figure out what's causing the turnover before we can find a solution.

Leader: That's a good point (*Regulating:* reinforcing). How might we discover the causes? (*Guiding:* probe)

Member B: I think these guys are just lazy and irresponsible. These days people are just interested in playing and are not committed to work.

Member C: Yeah, the values and character of young people today are just deteriorating. Does anyone have any ideas why?

Leader:	That's an interesting observation and question, John (*Regulating:* reinforcing participation), but I'm not sure it'll solve our turnover problem (*Regulating:* cutting off tangential discussion). What ideas do you have about how we can find out what's causing turnover in our shipping department? (*Guiding:* probe)
Member C:	Well, we could interview some of the people who have left.
Leader:	That's an interesting idea. (*Regulating:* reinforcing)
Member D:	I think it's better to talk to some of the people who are in the department now.
Leader:	That's also a good suggestion (*Regulating:* reinforcing). Any other suggestions? (*Guiding:* probe)
Member A:	I've a friend who's a foreman in the shipping department in another company. They used to have a high turnover, but they solved it by calling in a consulting firm.
Leader:	Are you suggesting that we contract a consultant? (*Guiding:* checkout)
Member A:	No. I meant that I could ask him what changes they made. I know whatever it was that they did, it was real successful.
Leader:	I see. Good (*Regulating:* reinforcing). What do the rest of you think of that? (*Guiding:* probe)
Member B:	It was just the Hawthorne effect. Do anything and production increases.
Leader:	That's an interesting phenomenon (*Regulating:* reinforcing), but (*Regulating:* cutting off tangent) I wonder if you have any suggestions about how we might discover the causes of *our* problem? (*Guiding:* probe)
Member B:	Ah, no.
Leader:	Are there any other suggestions? (*Guiding:* probe)
Members collectively:	No.
Leader:	So we've decided that before we can consider any solutions to the problem, we need to find out more about the causes (*Guiding:* summarizing). There were a number of good suggestions (*Regulating:* reinforcing). We can talk to those who have left the company or those who are still working in the shipping department. And we can talk to the foreman in another company that has successfully solved a similar problem. Are there any other suggestions? (*Guiding:* summarizing)

Members collectively: No.

Leader: Good. Let's consider each of these alternatives (*Regulating:* norm setting). What is the feasibility of interviewing past employees? (*Guiding:* posing a problem)

As can be seen, the leader simultaneously guided and regulated. The problem question initiated and focused the discussion. The probes elicited suggestions and indirectly moved members through the problem-solving process. The checkout aided in clarifying a suggestion, and helped the member to be more specific. And the summary pulled all of the relevant suggestions together and signaled that the group was ready to move into the next phase.

Evaluating Group Performance

Evaluation should not be left to the last meeting; it should be an ongoing process. When evaluation is not undertaken until the committee's termination, not much can be done if the results indicate less than satisfactory success. There are three basic underpinnings of evaluation: the metagoal, the behavioral objectives, and the baseline.

Committees are formed to produce a specific product or to effect a specific change in the behavior of employees, or both. When the metagoal specifies a product, such as the development of a procedure to reduce absenteeism, then objectives and metagoals are the yardstick of success. One reason objectives are stated precisely is to clearly determine when they are achieved. Accomplishment of objectives within the stated time period is an affirmation of success. If an objective is not attained, the committee knows immediately that something has gone astray; it does not have to go along for months wondering if it's making progress. For example, when a committee has clearly defined what specific policies it will review, and precisely what constitutes a review, it knows when one task is complete. When the metagoal has been accomplished, there is no further reason for the existence of the committee—it has successfully completed its task.

On the other hand, when the metagoal specifies a change in behavior, such as a specific reduction in absenteeism in a specific department, the baseline is the first measure in evaluation. A behavior change program may take weeks to produce the desired change specified by the metagoal. However, by constantly monitoring the frequency of the target behavior and comparing this with the baseline, the committee can determine if its program is effective: If the current absentee rate begins to drop compared with the baseline rate (the rate before the program was implemented), then there is concrete evidence that the procedure is working. It is helpful to chart the data, because it gives a clear picture of change or absence of change. Figure 8 illustrates the charting and evaluation of data collected on the rate of absences. By simple comparison, you can see that the rate of absences has declined steadily since the introduction of the new program.

Of course, the essential component in this type of evaluation is that the behavior be defined discretely enough that one can tell when it is or is not occurring. It is impossible to collect data on "morale," for example. Morale can be defined in terms of its component behaviors, such as making positive statements about the company, coming to work on time, smiling, infrequent absences, socializing with co-workers, and so forth. The utilization of objectives aids in focusing on specific behaviors. In short, objectives, metagoals, and baseline are the evaluation yardsticks and should be utilized throughout the life of the committee.

Figure 8. Rate of absenteeism before and after introduction of behavior change program.

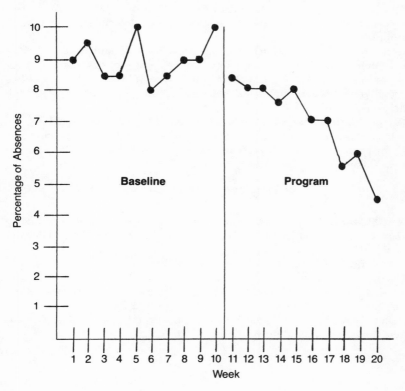

NOTES

1. K.W. Back, "Influence Through Social Communication," *Journal of Abnormal and Social Psychology*, Vol. 46 (1951), p. 9, and L. Berkowitz, "Group Standards, Cohesiveness and Productivity," *Human Relations*, Vol. 7 (1954), p. 509.
2. M. Deutsch, "An Experimental Study of the Effects of Cooperation and Competition upon Group Processes," *Human Relations*, Vol. 2 (1949), p. 199.
3. Carl E. Thoresen and Beverly A. Potter, "Behavioral Group Counseling," in George M. Gazda, ed., *Basic Approaches to Group Psychotherapy and Group Counseling* (Springfield, Ill.: Charles C. Thomas, 1975), pp. 433–467; Beverly A. Potter, Carl E. Thoresen, and Don Sorensen, *Behavioral Group Counseling* (Madison, Wisc.: Counseling Films, Inc., 1973); R. Liberman, "Behavioral Approach to Group Dynamics I. Reinforcement and Prompting of Cohesiveness in Group Therapy," *Behavior Therapy*, Vol. 1 (1970), p. 141.
4. B.H. Raven and J. Reitsema, "The Effects of Varied Clarity of Goals and Group Path upon the Individual and His Relation to His Group," *Human Relations*, Vol. 10 (1957), p. 29.
5. The labels "guiding" and "regulating" were first used by H.E. Gully, *Discussion, Conference and Group Process* (New York: Holt, Rinehart and Winston, 1960).
6. Reprinted with permission from John D. Krumboltz and Beverly A. Potter, "Behavioral Techniques for Developing Trust, Cohesiveness and Goal Accomplishment," in John Vriend and Wayne W. Dyer, eds., *Counseling Effectively in Groups* (Englewood Cliffs, N.J.: Educational Technology Publications, 1975), pp. 73–74.
7. Adapted with permission from Krumboltz and Potter, ibid., pp. 75–78.
8. For a detailed discussion of how to use structured exercises to prompt and shape problem-talk see Beverly A. Potter, "Using Roleplay to Shape Problem-Talk in Groups," *College Student Journal*, Vol. 9 (1975), p. 194.

SUGGESTED READINGS

Bower, Sharon A., and Potter, Beverly A., *Instructor's Manual for Asserting Yourself: A Practical Guide to Positive Change*. Reading, Mass.: Addison-Wesley, 1976.

Egan, G., *Encounter: Group Processes for Interpersonal Growth*. Belmont, Calif.: Brooks/Cole, 1970.

Gully, H.E., *Discussion, Conference and Group Process*. New York: Holt, Rinehart and Winston, 1960.

Michalak, Donald F., and Yager, Edwin G., *Making the Training Process Work*. New York: Harper and Row, 1979.

7

Managing Conflicts

CONFLICTS in the workplace are unavoidable. A conflict can be constructive in signaling a need for change, clarifying expectations (contingencies), preventing serious interpersonal deadlocks, building cohesiveness, and creating a problem-solving climate. In other words, conflicts per se are not a problem; the problem is how to manage them. A poorly managed conflict can reduce morale and motivation, impede control and coordination of subordinates, foster opposition to the manager, and provoke more conflict.

Conflicts emerge when a person believes that someone else is interfering with the pursuit of a desired goal. Ideally, disputants should negotiate a mutually agreeable compromise; typically, however, they go underground in attempting to pursue their goals and satisfy their needs. The result is a situation in which defeating the adversary and advancing one's position take precedence over attaining organizational goals.

A prime reason conflicts are mismanaged or pushed underground is anger. Anger is taboo in the modern business world: It is not businesslike or professional. It is considered "losing one's cool" or being petty. Consequently, airing conflicts openly and directly is avoided for fear of looking bad, incompetent, insecure, petty, or inappropriate. Fear of anger and conflict seems to be prevalent throughout society, and as a result few people have had opportunities to develop the skills necessary to negotiate a realistic settlement of differences. Manipula-

187

tions, subtle sabotage, and mocking insults become the means of solving the problem and getting what we want.

For managers who must resolve conflicts among subordinates, the problem can be even more complex. Often unable to effectively resolve their own conflicts, they must orchestrate resolution of other people's conflicts. Fortunately, the skills needed to manage conflicts can be learned. The approach presented in this chapter is one of information gathering and mediating.[1] Because it is a behavioral approach, its emphasis is on negotiating specific changes in disputants' behavior.

Managers must first find out what the problem is before they can take any action toward resolution. To accomplish this, the manager will typically meet with disputants one at a time to discuss the problem. This rationale is sound, but there are many hidden pitfalls in the procedure. Here is one such case.

Since Collin joined the staff of a small urban planning office two years ago, George, the director of the office, felt as if he were under constant scrutiny. Collin questioned his decisions, criticized the way he ran the office, and corrected his statements. George saw Collin as "just a punk kid with an authority problem." He was on the verge of firing Collin when Collin brought in an important federal grant. George was responsible for appointing the director of this project, and although he felt he had no choice but to select Collin, he took the opportunity to rein Collin in by requiring the formal appointment procedure, so that Collin had to go through the board interview and evaluation. George also had a number of serious talks with Collin about his work and their relationship. Afterward Collin stopped "needling" him but continued to get into conflicts with others in the office. Just the other day Collin and Stacy, the administrative assistant, had a terrible fight over a typewriter. George didn't know exactly what had happened, but he knew he had to restore peace in the office. He talked to Stacy and then called Collin in. The meeting with Collin went like this:

George: I talked to Stacy about that big blow-up yesterday. She says you've been needling her and she can't get her work done. She says you keep going into her office and taking the typewriter. Now what's going on here, Collin? Why are you taking her typewriter?

Collin: Wait a minute! I'm not taking *her* typewriter. It's the *office* typewriter and I need to use it, too. We had an agreement, and she's not living up to it. We agreed to leave the type-writer in the conference room right next to her office, so we could both use it. But no! She keeps taking it. It's bad enough that I have to come all the way across the building, but then she's got the damn machine in her office. She's not using it—it just sits there. But if I take it, she has a fit!

George: Come on, Collin, you know Stacy has things she must type. You don't have to type—you're a planner. Take your typing to one of the clerks.

Collin: You're always on Stacy's side. She can do *anything* as far as you're concerned. Well, she started the fight—she made an agreement and broke it.

George: You know she's very efficient and needs a typewriter at her fingertips. You don't *need* a typewriter. And you can get it from her when you do.

Collin: The hell I don't! I do a lot of writing—more than anyone else here. I *need* a typewriter. It helps me think. I know what's happening here. You resent me and the project. You're just trying to make me fail!

George: That's ridiculous! We're not going into that again. I want a peaceful office where we get work done. I want an end to your childish bickering.

Collin: OK, OK, George. You win. I'll end the "childish bickering." I was just trying to save $50 a month. I'll just rent one. We'll let the taxpayers pay for it. Does that make you happy, George?

George: You're blowing this way out of proportion. It's not a necessary expense.

Collin: Well, you don't have a lot to say about it. *I'm* the director of this project. I need a typewriter and I'll rent one. And I have the authority to do so. So, don't worry, George—Stacy can keep it. There'll be no more problems over the type-writer. I was willing to compromise, I was willing to go out of my way, and it didn't work. But now the problem is solved. Is there anything else, George? If not, I've got *work* to do! May I go now?

George: Just remember one thing, Collin. Project or no project, I'm still your boss. You're around here only because I gave you a second chance. I'm coming to the end of my rope. I want this needling to stop! Have you got that?

Collin: Yeah sure, *Boss!*

Rather than resolving the conflict between Collin and Stacy, George's efforts aggravated his shaky relationship with Collin, and laid the foundation for further conflict between Collin and Stacy. This happened because George violated several important principles of effective conflict management.

Principles for Gathering Information About the Conflict

Get All the Information First

Common sense tells us that we need to know what the problem is before we can solve it. In the example, George attempted to solve the problem before getting all the information. He didn't know about the agreement between Collin and Stacy and that the compromise was intended to save money. It would be easy for Collin to feel that George had already made a decision about the typewriter before their conversation took place. Not only is it difficult to make a good decision with incomplete information, but when one or both disputants feel that they haven't been able to tell their story, it is unlikely that the disputants will conscientiously implement any plan. Therefore, before considering any solutions, the first principle is to find out from all disputants the nature and scope of the problem.

There are two potential pitfalls: talking too much and asking leading questions. As in all interviews, minimize the amount of time you talk. When talking or asking questions, you are not gathering information about the conflict. Use effective interview techniques (described in Chapter 4) to draw out each disputant's story. Leading questions present a serious problem: Avoid questions that imply the answer you desire. Even more important is avoiding questions that lead disputants into areas that *you* feel are potential problems. The goal of the conflict interview is to find out how each disputant sees the problem. By asking leading questions, you may bring up areas that the disputants did not feel were problems. For example, consider this situation:

Tim: Carol doesn't complete the requisition forms. I have to go over them and fill in the missing information. This means a lot of extra work for me.

Manager: What about the sales reports? Does she fill them out correctly?

Tim: No! She makes a mess out of the sales reports. In fact, two weeks ago I had to. . . .

Carl:	Pete challenges everything I say. It makes me look like a fool around the office.
Manager:	What happens when you go out on calls together?
Carl:	He dominates the whole presentation. I can't say anything. And when I do, he corrects me. I'm sick of it!

By asking about other situations, the manager suggested problems. Typically, disputants want to build their cases against one another. Leading questions open up new problems for disputants to bring into the conflict. Avoid adding fuel to the problem; the disputants know what is bothering them. Even if you have observed or sensed conflict between them in other areas, avoid asking about it. Simply find out how each sees the conflict today.

Bring Disputants Together

Many managers question this principle, the idea of bringing the disputants together, because they believe it is best to interview the contending parties separately. On the face of it, separate interviews make a lot of sense: They eliminate the risk of losing control and of being caught in the middle of a verbal battle. However, without the other disputant present, each person is more likely to exaggerate if not deliberately distort the issues.

Separation actually creates more problems than it solves. First, it takes more time to interview each person individually. Second, each disputant is more likely to distort the conflict when the other is absent. Likewise, it is easier for the manager to be swayed by manipulative and persuasive tactics. But the third and most important reason has to do with trust and credibility. Interviewed separately, each disputant is likely to suspect that you have sided with the other. Not only do such suspicions encourage exaggerations and fabrications, but they make it difficult for you to assume the role of impartial mediator. Finally, when you interview separately, the implication is that *you* are going to decide what action will be taken. When you interview disputants in each other's presence you set the stage for their solving their own problems with one another.

Maintain Control

In any interview, whatever its purpose, maintaining control is an important concern. When interviewing two or more disputants, control is vital. Even if the disputants are not overtly angry at the beginning of the interview, their anger is likely to be reignited when they hear their adversary stating the other side of the dispute. Angry people often forget their manners: They rudely interrupt in an attempt to correct the other's version and sway the interviewer's opinion; they raise their voices, call people names, and sometimes make threats. Such outbursts are obviously counterproductive, but you should expect them to occur and be prepared to control them. Of course, the prospect of controlling emotional outbursts is precisely what is frightening about conflicts. Fortunately, there are specific control techniques that are easy to learn and that in most cases will eliminate this threat. You have several control tools available: your authority, ground rules, your body itself, and your voice.

Using your authority. It is not advisable to assert your authority too blatantly. When confronted head on with authority, people have a tendency to rebel. Naturally, you want to avoid this because it makes your task harder. Instead, communicate authority through your manner in handling the interview. Subtly but firmly convey the message, "I expect you to cooperate by following my instructions." This message, combined with the awareness that you can enact negative consequences (termination, reprimand, withholding promotion or privileges), is very effective. Use the setting to emphasize your authority. Whenever possible, meet with disputants in your office. Make a formal appointment.

In most cases the disputants will want you to see them as being reasonable and justified in their complaints. This is a powerful weapon for you, because they will realize the danger of undermining themselves if they become unruly or obstinate. On the other hand, disputants often try in subtle ways to enrage their adversaries so as to make them look bad. This is what you must control.

Setting ground rules. It is easier to establish control immediately than to regain it once it has been lost. Don't wait until control becomes a problem—use a preventive approach. Ground rules are invaluable. A ground rule is an explicit statement of what you expect and what the disputants can expect from you. I suggest that you begin all conflict resolution sessions with a ground rule stated something like this: "I'm going to begin by finding out what's been going on. I will talk to you one at a time. I want to know how each of you sees the problem. OK, I'm going to begin with Joe and then I'll talk to Sam." Often this is all that is necessary. The disputants know that if they interrupt or argue, they will be breaking your explicit prescription. If you begin to lose control, stop and restate the ground rules: "Sam, right now I'm listening to Joe's side. I will get to you next" or "Joe, I heard your side —now I want to hear Sam's story." Naturally, you need to use a firm voice so that you project the message, "I expect you to be quiet and listen."

Under most circumstances, have disputants tell their stories *to you.* While one disputant is talking, the other should be listening—but *not* participating. Allowing disputants to talk directly to one another requires too much risk of losing control. Set the ground rules for this procedure: When the disputant you are interviewing begins talking to the other, say something like, "Talk to me, Joe." Sometimes you may have to repeat the phrase: "Talk to *me,* Joe. Talk to me!"

Using your body. Where and how you sit or stand and the way you use physical gestures can help control disputants. Sitting behind your desk may enhance your authority and give you a sense of security, but it makes the job of control more difficult. From behind the desk, it is almost impossible to use physical control: If the disputants should get out of hand by bickering angrily or making physical threats, you will be caught behind the desk. Avoid this; place yourself physically between them (Figure 9). In this position you can quickly lean forward to block the disputants' view of one another, and because it is difficult to shout at someone who can't be seen, the disputants will then direct their remarks to you. This will allow you to regain control quickly with little interruption. Sitting between disputants allows you to stand up when the more subtle control methods fail.

Seat disputants in comfortable chairs, if possible. It is best for you to sit on the edge of a straight-back chair. Such an arrangement allows you to employ the maximum control potential of the environment.

Figure 9. Seating arrangement and control.

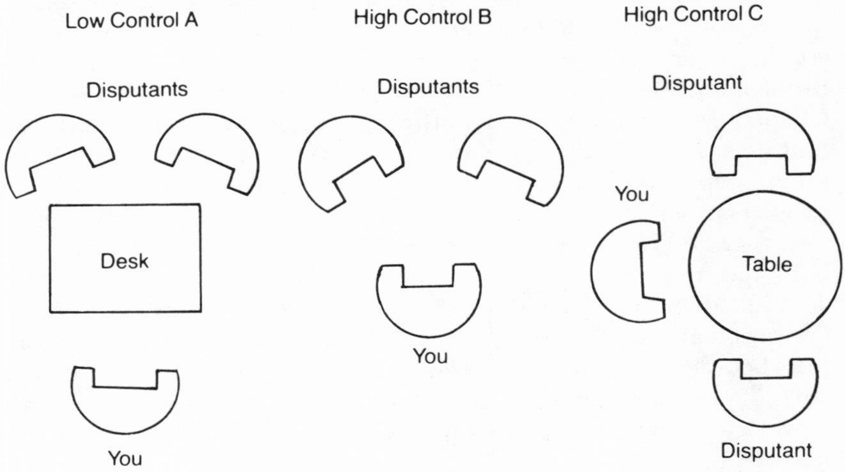

Low Control A

High Control B

High Control C

Disputants are more inclined to relax in comfortable chairs and less likely to jump up. (If you have only one easy chair, place the angrier disputant in it.) On the other hand, sitting on the edge of a hard chair allows you to move rapidly. Position C in Figure 9 when you fear that disputants may present a physical control problem: You and the table create a barrier between the two rivals.

Your hands and the gestures you make with them are an important control tool. The standing figure (see Figure 10) illustrates a gesture that communicates "wait" or "quiet." Often this simple gesture alone is sufficient to calm disputants, and it can be used without either looking at the disputant or interrupting the interview. (Observe the position of the left hand on the seated leader.) Encourage disputants to speak by leaning toward them and gesturing upward with your palm (see the right hand on the seated figure). Most of us use such gestures spontaneously. Avoid pointing or shaking your finger, since people tend to feel demeaned and antagonized by such gestures.

Your voice. The pitch and volume of your voice can be modified to exert more or less force. In general, the louder the volume and the lower the pitch, the more force or control you will exert. It is important that your control level be appropriate to the situation. Once you have made a strong display of force by raising your voice, it will be difficult to back down. As a rule of thumb, start in a low tone and increase the degree of force in your voice or gestures to match those of the disputants.

Keep Disputants on the Topic

In an employment interview you know what topic areas to explore, but this is generally not the case in a conflict interview, where frequently you will know nothing about the problem. The goal of the conflict interview is to find out each disputant's perception of the problem. (Please review the interviewing techniques discussed in Chapter 4—I will refer to them throughout this chapter.) If a disputant gets sidetracked into telling the adversary's story or describing other people's opinions, get him or her back on the topic. "What is the problem as *you* see it?" you can ask. When disputants get off the topic, interrupt and use a probe to bring them back. In general, maintain a here-and-now focus: Angry people often go into lengthy historical accounts of previous conflicts; you can interrupt by saying, "What's the problem *today?*" Even when there's a backlog of unresolved conflicts between disputants, it is best to focus on one problem, the most current one. Successful change in one area will encourage disputants to work toward resolving other problems.

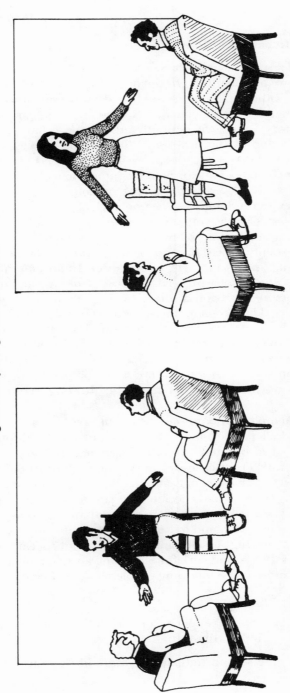

Figure 10. Physical gestures and control.

Remain Impartial

Avoid jumping to conclusions. Everyone knows that a mediator must be objective and neutral. On the face of it, this seems simple. Often, however, without realizing it you may draw unwarranted conclusions and communicate your bias. Some disputants will fear your reactions to their story; others will doubt that they have a chance for a satisfactory resolution of the problem. When this is the case, they will be sensitive to subtleties in your speech and behavior. Casual remarks on your part could lead one or both disputants to feel cornered. When a disputant feels backed into a corner by both you and an adversary, you can expect a defensive reaction such as withdrawal, hostility, or guardedness. Clearly, you want to avoid this.

Drawing conclusions seems to be a natural tendency. Most people find uncertainty unsettling, and to escape it they will draw conclusions from vague and incomplete information. In an employment interview, this is a serious problem because it often leads to hiring the wrong person. In a conflict interview, leaping to conclusions destroys impartiality. This problem can be reduced by using effective interview techniques to get specific information. Use probes, repeats, and checkouts to find out exactly what happened. The more you get down to specific behaviors, the better. What did the person do? What did the person say? When and where did it occur? By focusing on the antagonizing behaviors, you minimize drawing erroneous conclusions.

For example, suppose one disputant says, "When I came in this morning, Bill jumped me." Did Bill confront the disputant with a grievance? Did Bill make an insulting remark? Or did he startle the disputant with a practical joke? Even though drawing out information about specific behaviors may at times be tedious, it is important to do so. Probing specifics and checking out your understanding communicates that you want to understand the employee's point of view. This will reduce suspicion and aid in enlisting the disputants' cooperation in problem solving. Finally, information about specific offensive behavior lays the groundwork for mediating an action plan for behavior change. Compare the following problem statements:

Vague: "She's inconsiderate."
Specific: "She takes pens from my desk without asking and then forgets to return them."

Obviously, the second statement is more likely to lead to successful mediation.

Accept each disputant's view. Remember that the goal of the interview is to find out each disputant's perception of the problem. Judging or evaluating a disputant's story destroys impartiality and makes it difficult to accomplish this goal. When you question or evaluate disputants' stories on the spot, you are negating their perceptions. This is an important point and one that many managers have difficulty accepting. Some feel the necessity to "get to the truth of the matter" to determine the correct version of the problem. But this approach can have several pitfalls. When people feel judged, they become defensive and edit out parts that may make them look bad and exaggerate aspects that they think will be looked on favorably. Likewise, feeling judged can set off a host of emotions: anxiety, suspicion, hostility, fear, and anger. Obviously the person doing the judging cannot remain impartial for long, because judging requires taking a stand and evaluating each story from the perspective of that stand. Obviously, a judgmental climate is not conducive to finding out how each disputant sees the conflict.

Another more subtle problem with judging is that it tends to shift responsibility for resolving the conflict from the disputants to you. If you assume this responsibility, you will have made your job more difficult and reduced the chances that the conflict will be resolved. Disputants will attempt to get you to assume responsibility. They usually prefer to go to you as the all-knowing monarch who will review the facts and issue an edict. When the decision comes out in their favor, they gloat over their adversary's loss. If they don't like your decision, they will try to prove you incompetent by destroying your attempts at resolution. In either case, future conflict is likely because blame for the failure of the resolution attempt can be placed on you.

The key word here is *acceptance*. Accept each disputant's statement of the problem. You may want to question for clarification and specific information, but don't question the validity of the disputant's perceptions. It is futile and counterproductive to attempt to arrive at "reality" or the "truth." For example, when questioning several eyewitnesses, police frequently get dramatically different descriptions of the suspect or of the getaway car. One witness may report that the car was blue; another, that it was green. If discrepancies of this magnitude can occur when several people have observed the same objective event, you can imagine the range of differences possible when people are describing their perceptions of an interaction in which they have considerable emotional investment. One person will interpret a look as sneering, another will see it as disapproving, and a third may view it as joking. Avoid becoming a detective who attempts to determine which story is right. Obviously the disputants' stories will differ in many places. If there were no differences, there would probably be no conflict. It is not necessary to identify reality to resolve the conflict, but it is necessary for each disputant to hear how the other sees the problem. Sometimes this alone is sufficient to resolve the problem. Although this is somewhat rare, there are times when the entire conflict is grounded in a misunderstanding. When that misunderstanding is rectified, the conflict disappears.

The problem most managers face is the confusion between acceptance and agreement. Because you accept a person's perception of a situation does not mean that you personally agree with that perception; in fact, you may totally disagree. But you should not say this to either disputant—to do so would destroy your position of impartiality. It is important to remember that even when a disputant is completely wrong in his or her perception of the conflict, *subjectively* that person is right. People make decisions and act upon their perceptions of the world—it is their personal reality. Therefore even though their statements and views may seem exaggerated or absurd to you, they are real to the disputants, because that is the way they see things, and this information forms the basis of their actions. And most people are inclined to believe their own perceptions rather than someone else's arguments. In short, the goal of the conflict interview is to find out how each disputant sees the problem. This is best done by remaining impartial and accepting each disputant's version. Disagreeing, judging, and criticizing should be avoided. Likewise, interpreting, analyzing, and diagnosing should be avoided, since they also indicate disagreement with the disputant's view. For example:

Mary: He bosses me around constantly.
Manager: You're just saying that because you feel threatened.

The manager's interpretation suggests that Mary's view of the problem is inaccurate.

On the other hand, agreeing with either disputant should also be avoided. When you agree with one, you implicitly disagree with the other. Disputants always attempt to get you to agree with them—this is a way of pulling you over to their side. Here is a typical example:

Manager: What's the problem as you see it?
Jim: She lost the requisition and the order wasn't filled. The client was furious. Naturally, I had to chew her out. You'd do the same thing, wouldn't you?

Avoid this trap. If you fall into it, you'll be pulled into the conflict. By the same token avoid reassuring, sympathizing, consoling, or supporting either disputant. As well-meaning as your actions may be, they will cause the other disputant to interpret them as being a vote of confidence for his or her adversary's position.

Don't Make Suggestions

As well as attempting to get you to agree and to commiserate with them, disputants will often ask for suggestions. Always avoid giving suggestions, because as soon as you offer a suggestion, you lose control of the interview: You have been sidetracked from getting information into giving information, and *you* have assumed responsibility for solving the problem. During the interview, do nothing but gather information on how each disputant sees the problem. When disputants request suggestions or push you for agreement, don't respond; ignore the request and proceed with the interview. Don't worry about being polite—this is not a social situation. At all times keep sight of your objective and maintain control.

Encourage Disputants to Express Their Feelings

Whether the conflict is grounded in substantive issues—such as disagreements over policies and practices—or in personal issues, there is always a layer of emotion that insulates and obscures the basic conflict. As I stated earlier, most people are reluctant to express negative emotions (fear, resentment, distrust, rejection, and hostility), and very often disputants will attempt to mask these feelings behind seemingly reasonable complaints. In the dispute between Stacy and Collin, for example, there were certain personal antagonisms that underlay the conflict about the typewriter. Collin went to lunch with the other planners in the office nearly every day, and they would often get together again after work for a couple of beers. Stacy was never invited along, and she believed that Collin was responsible for her being excluded. Once or twice she timidly hinted that she would like to be included. Collin responded by laughing and saying, "You're not a planner. You're just a high-class secretary."

Stacy was hurt by his offhand comment. She ruminated over it, and began watching Collin's every move. Soon she began to feel intense resentment toward him. As she watched him, she saw that he always stretched the rules: He made personal long distance calls on the office phone, and sat around his office reading the newspaper in the morning. When she confronted him on wasting time, he claimed he was thinking. When he got the grant he became intolerable. He acted as if he were her boss. All of these things added to Stacy's resentment.

Stacy prided herself on being efficient—she was organized and had everything at her fingertips. One of the things she needed was a typewriter, and she could see no reason why she—the administrative assistant in charge of the typing pool—shouldn't have a typewriter in her office. She made an agreement with Collin about leaving the typewriter in the conference room, but it just didn't work out, because it took too long to go into the conference room several times a day. And Collin didn't need the typewriter that often, anyway. At most, he used it once every other day. They finally had a big argument over the typewriter. Stacy had several letters she had to get out by the end of the day. When she came back from lunch, Collin had the typewriter, but he wasn't using it. For nearly an hour and a half, he had it on his desk but didn't type. Stacy was certain about this—she had timed him. When she politely asked him to hurry, he made some nasty remark about getting his fair share. Then he spent 22 minutes talking to Bill, another planner. When Stacy went a second time to prompt Collin, she heard Collin and Bill laughing and making plans to meet after work. She told Collin that she had work to do. He threw a tantrum and started shouting at her. As far as Stacy was concerned, that was the limit—she went straight to George.

Stacy's hostility toward Collin went beyond the immediate problem of sharing the typewriter. In fact, the typewriter was not the primary problem at all; it was merely a pretext. But when Stacy told her story to George, she didn't mention her feelings about being excluded from the office social activities. Stacy herself might not have been entirely aware of her feelings—most people don't like to admit, even to themselves, that they feel resentment. Negative feelings toward others tend to attach themselves to one event after another. Insignificant things become antagonizing.

Always encourage disputants to express their feelings. Many times they are not aware of how another is reacting to them. Collin knew Stacy watched him constantly, but he didn't realize that she felt he was excluding her. Usually, disputants will attempt to cover up their feelings, because they don't want to look petty or immature. But in attempting to mask their feelings, they frequently fail to state the problem in its entirety. They tell the most acceptable part of their story, and their withholding makes resolution of the problem difficult.

Being impartial helps considerably here. Listening to the disputants' feelings without suggesting your personal reaction will make it easier for them. But don't expect this to happen spontaneously: Hostility and other negative emotions are easier to express than hurt feelings. It is much easier for Stacy to say, "You irritate me because you're selfish" than for her to say, "I was hurt because I was not invited."

Even when a conflict has a substantive basis, there is invariably an emotional overlay. When these feelings are ignored, they can interfere with problem solving and take on a life of their own. That is, once the original problem has been resolved, the feelings remain and color future interactions.

The feeling checkout discussed in Chapter 4 is very effective. This technique involves a reflection, presented tentatively, of the feelings you are sensing. Reflecting can be a little tricky. It is easy to inadvertently comment on the feeling rather than simply to reflect. You cannot comment on another's feeling without implying an evaluation. Compare the following examples:

1. I've tried to talk with Sally, but I always end up at odds with her, because she takes any expression of opinion as a personal attack.

   Poor Response: Perhaps you come across as attacking her and you just don't realize it. (*Analyzing*)

   Better Response: Do you mean you feel frustrated because your intentions are misunderstood? (*Reflecting*)

2. When I see Don smoking, I just feel like grabbing the filthy thing right out of his mouth!

   Poor Response: Breathing someone's smoke is pretty unpleasant. (*Agreeing, sympathizing*)

   Poor Response: You feel like grabbing the filthy thing out of his mouth? (*Restating*)

   Better Response: Do you mean the sight of Don smoking makes you angry? (*Reflecting*)

3. If he does that again, I'll let him know who's boss. One bit of flack and I'll pop him one!

   Poor Response: Seems a little extreme. (*Evaluating*)

   Poor Response: That'll make things worse. (*Moralizing*)

   Better Response: Do you mean you're so angry that you'd consider having it out with him physically? (*Reflecting*)

4. She's a fool because I have more on the ball than she realizes. If she'd just give me a little freedom and responsibility, I could do a lot more.

Poor Response: You don't like a woman boss. (*Analyzing*)
Poor Response: Be patient. (*Giving suggestions*)
Better Response: Do you mean you can do something but don't have the chance to show it? (*Reflecting*)

There are three places in the conflict interview where feeling checkouts are helpful. First, it is useful when there is a discrepancy or inconsistency in what the disputant is saying. Sometimes the discrepancy is between the verbal and nonverbal communications—for example, sneering while saying, "I think Joe does a good job." A feeling checkout response might be, "I sense you have some negative feelings about Joe's work." Second, it can be helpful when one thing the disputant says contradicts something else he or she said. For example, a disputant might say, "I like working with Margaret," and then might complain about Margaret. An appropriate feeling checkout would be, "Do you mean that though you like Margaret, there are some things she does that bug you?" A third situation in which a feeling checkout works well is when a strong emotion is implicit in the disputant's remarks. For example: "I'll tell you one thing. You won't catch me sticking my neck out again in staff meetings." To this one might say, "Do you mean you took a risk and now you're sorry you spoke up?" You will encounter times when the emotion is strongly expressed, but the disputant can't speak about it. Crying is a good example. You might say, "You seem to feel hurt and don't seem to know how to talk about it."

Don't belabor the point. If after three or four attempts to encourage the disputant to express feelings, that individual is still reticent, then it would be best to let it drop. Some people find it extremely difficult to talk about their emotional reactions, but even when they don't respond in a way you might want them to, the feeling checkout communicates your willingness to listen.

Sum Up Often

The sum-up technique described in Chapter 4 is one of the most valuable tools in the conflict interview. It tells you when the interview with the first disputant is complete and when to move on to interviewing the second disputant. When you think you have the first disputant's complete story, summarize and ask, "Is there anything else?" A "no" response is your signal to move on to the next disputant. If the answer is "yes," continue with the interview.

After you have completed interviews with all disputants, summarize each disputant's story again before going on to the mediation phase. It may seem redundant to sum up each story so many times, but the repetitiveness will help you in the long run. First, it is an insurance against cutting disputants off prematurely. When they haven't told their entire story, they are more likely to interrupt when others are speaking. Things can become confusing when you find yourself going back and forth between disputants and getting only pieces of stories each time. In short, the sum-up technique helps you to keep things orderly and under control. In addition, disputants get to hear their stories in an encapsulated form. This sets the stage for you to move into mediation.

In the following example, George will use conflict interview techniques to find out how Collin and Stacy each view their argument. I will act as the coach and assist George when he gets off the track.

Coach:	*OK, George, begin by laying the ground rules.*
George:	Stacy and Collin, I want to find out how each of you sees the problem. I'm going to talk to you one at a time. I'll begin with Stacy, then I'll listen to Collin's story.
Coach:	*Good, George. Begin the interview with a probe or open question.*
George:	Stacy, how do you see the problem? (Probe)
Stacy:	Collin is just impossible!
George:	Impossible? (Repeat)
Stacy:	Yes, he's selfish and inconsiderate. Like yesterday, with the typewriter. That's a good example.
George:	He took your typewriter?
Collin:	Hey, just a minute. It's not *her* typewriter. I'm not going to sit here and listen to this.
Coach:	*Hold on a minute, George, that was a leading question. You put words into Stacy's mouth and it looked as if you were taking sides. Just find out how Stacy sees the problem. Begin again with a probe.*
George:	What happened with the typewriter? (Probe)
Stacy:	I had a lot of work to do and Collin was monopolizing the typewriter.
George:	Monopolizing? (Repeat)
Stacy:	Yes, he wasn't typing at all. For an hour and a half he had it on his desk but he didn't type at all. I know because I timed him.

Collin:	Oh, come on!
George:	(raising his hand toward Collin) Hold on, Collin, I'll get to you in a minute. (Repeated ground rules and used hand gesture to reestablish control)
George:	Go on, Stacy.
Stacy:	I asked him to hurry up. I was very nice.
Collin:	The hell she was!
George:	(looking at Collin) Collin, I'm listening to Stacy's side. I want you to be quiet until I'm finished. Then I'll listen to your story. (Escalated force in repeating ground rules)
Coach:	*Perfect, George, you stopped Collin's intrusion without being sidetracked.*
Stacy:	Yes. After I spoke to him he deliberately wasted time talking with Bill about his social life. I went back a second time to urge him to hurry. When I heard the two of them planning their evening drinking party (Stacy sneers at Collin), I told him I thought he was wasting time. He got furious and had a fit.
George:	Do you mean he yelled at you? (Checkout)
Stacy:	Yes, he told me that he was going to get his fair share. I don't have to take this—I have work to do! Collin and his friends (Stacy sneers) just party around here when I'm trying to work. They don't care about work—all they care about is joking and drinking. Well, I'm sick of listening to them.
George:	I can understand that. We're being paid to work.
Coach:	*Wait, George. You're agreeing with Stacy. This is going to get you into trouble. You'll lose your impartiality.*
George:	Have you had this kind of problem with Collin in other areas? Like the dictaphone, for example?
Stacy:	Well, yes. He finds some way to needle me. Last week I wanted to use the dictaphone but he'd taken it with him into the field.
Coach:	*What's happening here? Who brought up the problem with the dictaphone?*
George:	*I guess I did.*
Coach:	*Yes, that was another leading question. Don't lead her into other areas. Just find out how Stacy sees the problem. Sum up now and see what happens.*
George:	So as you see it, you needed to use the typewriter but Collin had it and wasn't actually using it. You asked him a couple of times to hurry. Then he insulted you. Is there anything else?

Stacy:	Yes, I don't see why Collin should be able to use this place as a social forum.
George:	*I'm stuck. What do I do now?*
Coach:	*Stacy mentioned the socializing a couple of times. It seems somewhat unrelated. What do you suppose this means? How do you think she feels?*
George:	*I don't know. I suppose she feels left out.*
Coach:	*Good, try that out on her with a feeling checkout.*
George:	I get the feeling that you sometimes feel left out of the social activities.
Stacy:	Well, I really wouldn't want to go *anywhere* with those guys. It's just that I can't stand the way they talk about it all the time in front of me!
George:	Do you mean you feel it's rude and you wish he'd make his social plans outside of your hearing? (Feeling checkout)
Stacy:	No, it's not that. I'm new here. I mean, we all work together, don't we? I like to go out to lunch or have a couple of beers, too. Collin seems to think he's better than me. I just don't like his attitude.
George:	Do you mean you'd like to be asked along? (Feeling checkout)
Stacy:	(hesitantly) Well, yes. I do want to be included.
George:	Let me see if I've got this now. As you see it, Collin had the typewriter when you needed it and when you asked him to hurry, he was rude. Also, he often makes social plans with other people in front of you but doesn't ask you along. Is there anything else?
Stacy:	No, that's about it.
George:	OK, Collin. Stacy says that you're excluding her and that you kept the typewriter when she needed it. What's your side?
Collin:	There's no point in saying anything. You don't listen to me. You're always on her side. And I *don't* exclude her!
Coach:	*What happened, George?*
George:	*I don't know. I was just trying to find out what Collin thought of Stacy's story.*
Coach:	*That's the problem, George: You asked Collin to answer Stacy's story. This puts Collin on the defensive. Don't mention Stacy's story—he heard it. Your objective is to find out how Collin sees the problem. You've been doing a good job so far. Let's start again.*
George:	How do you see the problem, Collin? (Probe)
Collin:	There's only one typewriter here for all the planners and Stacy. It's ridiculous. I need to use a typewriter. I do a lot of

writing and I can think better with a typewriter. Well, Stacy
and I had an agreement that we'd leave the typewriter in
the conference room, so that we could both use it. This is a
big inconvenience to me. It means that I have to get all my
stuff together and bring it across the building. Stacy only
has to go a couple of feet. If I get a call or forget something,
I've got to go all the way back. Well, I was willing to compromise, but she didn't keep her part of the bargain.

Stacy: That's not true!

George: (raises hand toward Stacy to maintain control) What happened? (Probe)

Coach: *Good, George.*

Collin: Every time I came over to use the machine, it was on her
desk. When I'd try to get it from her, she'd get angry and
tell me she had to use it. But it would just sit there. Well,
she broke the agreement, so I figured what's good for the
goose is good for the gander. Yesterday I took the typewriter—just like she does. That's what made her so angry.
When she came over to get it, I just happened to be talking
to Bill for a moment about the park on the West Side.

George: Stacy said—

Coach: *Careful, George, you're asking Collin to answer Stacy's story.*

George: Do you mean that since Stacy broke the agreement by taking the typewriter into her office you felt it was OK for you
to do the same? (Checkout)

Collin: Exactly. Do you expect me to compromise when she won't?
What would you do, George?

Coach: *Ignore that question, George.*

George: Go on.

Collin: You heard her—she *timed* me! That's ridiculous. I can't
work under these conditions. She talks about wasting time
when *she* wastes time spying on me. I've had enough of it—
I want her off my back.

George: What do you suggest?

Coach: *Hold off with that for now. By asking for suggestions you'll get off
the track. Just find out how Collin sees the problem.*

George: Do you mean Stacy is watching and judging your work?
(Checkout)

Collin: That's right. Just like she said, she timed me. She tells me
exactly how many minutes I'm late. She even listens in on
my calls.

Stacy: I do not!

George: Stacy, we heard your side. (Repeat ground rules for control.) Go on, Collin.

Collin: Well, I haven't been excluding her. I just don't like to be around her. I like to go out with Bill and a couple of the other fellas. They don't hassle me. And we talk about the projects. Stacy doesn't know anything about that stuff— she'd just be bored. Besides, she's got the secretaries to hang out with.

George: Wait a minute, Collin. That's a little unfair, isn't it?

Collin: Oh, what's the use! I knew you wouldn't understand. I don't have anything else to say.

Coach: *What happened?*

George: *I said something wrong. Oh, I know—it was that comment about being unfair.*

Coach: *Yes, George. You evaluated Collin's feelings. Try summing up to get back on the track.*

George: So as you see it, you made an agreement with Stacy about keeping the typewriter in the conference room. But when Stacy took it in her office, you felt the agreement was off. Yesterday you were using the typewriter and Stacy wanted it. Is there anything else?

Collin: Yes, I don't ask her to go out with us for beers because it's bad enough having a watchbird watching me all day; I don't need it when I'm trying to relax and enjoy myself.

George: Watchbird? (Repeat)

Collin: She watches me. If I'm a little late, she tells me exactly how much. She tells me about deadlines. I'm tired of her trying to be a self-appointed time manager.

George: OK, tell me if I understand correctly: You and Stacy had an agreement about the typewriter. When you found she was taking it into her office, you figured the agreement was off and it was OK for you to do the same. Also, you feel she is monitoring your work by telling you when you are late. This makes you uncomfortable, and this is why you don't ask her along with your friends after work. Is there anything else? (Sum-up)

Collin: No, that's all. Isn't it enough?

George: Stacy, what about this agreement? You didn't mention an agreement with Collin. How did you see the agreement?

Coach: *You'll get yourself into trouble with that question, George. Now you're asking Stacy to answer Collin's story. Stacy didn't mention the agreement. That must mean she didn't see it as part of the problem. You've got both stories. Now sum up both stories quickly and you'll be ready to move into mediation.*

George: (to Collin) Stacy sees the problem as. . . .

Coach: *Sum up Stacy's story to Stacy and Collin's story to Collin. Try again.*

George: (looking at Stacy) You needed to use the typewriter yesterday and Collin had it on his desk. When you didn't hear him typing, you asked him to hurry up. Also, Collin often makes social plans with the others but doesn't include you. This makes you feel left out. (Looking at Collin) And Collin, the way you see the problem is that you made an agreement with Stacy to leave the typewriter in the conference room. Several times Stacy took the typewriter into her office, so you figured the agreement was off. You took the typewriter into your office. When you did this, Stacy came and asked for the typewriter. Also, Stacy often tells you when you're late and points out your deadlines. Because of this you prefer not to be around her after work because you don't like feeling watched. Is there anything else?

Stacy: That's it.

Collin: You've got it.

By conducting the interview in this fashion, George sidestepped the trouble spots he had encountered before. Now it becomes apparent that bringing disputants together for the interview sets the stage for problem solving. With the conflict stated as it was in the final sum-up, George stands a good chance of facilitating a successful negotiation between Collin and Stacy.

Decision Point

At the end of the interview you must make a decision on the basis of the information you have gathered. In general, you have six broad decision categories. You might decide to *reprimand* or in some cases *terminate* one or both disputants; recommend that one or both be *transferred;* think things over and *issue a directive* for resolving the problem; and in some rare cases decide to *do absolutely nothing.* I say in rare cases because if the conflict has gotten to the point of a formal interview, some decisive action usually is in order.

The final option is to *mediate an action plan.* Since you have already succeeded in getting the disputants to state their problem, the next step seems obvious: Guide them in resolving their conflict. Don't jump to conclusions about the insolubility of a conflict; disputants often arrive at a mutually agreeable solution, perhaps one that you may never have considered. After all, barring termination or transfer, they must continue to interact. The fact that you are conducting the mediation implicitly communicates to them that you expect them to arrive at some compromise. It is an effort well worth the time it takes.

Mediating an Action Plan

The goal of mediation is to facilitate the disputants' negotiating a mutually agreeable resolution. Generally, the outcome represents a formal statement of a compromise. Sometimes it will be a 50-50 give and take; at other times, it may appear that one party is compromising more than the other. But don't concern yourself with who is giving in more: What may appear to be a large concession to you may not be to the disputants. The important thing is that they arrive at the agreement. In extreme cases disputants may remain entrenched in their positions. Should this happen, you can fall back on one of the other potential resolution tools mentioned above. Attempting mediation is almost always worth the effort, however, because the time involved is minimal compared with the potential gains.

How to Mediate

Elicit suggestions. Turn to one of the disputants and request a suggestion with a probe, such as "What do you suggest?" Often your first request will meet with a denial, a reversal, or an extreme. An example of a denial is "I don't know" or "I don't see any way to solve this." Ignore denials. Simply restate the request for a suggestion, perhaps a bit more firmly. If you request a suggestion three times and don't get a response, turn to the other disputant and repeat the process. A disputant may attempt a reversal, such as "I don't know. What do you suggest?" Clearly this is a ploy to shift the responsibility for solving the problem to you. Once again, sidestep this by ignoring the question and restating the request for a suggestion.

Sometimes the disputants will offer extreme suggestions, such as that their adversary acquiesce; that you take some radical action such as terminating their adversary; or that they be given some unreasonable privilege. Simply accept the suggestion and ignore the unreasonable aspect. If you fall into the trap of commenting on the validity of the suggestion, you will destroy your impartiality and reduce the chances of a successful mediation. Leave evaluation of the suggestion to the other disputant, who won't agree to something extreme.

In most cases if you remain firm in communicating that you expect the disputants to solve the problem, one of them will offer a suggestion. Remember, disputants don't want to appear unreasonable in your eyes. When the first disputant refuses to offer some suggestion, that person is running the risk of the second disputant's offering an acceptable one. The first disputant knows that refusing makes a person appear to be a troublemaker and thereby undermines the reasonableness of his or her side of the story. By remaining firm in your insistence on a suggestion and by avoiding the urge to offer one, you can capitalize on this unspoken undercurrent.

Don't accept vague suggestions; use the interview techniques described in Chapter 4 to clarify exactly what the disputant means. Find out what specific behavior change is being requested. For example, a suggestion such as "I want him off my back" is not workable. What exactly is being requested? If the adversary agrees, what exactly has been agreed to? "Tell him to stop commenting on my spelling" is workable because it requests a specific behavior change.

The need for specificity cannot be overemphasized. When a final agreement is arrived at, the specificity will make accountability possible. Both parties will know exactly what they have agreed to do, and whichever party does not follow through will look bad. Specificity exerts a strong pressure to carry out the agreement.

Check out suggestions. Once you get a specific suggestion, check it out with the other disputants. "Tom suggests that you stop commenting on his spelling. What do you think of that?" The pressure is on the second disputant either to accept the suggestion or to offer a substitute. When you get an alternative suggestion, take it back to the first disputant. "Bill suggests that you proofread the draft before giving it to him. What do you think of that?" Continue this back-and-forth process until the disputants arrive at an agreement.

Be impartial. For mediation to work, it is imperative that you remain neutral. Accept the disputant's suggestion without comment. Don't criticize or evaluate it—and above all, don't offer suggestions. As soon as you offer suggestions, you will become responsible for solving the problem. People are more likely to conscientiously follow through on their own suggestions. When the solution is yours and the plan fails, you can be blamed.

Sum Up the Agreed-Upon Action Plan

When it appears that the disputants have arrived at an agreement, sum up the behavior changes each has agreed to make. Mediation should end with a behavioral contract. This is an if-then contingency statement (see Chapter 2)—for example, "I (Tom) will proofread all my reports and correct all the spelling errors if Bill will make comments on the content of the reports only and say nothing about the spelling." Such a resolution statement specifies what each disputant will do. Sum up the resolution and get a final agreement from all disputants. For example, while looking at Tom, you say, "Tom, you will make sure that the final copy of the monthly report is typed without errors if Bill makes no comments on your spelling when he reviews the draft. Is that agreed?" Then, turning to Bill, you add, "Bill, you will read the drafts of the monthly report and make no comments on Tom's spelling if he agrees to make sure the final copy is typed without errors. Is that agreed?"

Write a Behavioral Contract

Put the agreed-upon plan in writing in the form of an if-then behavioral contract. Have all parties, including yourself, sign the contract. You don't have to call it a contract. If you prefer, you can say, "To avoid confusion I will write a memo confirming this agreement. Please initial the memo. I will send you a photocopy for your files." What you call the process doesn't matter; the important thing is that it is written and signed—this emphasizes commitment. The message to disputants is, "I expect you to follow through." With a signed written agreement, accountability is easy, and the disputants know this. Set up an appointment for a follow-up talk or interview with both disputants together. Also write this into the contract.

To get a better idea of how the mediation process actually works, let's look in again on George and his two problem employees. George has just summed up Stacy and Collin's stories.

George: (to Collin) What do you suggest?
Collin: What's the use? You're the boss, what do you suggest?
Coach: *Ignore that, George. Just restate the question.*
George: Collin, what do you suggest?
Collin: Tell her to get off my back.
George: What are you suggesting that Stacy do? (Using a probe to clarify specific behaviors)
Collin: I want her to just mind her own business and completely ignore me.
George: Do you mean you don't want Stacy to speak to you? (Checkout)
Collin: Yes, just tell her to keep her mouth shut!
George: Be reasonable, Collin, you can't expect Stacy never to speak to you!

Collin: Can't I? Well, then, what do *you* suggest? It doesn't matter what I want.

George: Listen, Collin, I expect you to cooperate.

Coach: *Hold on, George. You got into trouble when you evaluated Collin's suggestion. Then you threatened him. Just take his suggestion to Stacy.*

George: Stacy, Collin suggests that you not speak to him. What do you think of that?

Stacy: That's stupid. He's totally unreasonable. What am I supposed to do—pass him notes?

George: What do you suggest?

Coach: *Good, George. When Stacy rejected Collin's suggestion, you asked her for one.*

Stacy: All I care about is having the typewriter when I need it. I have to use it several times a day. I can't spend all day getting it from Collin.

George: What are you suggesting?

Stacy: That I keep the typewriter in my office. Collin can take it into the conference room if he needs it.

George: Collin, Stacy suggests that she keep the typewriter in her office and that you take it into the conference room if you need it. What do you think of that?

Coach: *That's it, George. You didn't evaluate Stacy's suggestion. Instead, you took it without comment to Collin.*

Collin: I won't agree to that. Why should she have her way?

George: What do you suggest?

Collin: All right, all right. I'm willing to compromise. Let her keep the stupid thing. I don't want to go through a big hassle, though. If I need it, I want to be able to get it without a problem.

George: Do you mean it's OK with you if Stacy keeps the typewriter in her office as long as you can take it whenever you need it? (Checkout)

Coach: *Good clarification, George.*

Collin: Yes.

George: (to Stacy) Collin says he'll agree to leave the typewriter in your office as long as he can take it whenever he needs it. What do you think of that?

Stacy: No. What if I'm in the middle of using it? He just can't have it *any* time.

George: What do you suggest?

Stacy: Well, if he tells me in the morning on the days that he needs it and for how long, I'll work around it.

George: Do you mean that if Collin lets you know in advance when and how long he needs the typewriter, he can get it without comment? (Checkout)

Stacy: Sure. It can be like making an appointment, but I want him to stop treating me like a social outcast.

George: Outcast? (Repeat)

Stacy: Like I'm not good enough to drink beer with them.

George: What do you want Collin to do? (Probe)

Coach: *That's right. Insist that she be specific.*

Stacy: I don't know. I just don't like being excluded. I mean, I'm not hot to be around him. I just don't like hearing about plans and being left out.

George: Do you mean you want Collin to invite you, too? (Checkout)

Stacy: Well, I probably wouldn't go, of course. But I'd like to be able to decide myself. Yes, I *do* want to be invited!

George: Let's see if I understand: You are willing to let Collin take the typewriter without comment if he agrees to make arrangements in the morning about what time and for how long he needs to use it, and you want him to invite you along when he makes social plans with others in the office. Is that right?

Stacy: Yes.

George: Collin, how does that sound to you? (The disputants have calmed down and are negotiating reasonably. When this occurs, abbreviate the process as long as you continue to maintain control.)

Collin: All right, I agree to make advanced arrangements. But she'd better stick to her agreement. And as far as inviting her along—well, I can't always do that.

George: What do you suggest?

Collin: Sometimes Bill and I get together and we don't necessarily want anyone along. I mean, if it's a bunch of us going somewhere, then OK—I'll make sure she's invited. But I want her to keep her mouth shut about my being late.

George: Stacy, Collin agrees to arrange to use the typewriter and also to invite you to general social activities if you agree to stop commenting on his being late. (Notice how George "cleans up" Collin's suggestion. He changed "keep her mouth shut" to "stop commenting." In general, it is best to change potentially irritating language into a more neutral suggestion.)

Stacy: OK, I agree.

George: Well, I think we have reached a solution here. Let me review it. (To Collin) You agree that Stacy can keep the type-writer in her office, and that in the morning of days when you need to use it you will make arrangements about when and for how long you'll need it. (To Stacy) Stacy, you agree to let Collin take the typewriter at the arranged time with-out comment. (To Collin) And Collin, you agree to invite Stacy to go along with the group to lunch and so forth if (to Stacy) you, Stacy, agree to stop commenting on the time Collin arrives at work. (Looking at Collin) Is that agreed?

Collin: Yes.
George: (looking at Stacy) Is that agreed?
Stacy: I guess.
George: I feel good about this. I think you've reached a workable plan. Just to make sure there is no confusion, I am going to write this down in a memo. I'll initial it and I want both of you to initial it and return it to me. I'll give you each a copy. This way we'll all be straight on what's expected. Is that agreed?
Stacy: Yes.
Collin: Yes.
George: Good. I want to meet with both of you again in a week to see how things are working out. Come into my office first thing next Friday morning.

As you can see, the interview-mediation approach to managing conflicts is straightforward. The amount of time required to manage a typical conflict between two subordinates is surprisingly minimal. In most cases you should be able to complete the entire process in a half hour or less.

The Follow-up Session

The follow-up session augments accountability. Disputants know that they will have to account for ways in which they did not adhere to their agreement. This exerts additional pressure to carry out the plan conscientiously.

During the follow-up session, adjustments can be made to the plan. Perhaps the agreement was unrealistic. Sometimes one or both disputants will agree to a greater behavior change than they could accomplish. When this occurs, conduct another interview and me-diate a modified action plan. At other times, the action plan will have been carried out successfully by both parties. Such success usually sets the stage for resolving other interpersonal problems between the disputants. If they are receptive, you might try probing other problem areas. Avoid leading questions and simply ask, "Are there any other problems which you care to discuss with me?" Control is usually not as big an issue here. Often the disputants will carry the major responsibility for negotiating; you merely have to intervene occasionally to keep them on track.

A successfully resolved conflict can have ramifications that far exceed the immediate conflict. Others in the work area will see that the disputants have solved a conflict through a mutually agreed-upon behavior change. They will get the implicit message that you expect all personnel in your unit to be responsible for solving their own problems. In short, each time you guide disputants through the resolution process, you are actually conducting a teaching session. If you consistently use this approach, you'll discover that over time disputants will spontaneously use negotiation and contracting without your having to intervene. This will take a tremendous burden off you and will set the stage for more harmonious work relationships.

Reinforce Disputants

Monitor disputants and reinforce them any time you notice that they are acting in accordance with their action plan. All that is required is an occasional positive comment about specific actions they have taken. After all, it is difficult for people to change, and it is especially difficult to change a person's actions toward someone who has antagonized him or her. Therefore it is important that changes— no matter how small—be noticed and reinforced. This is your responsibility in helping to insure that the action plan will work. Some managers become moralistic. They believe "He agreed to . . .; therefore he should. . . ." It is true that people "should" adhere to their agreements, but the fact is that they sometimes slip, and it is the wise manager who seizes every opportunity to reinforce change.

More Than Two Disputants

The procedure for resolving conflicts remains the same no matter how many disputants are involved. Control is the major difficulty. As the number of disputants increases, loss of control is more likely and reestablishing control once it has been lost is more difficult. Attention to the seating arrangement is important. Place yourself in a position where you can move rapidly between any two disputants. Keep the most hostile disputants apart and the less hostile disputants in the middle. Be firm in laying ground rules and in adhering to them. Systematically interview each disputant one at a time. Even when two claim to have the same story, interview each one. Before moving into mediation, sum up *all* the stories. Mediation is conducted in the same manner as with two disputants. Elicit suggestions from each one and check out each suggestion with all disputants.

When Mediation Fails

In a high percentage of office conflicts, a resolution is possible. All that is required is conscientious negotiation between the disputing parties. On the other hand, it would be naive to think that all conflicts will be resolved. Situational factors, personal sensitivities, and stubbornness will at times defeat your best efforts. When this happens, you must fall back on one of the other decision tactics open to you. Occasionally you can rid yourself of the problem entirely by terminating, transferring, or referring one or both disputants elsewhere. More frequently, however, you are stuck with choosing between doing nothing and issuing a directive. Issuing a directive is a control strategy—that is, if the directive is followed, the conflict may continue to exist, but its expression will be controlled. As with all behavioral sequences, conflicts have three intervention points: events that trigger the conflict (antecedents), the conflict behaviors themselves, and the consequences of the conflict. Office arguments can be controlled by altering any one of these events.

Remove conflict triggers. To use this strategy, you must understand which factors trigger the conflict and which factors inhibit it. This is best done through careful observation and by interviewing disputants as to what events immediately precede an outburst. (Follow the guidelines in Chapter 2 for conducting a functional analysis.) When the factors have been isolated, issue a directive aimed at preventing or eliminating the occurrence of these triggers. Sometimes this will involve creating a buffer between conflicting parties. For example, Sally felt that Beth's requests for clerical services were condescending. After several attempts at resolution failed, their manager, Joe, issued a directive that all requests for Sally's services go through him. This procedure stopped Sally and Beth from interacting directly and thus, by removing the triggering event, stopped expression of the conflict.

Control conflict behaviors. In this strategy, the way in which the conflict is expressed is controlled. In essence, your directive specifies "fair fight" tactics. Harriet and Randy, two floor supervisors, were constantly bickering in front of subordinates over minute interpretations of departmental procedures. The manager felt that this confused employees and undermined Harriet and Randy's authority. The conflict was controlled by imposing limitations on where and when they could argue. They had to leave the floor and discuss the disputed issue in one of the closed offices. Examples of other fair-fight tactics include injunctions against two-on-one fights, personal attacks ("Maybe if you were doing a better job at home, you wouldn't be such a bear at work!"), or attacks through a third person ("Bill says you've reached your level of incompetence"). In short, your directive states when, where, and how disputants are permitted to fight. This is similar to the street gangs who agree to fight it out in the boxing ring, or (on an international level) to nations who agree to eschew the use of nuclear weapons.

Alter the consequences of a conflict. Often there are hidden secondary gains in a conflict. For example, one disputant may receive a lot of sympathy ("Gee, Ralph, that was awful. Let's go to lunch and talk about it. I know just how you feel") or praise ("Boy, I've got to hand it to you—you sure can come across when the chips are down"). You yourself may inadvertently be giving positive reinforcement that helps maintain the conflict. Once again, careful observation of events occurring after the conflict is necessary to identify possible consequences. As a rule of thumb, strive to eliminate the positive consequences and substitute a neutral or negative one. If you notice that one disputant runs to you for sympathy, employ the extinction process by withholding that sympathy—change the subject. Often, however, it is the response of co-workers that feeds the conflict. You might experiment with a procedure whereby all employees will be reinforced for a reduction in conflicts. For example, if a conflict-free week resulted in everyone's being able to leave an hour earlier on Friday, co-workers would be less likely to respond positively to conflict behavior.

Managing Conflicts When You Are a Disputant

A different approach to managing conflicts is needed when you are involved personally. The most practical and effective method I have encountered is the assertive negotiation technique developed by Sharon Bower.[2] The first step is to prepare a DESC script. The DESC message is a behavioral statement of the problem as you see it, how you feel about it, what change you desire, and what you plan to do if change does not occur.

D   Describe the problem behavior
E   Express your feelings or thoughts, or both.
S   Specify the behavior change you desire (If-statement)
C   State consequences of change and no change (Then-statement)

Preparation of the DESC is the step that requires the most thought. Here the problem is translated into observable behaviors. DESC guides you in thinking through the problem, your reaction to it, your needs, and the options open to you. DESC should be written in verbatim form—that is, write down the exact words you intend to say when you meet your adversary. This will help you pinpoint and remove provocative or passive language. The guidelines for using authoritative language (see Chapter 5) are helpful in writing an assertive script. Practice your completed script several times. A tape recorder and mirror are helpful practice aids. Finally, meet with your adversary and deliver your script.

Presenting the conflict to your adversary with a DESC script sets the stage to begin negotiating a resolution. Often the other disputant will not accept your suggested resolution plan in toto. If it is rejected, ask, "What do you suggest?" Then use effective interviewing techniques (probes, repeats, checkouts, and sum-ups) to clarify exactly what behavior changes the other disputant suggests will resolve the problem. A resolution plan should be an if-then statement. You and your adversary should both know what to do and what to expect. Write your agreement down, and each of you sign it. It is a good idea to schedule a follow-up meeting to discuss the progress of your plan. To get a better idea of how DESC sounds in practice, let's look at an example:

Manager: Donald, there is something I'd like to talk to you about.
(Describe) Three times this week you've interrupted me when I've been conducting the sales meeting. Today you interrupted to ask me who to contact about the Shubird project.
(Express) I think these interruptions undermine my credibility with the sales staff, and I feel distracted.
(Specify) In the future I'd like you to either save your questions until I'm out of the meeting or ask my secretary to help you.
(Consequences) If you do this, I'll make it my first priority to help you get what you need. What do you think?

Donald: That won't work! If you're not in the sales meeting, you're out of the office. There are times when I've come over here or called five or six times. And your secretary isn't much help.

Manager: What do you suggest?

Donald: I don't know. Maybe give me a call once or twice a day.

Manager: Do you mean check in with you?

Donald: Yes, that would help a lot.
Manager: A couple of times a day is too much. But I can do it once a day.
Donald: That might work.
Manager: I'd like to set a specific time. How about just before lunch at 11:45?
Donald: That's fine.
Manager: OK, Donald, I think we've reached an agreement. I'll put it in a memo and send it to you this afternoon.

DESC scripts work equally well with subordinates, peers, superiors, and clients. The direct problem statement and negotiation process tend to balance the power between yourself and the adversary. Resolving conflicts with others in this way conveys respect and cooperation. DESC scripts help open communication channels. Thus, general working relationships tend to improve. As you gain confidence, you can negotiate for change (yours and theirs) before problems get to the conflict stage.

Effectively managed conflicts can create profound changes in employee relations. By shifting the responsibility for change to the persons involved in the conflict, you the manager become a successful mediator, eliciting employee participation and cooperation.

NOTES

1. This approach for handling conflicts grew out of the interview-mediation procedure I was introduced to when I was a training consultant with Law Enforcement Training and Research Associates (LETRA), Mountain View, California.
2. DESC scripting was developed by Sharon Bower and is described here with permission. See Sharon A. Bower and Gordon H. Bower, *Asserting Yourself: A Practical Guide for Positive Change* (Reading, Mass.: Addison-Wesley, 1976), pp. 87–105.

SUGGESTED READINGS

Bower, Sharon A., and Bower, Gordon, *Asserting Yourself: A Practical Guide for Positive Change.* Reading, Mass.: Addison-Wesley, 1976.
Gordon, Thomas, *Leader Effectiveness Training.* New York: Wyden Books, 1977.
Walton, Richard E., *Interpersonal Peacemaking: Confrontations and Third Party Consultation.* Reading, Mass.: Addison-Wesley, 1969.

8

Applications

BEHAVIOR change programs have been implemented successfully in a variety of organizational settings. Representative case histories are presented here to illustrate how behavior change techniques have been applied in the workplace and to help you generate ideas for improving performance in your organization. Applications of single intervention techniques are described first, followed by programs that include several interrelated change techniques. Evaluation has been highlighted throughout to emphasize its central place in behavior change programs and to illustrate how data collection can be integrated into the program to become one of the vehicles of change. The first case history illustrates the simplest intervention: adding a contingent reinforcer.

Adding a Reinforcer as an Incentive for Performance

Annual bonuses ranging from $24 to $40 proved ineffective in increasing punctuality and attendance in Ideal Standard S. A., a plant in Mexico City. Likewise, disciplinary interviews and one-day suspensions without pay failed to reduce tardiness. Jaime Hermann and his associates (1970) tested an incentive program over a period of 77 weeks with six chronically tardy semiskilled male laborers.[1] The incentive system was simple: Each day that the worker punched in on time or earlier, he was given a slip of paper stating that he had earned approximately two pesos. At the end of each week, the men went to the Supervisor of Industrial Relations and exchanged their slips for cash. Statistical analysis revealed a significant decrease in tardiness when the incentive program was in effect.

This program employed a number of reinforcement techniques. Most notable is that a small and more frequent (once a week) monetary reinforcement was substituted for a larger ($24–$40), less frequent (once a year) one. From learning theory we know that the shorter the time between the reinforcement and the behavior, the more power the reinforcement exerts over that behavior. The slips of paper, which functioned as tokens (see Chapter 2), closed the time gap even more. As soon as the worker performed the desired behavior of punching in on time or before the required time, he was reinforced with a token. The Supervisor of Industrial Relations (who conducted the study) probably also reinforced the workers with praise or smiles when they exchanged their slips.

Two procedures were followed to evaluate the program. First, data on tardiness rates were collected for six workers who had similar tardiness patterns but did not receive incentives. Tardiness among these control workers averaged 9.8 percent over the 77 weeks of the study. In contrast, the average rate for target workers when incentives were being administered was less than 2 percent. The second control for comparison was the target workers themselves. The study used a reversal design in which the target workers were used as their own controls. After the baseline period, the incentive program was implemented and discontinued (reversed) three times. This procedure allowed a comparison between tardiness rates when the program was in effect and when it was not. There were three incentive periods and two reversals. The results are shown in Figure 11.

The results point to two conclusions: First, reinforcing workers who punched in on time increased punctuality; second, behavior that is not reinforced will stop being performed. That workers knew what was expected of them and were capable of performing appropriately was substantiated by the increase in punctuality when the incentive program went into effect. Yet, when reinforcement for being on time was stopped, the workers stopped performing the desired behavior.

It should also be noted that the workers were reinforced for punching in on time. The incentive did not reinforce *starting* work on time. One could argue that if the workers were in the factory on time they were more likely to begin working on time, but this leaves per-

Figure 11. Reducing tardiness in a Mexican factory.[2]

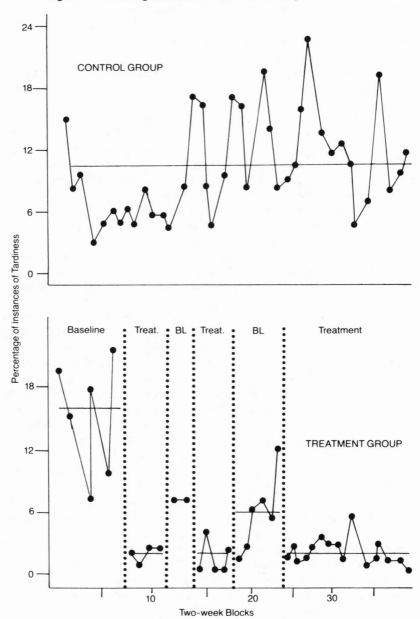

formance of the desired behavior to chance. To be effective, the reinforcement should be linked to the desired behavior. To increase beginning work promptly, incentives might have been given for being at the work station and beginning work on time.

Another interesting result was that although the rate of tardiness was reduced, the length of a tardy period did not change. In other words, there was no reinforcement for being less late. Incentives for a reduction in the length of lateness would be expected to reduce the average length of tardiness.

The difference in tardy rates between the target workers was interesting. During the three incentive periods, percentage rates for the least tardy worker were 0, 2, and 1.2 compared with 6.2, 5.6, and 5.4 for the most tardy worker. This difference indicates that the power of the incentive as a reinforcer was not the same for the two workers. Other reinforcers—such as longer breaks, cigarettes, or praise—might have been more effective than money in motivating the most tardy worker to get to work on time. Many behavior change programs employed in industrial settings neglect to tailor reinforcement to the individual. Of course, tailoring is difficult when using an incentive program with several dozen people. One way to solve this problem is the reinforcement menu technique (see Chapter 2) in which the worker selects one of many possible reinforcers in exchange for a token.

To reduce absenteeism, a similar program was implemented in a garment factory in Cape Town, South Africa. In the year preceding the program, the average weekly absenteeism rate had been 3.06 percent. Once again, an annual bonus (for fewer than three absences a month) had failed to control the problem. Christopher Orphen tested an incentive program with 46 female workers. Half the workers received a weekly bonus for perfect attendance and half did not. A reversal design with two baseline periods and two incentive periods was used.[3]

The incentive program was identical to the first program described. Each worker was given a slip of paper (token) indicating that she had earned a small bonus when she arrived at work. The workers were told that the bonus was for coming to work rather than for being on time. Workers in the control group knew nothing of the program and continued under the annual bonus system. When the incentive program was in effect, the absenteeism rate was considerably lower among workers receiving incentives than among those in the control group. It increased again when the incentives were removed (see Table 6).

TABLE 6.

Phase	Number of Weeks	Average Target	Absenteeism Rate Control
Baseline (A)	4	3.94%	3.76%
Incentive (B)	8	2.56	3.70
Baseline (A)	4	3.74	3.71
Incentive (B)	8	2.01	3.68

Both programs demonstrated that reinforcement of arriving at work on time can effectively reduce tardiness and absenteeism. On an ongoing basis, however, these programs as they were administered had a common drawback: The desired behavior was reinforced each time it occurred. Although the most rapid change occurs when the behavior is continuously reinforced, a continuously reinforced behavior extinguishes rapidly once the reinforcement is discontinued. This is exactly what happened in both programs: When the incentive programs were discontinued, the amount of absence from work and of lateness among the labor force returned to its former levels.

Walter Nord reported two long-term programs designed to reduce absenteeism and tardiness.[4] In one, a $50 bonus had been given at the end of each semester for five years to all teachers who had perfect attendance during the semester. In the second, a lottery system had been in effect for 18 months to reduce tardiness and absenteeism among secretaries, sales and stock personnel, and porters. The same phenomena were seen in both programs: Initially, they were highly effective, but over time their effectiveness dropped considerably.

Contingencies that maintain behavior are different from those that promote change. Consequently, the final step in a behavior change program is maintenance. One maintenance strategy is fading or stretching out the reinforcement—that is, switching from a continuous schedule to an intermittent one (see Chapter 2). In an attempt to operationalize this principle, Ed Pedalino and Victor Gamboa tested a lottery incentive system with 215 hourly employees of a manufacturing/distribution facility.[5] The lottery worked like this: Each time employees came to work on time, the supervisor asked them to pick a card from a poker deck. The card was recorded on an individual sheet and on a game sheet posted in the work area. At the end of the week, the worker who had the best "hand" in each of the eight participating departments won $20. This way, each time workers came to work on time, they were reinforced with the opportunity to play the game. The evaluation design was similar to those used to evaluate the other incentive programs.

The results revealed that prior to the lottery, the average absenteeism rate had been 3.01 percent but that when the lottery was introduced, the absenteeism rate dropped to a weekly average of 2.38 percent. As expected, when the lottery was discontinued, the rate jumped back to the baseline rate. During the second test phase, reinforcement was stretched by having the lottery in effect every other week. The absenteeism rate dropped to a weekly average of 2.51 percent. After the program was terminated, absences were recorded for an additional 22 weeks, and the rate eventually returned to the baseline level. Interestingly, over the same five-month period, absenteeism rates among control employees in four nearby plants increased 13.79 percent.

The results of the lottery incentive program showed that stretching worked. During the first phase, attendance was increased with the use of continuous reinforcement. The second phase demonstrated that a high attendance rate could be maintained by intermittent reinforcement. The transition from the change phase to maintenance may require several stretching steps. (For example, the next step might be a lottery every third week.)

An alternative maintenance strategy is to rearrange existing contingencies so that reinforcers already present in the environment are made contingent on the desired behavior. The following program illustrates how contingencies were arranged so that having the opportunity to perform more desired work was made contingent on performing less desired work.

Using the Premack Principle to Reinforce Work with Work

The incentive programs used to reduce tardiness and absenteeism illustrated the effectiveness of one of the simplest intervention strategies—the addition of a reinforcer. The feasibility of this strategy for first-line managers concerned with individual employee behavior problems is limited: Most managers do not have discretionary funds from which to draw incentives, and there are potential problems in placing one or two employees in a division or office on an incentive system. Rearrangement of existing contingencies is a simple reinforcement strategy that bypasses these problems. Here, there is no addition; rather, the sequence of events is rearranged so that an existing reinforcer follows the behavior to be increased.

One often overlooked reinforcer is favored work—tasks that employees tend to do first can be used to reinforce those they tend to leave until last. Salespeople, for example, often call their old clients first and put off calling new clients. This can be reinforcing, because old clients are probably easier to sell to. Consequently, it is often difficult for the sales manager to motivate salespeople to call on new clients.

Ted Gupton and Michael LeBow demonstrated how to use the Premack principle (see Chapter 1) to solve this problem.[6] Two part-time telephone solicitors were employed to sell new appliance service contracts (warranties) and to renew old ones. During the first ten sessions the salesmen could phone warranty and renewal customers in any order they chose. As expected from previous experience, the percentage of calls which resulted in sales was higher for renewing old contracts (31 and 27 percent, respectively) than it was for selling new contracts (13 and 10 percent, respectively). In other words, renewing previously existing contracts that were about to expire was a high-probability behavior, whereas selling new contracts to new customers was a low-probability behavior.

During the next ten sessions the salesmen's opportunity to make five renewal calls was made contingent on their selling a new contract, not just calling a new customer. Each salesman was instructed that after he made one warranty sale he could make five renewal calls (five renewal calls usually resulted in a sale). Using renewal calls as a reinforcer had a significant impact on the percentage of warranty sales made. Both salesmen increased the number of warranty sales (10 and 21 percent, respectively). Unexpectedly Gupton and LeBow discovered that both salesmen made more renewal sales as well (4 and 22 percent, respectively).

During the final ten sessions the men were told that they could once again call customers in any order they chose. The percentage of warranty sales took a dramatic nose dive. After the contingencies for warranty sales were removed, neither salesman made any warranty calls. The number of renewal sales also dropped. For the first salesman, the percentage dropped only one percent, whereas the percentage of renewal calls by the second salesman dropped by 21 percent. (See Figure 12.)

Although there are few systematic evaluations of the application of the Premack principle in organizational settings, this study points to its potential cost-effectiveness. Not only did the low-probability behavior of making warranty calls increase substantially, but the high probability behavior of making renewal sales increased as well. In other words, productivity increased in both cases, and there was none of the expense involved in giving bonuses.

Interestingly, the intervention had more of an impact on one of

Figure 12. Increasing new and renewal sites.[7]

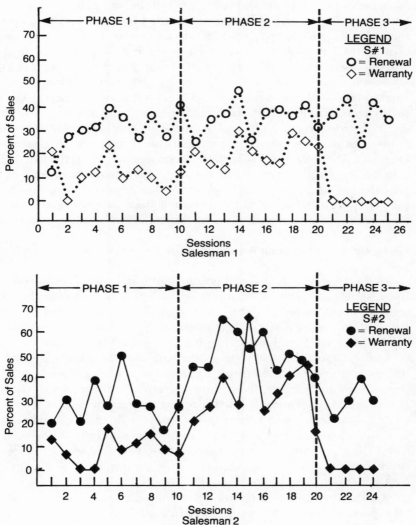

Sessions
Salesman 1

Sessions
Salesman 2

the salesmen: The second salesman's performance increased more than did the first one's. Stated another way, the reinforcer was more effective with the second salesman. This once again points to the importance of tailoring the reinforcers to the individual.

An interesting feature of the Gupton-LeBow study is that they did not tell the salesmen how sales should be accomplished, only that they must be closed before the salesmen could call the renewal customers.[8] Although one salesman showed a greater increase than the other, both showed a significant increase compared with their previous performance. Leaving it up to the individual salesmen to determine their own method of improving their efficiency not only resulted in increased sales, but the salesmen reported that they felt they were being allowed to follow their own unique styles rather than being encouraged to imitate that of someone else. The company was perceived as finally recognizing their individual talents, and the salesmen actually enjoyed producing a higher sales rate. This contrasts with the commonly reported feeling of being made by the company to run faster to keep up. They reported that their success genuinely reflected their own talents. On the other hand, the salesmen's program did not employ the use of goal-setting. Goal-setting has a powerful positive impact on performance. Had the salesmen been assigned goals, their percentage of warranty sales may have increased even more.

Using Goal-Setting as an Antecedent for Performance

In this strategy, an assigned objective or goal acts as an antecedent (see Chapter 2) which elicits improved performance. The new higher level of performance is then reinforced. Gary Latham and Sydney Kinne demonstrated the effectiveness of goal-setting in a program conducted with 20 pulpwood-logging operators.[9] Half of the producers were trained in goal-setting and half were not. Each week the trainer and producer determined minimum production goals. Using the goal-setting training, the producer converted the goal into cords-per-sawhand-hour and assigned it to the workers who directly controlled that production variable—the sawyers themselves. The sawyers were told that the goal was a minimum standard. They monitored their performance with tally meters. Both control and target producers recorded production, turnover, absenteeism, and injuries for their crews.

Results after 12 weeks revealed that compared with control producers, producers who set goals increased their production and decreased their absenteeism significantly. There was no change in turnover or injury rates. Latham and Kinne hypothesized that it was the sense of satisfaction that comes with accomplishing a goal that led to a reduction in absenteeism. Work becomes more rewarding and consequently worker attendance increases.

Let's take a closer look at each aspect of this more complex intervention. First, the goals set were clear, specific, and attainable. Goals were stated in terms of workers' tasks: Sawyer goals were set in terms of cords-per-sawhand-hour and producer goals were in terms of cords-per-man-hour. The goals clarified for both supervisor and subordinate what they were to get done. By providing specific knowledge about job tasks and priorities, the goals prompted improved performance. But improved performance must be rapidly and frequently reinforced if it is to be maintained and if goal-setting is to be established as a controlling stimulus (see Chapter 1). The data collection and self-monitoring procedures solved this problem. Sawyers recorded how much wood they cut, and producers recorded the collective productivity rates of the sawyers they supervised. In the process of recording, each received immediate feedback on performance.

Comparisons between the goal and feedback tend to have two results: When people attain or surpass a goal, they tend to reinforce themselves with positive thoughts—a sense of satisfaction. If they fall short of the goal, their tendency will be to exert more effort to improve performance, provided that positive consequences seem probable—that is, people must see the goal as attainable and believe that they will be reinforced for achieving it. In this program the goals were determined from an assessment of the harvest area and time studies made under similar conditions. There were no penalties for failure; rather, praise was given for goal attainment. Thus, producers and sawyers alike were likely to have viewed their goals as attainable and were motivated to achieve them. When they did reach the goal, they were reinforced externally with praise and internally with self-reinforcement. In this way, goals became antecedents that elicited improved performance.

We would expect that goal-setting plus self-feedback would promote the learning of self-management or of self-directed behavior. The intervention sets the stage for employees to learn to set their own task goals and to reinforce themselves for reaching them. The supervisor seems to be a critical factor in this process. Ronan, Latham, and Kinne conducted another program with loggers which demonstrated that high-productivity crews had supervisors who were more accessible and who gave more training, instruction, and explanation, whereas crews with inaccessible supervisors had higher turnover rates.[10] Supervisors can teach subordinates to set individual task goals and thus reinforce their accomplishment. In other words, in the process of setting goals with employees, the supervisor probably informally arranges the conditions for learning of self-management to occur.

Participative Goal-Setting

Yet another logger project conducted by Gary Latham and Gary Yukl supported the notion that the nature of the supervisor-subordinate relationship is critical in the success of goal-setting programs.[11]

The target of the study was 48 logging crews, half of which were classified as marginal or educationally disadvantaged (workers were primarily black with educational levels below the ninth grade) and the remainder of which were classified as educated (white workers with at least a high school education). The intervention was similar to those in the other logger programs. Producers handled goal-setting with their crews in one of three ways: Those who used participative goal-setting required their crew to determine difficult but attainable weekly production goals; those in assigned goal groups set specific goals without consulting their crews; those in control groups urged their crews to do their best (vague goals). Sawyers in goal-setting crews monitored their performance with tally meters.

The results after eight weeks revealed that among the uneducated sawyers, those that participated in goal-setting set higher goals, accomplished their goals more often, and produced more than sawyers in the other groups. This finding supports the hypothesis that by allowing workers to participate in goal-setting, the supervisor informally trains the subordinate in goal-setting and reinforces improvement. The data from the educated crews showed that there were no differences among the three kinds of goal-setting. Latham and Yukl reported that the management in the company with the educated crews did not support the program. Consequently, although goals were set, educated crews did not receive "stimulation, counseling, and encouragement." The failure of the program with educated crews emphasizes the significance of the supervisor as well as the importance of top management support.

Most organizational goal-setting programs focus on production goals. To meet production goals, however, workers must complete individual tasks. Completing tasks requires engaging in a series of behaviors, yet goal-setting programs in organizational settings often overlook behavioral-based objectives or goals. Gary Latham, Terence Mitchell, and Dennis Dosset found the behavioral objective approach (see Chapter 2) effective in increasing the productivity of engineers and scientists provided that they participated.[12] Again the procedure was similar to those used with the loggers: Thirty-eight managers were trained in goal-setting, and 76 subordinate engineers participated in goal-setting or were assigned goals by their managers. Engineers monitored their performance with behavioral checklists. Findings revealed that engineers in both assigned and participative groups were equally committed to their goals and saw them as advantageous, relevant, and potentially satisfying. The main difference was that those who participated set higher goals.

In a second phase of the program, data were collected on 132 engineers and scientists six months after goal-setting. Engineers with specific goals, regardless of whether they were assigned or participative, produced more than those who were urged to do their best (vague goal) or those who had no goals at all (control group). In other words, the more specific the goal, the higher the performance. As in the case of the loggers, engineers who participated set more difficult performance goals and produced more.

Let's summarize the outcomes of the goal-setting programs. Most notable is that when combined with feedback, goal-setting resulted in increased levels of productivity. Specificity was important: Specific goals led to more productivity, whereas a vague goal (to "do one's best") did not. Subordinates' participation in the goal-setting process was a critical variable. Participation led to more difficult goals, which were accomplished more often and resulted in higher productivity. Beyond specificity and participation, little is known about the impact of goals on performance. A functional analysis (see Chapter 1) revealed that goals function as an antecedent for improved behavior which is then reinforced with feedback.

The supervisor plays a critical role in setting this process in action. When given a vague goal and little supervision, a subordinate is likely to set inappropriate goals (too low or too high). Supervisors can guide subordinates in setting specific, appropriate (difficult but attainable) goals. During this process, subordinates can learn the behaviors involved in setting a goal. The supervisor can also provide positive consequences for improved performance. Once set in motion, self-monitoring provides feedback which prompts self-reinforcement and additional goal-setting. At this point the supervisor can maintain the process with intermittent reinforcement for setting goals, recording data, and improving performance.

One program demonstrated that goals expressed in terms of behavioral objectives can be used to improve productivity. Behavioral objectives have many advantages. First, task or production goals specify an outcome, but not how much of what behavior is required to accomplish that outcome; behavioral objectives do this. Second, when subordinates participate in setting their own behavioral objectives, they have an opportunity to learn work performance. They learn to focus on their own behavior and its relationship to outcome. Providing consequences to oneself for performance is another self-management technique (see Chapter 3). The self-monitoring procedures help maintain a focus on one's own behavior, provide immediate feedback, and prompt self-reinforcement.

Using Participative Goal-Setting to Teach Self-Management

Ivancevich, McMahon, Streidl, and Szilagyi evaluated the broad-based Tenneco, Inc., performance planning and evaluation system for management development.[13] The premise behind the program was that constant management is important and that an ongoing dialogue between manager and employee at every level of the organization is the basis for such continued development. Three overriding program goals were established: (1) improved on-the-job effectiveness by each employee in his or her present position; (2) self-development of each employee to promote future effectiveness and career growth; (3) identification of managers who were capable of handling greater responsibility.

To accomplish these goals, a task force representing each divisional company developed a flexible program that could be tailored to individual needs and circumstances. Top-level commitment and support were demonstrated through publicity statements and the active participation of the president. Fifteen thousand managers were trained in the identification of job responsibilities (outputs expected) and performance planning (setting personal development goals). Five thousand managers of managers were trained in performance evaluation, coaching, and counseling. Once a year, employee and supervisor met for performance planning. During their dialogue, specific aspects of the job were discussed and performance goals were agreed upon and recorded. Periodically the supervisor checked progress, gave feedback, and suggested ways to improve. At the end of the year a formal performance evaluation was made. In this meeting, actual performance was compared with the stated behavioral objectives. Employees discussed with the supervisor how they were doing, and participated in developing a self-development plan for the next year.

The available results on the effectiveness of the Tenneco approach are limited to measures of attitude change after the first six months of implementation. A survey was made of a random sample of over 4,000 managers, half of whom were using goal-setting and half of whom were not. Users reported that goals were clearer, that they participated more in goal-setting and received more feedback on goal accomplishment. Users also reported having more job autonomy and variety, more work group cohesion, satisfaction with pay, and promotional opportunities, and less job tension than did nonusers.

The supervisor-employee dialogues provided an on-the-job opportunity for supervisors to develop and refine their management skills. This process was repeated at every level of the company. Thus, each manager was constantly involved in self-development activities. On the one hand, each manager had a personal yearly performance plan; on the other hand, each practiced and perfected his or her supervisory skills with subordinates. The locus of this development was the goal-setting and evaluation meeting.

Multifaceted Programs: Putting All the Pieces Together

The majority of industrial accidents are a result of unsafe acts. Yet most occupational safety programs focus on avoiding accidents rather than on motivating employees to perform in a safe manner. To reverse a dramatic increase in injuries in a wholesale bakery, Judi Komaki, Kenneth D. Barwick, and Lawrence R. Scott implemented a program that concentrated on specific employee behavior.[14] Two shifts with the highest injury rates—wrapping and makeup—were selected as targets. A functional analysis revealed that commercial posters and posted in-house accident statistics were ineffective antecedents. When they did elicit safe performance, it went unnoticed and unreinforced. There was no training program, and new employees learned informally on the job what precautions to follow. Using input from supervisors and workers, Komaki's team pinpointed 35 specific safety items. Depending on the nature of the task, either an outcome or a specific behavior was clearly defined for each safety item. Following a sampling procedure (see Chapter 2), a trained rater observed and rated workers on the safety items to establish a baseline for comparison. The rating periods were of the same duration, but occurred at different points in the shift.

The new safety program began with the training of all workers in the target department. Each pinpointed safety item was demonstrated and discussed. At the conclusion of the training session, a graph was posted in the work area. The baseline data were explained, and a 90 percent performance goal was assigned. Observers continued to collect data and to provide feedback by posting the percentage of safely performed tasks on the graph. Supervisors were instructed to watch for and comment specifically on safe performance. To prompt this, the supervisor was requested to indicate on a checklist each day how often he had commented on five selected incidents. The list of incidents changed daily.

Eight and a half weeks after the program began in the wrapping department, it was introduced in the makeup department, and the same procedures were followed. After eleven weeks in wrapping and three weeks in makeup, the program was discontinued. Data were collected for evaluation after the program ended, but no feedback was posted on the graphs. The results were exactly what one would predict: When the program was introduced in the wrapping department, the average percentage of safely performed incidents jumped dramatically (70–96 percent). During this period there was no comparable increase in the makeup department. When the program was implemented in the makeup department, it evidenced a similar increase in safe performance (78–99 percent). When the program was terminated, safe performance dropped to the baseline level. (See Figure 13.)

Following the end of the formal evaluation period, an in-house rater observed workers and posted feedback on a weekly basis. In less

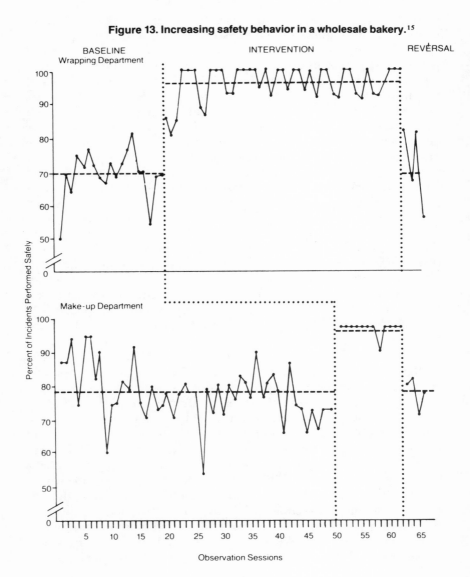

Figure 13. Increasing safety behavior in a wholesale bakery.[15]

than a year, the injury rate was stabilized at a low level, and the plant's safety statistics jumped from lowest to highest in the company.

The program was well received by the on-line workers. Workers applauded and cheered the first time the feedback indicated an improvement. They were observed reminding one another about the safety procedures. When the second program was implemented, a spontaneous competition arose between the two departments.

The core strategy was an assigned goal plus feedback on performance to the entire group and reinforcement of individual workers (goal + feedback + reinforcement). The program illustrates an important first step in setting up a behavior change program: translating the problem into a desired behavior to be increased. Rather than focusing on preventing injuries, the goal was stated in terms of increasing safe performance. The next important step was pinpointing (see Chapter 2), in which specific safe behaviors and outcomes were identified. For example, "When lifting or lowering dough trough, hand holds and at no time loses contact with dump chain" (safe behavior), and "Roll pans are stacked no higher than the rear rail of the pan rack" (safe outcome). Notice that the behavior/outcomes are clearly defined in observable terms. This serves two purposes: First, specificity allows for feedback and evaluation; second, workers know exactly what behaviors to perform and supervisors know what behaviors to monitor.

Komaki, Barwick, and Scott reported a breakdown in implementing a portion of the program. The two supervisors did not complete their checklists consistently. If a change program is to run smoothly, persons at all levels of the organization must be reinforced. Obviously, in this case, reinforcement to supervisors was not powerful enough to motivate them to reinforce safe behavior and to record it on a checklist. If a program is to succeed, provisions must be made for reinforcing and maintaining the behavior of each change agent. On the other hand, the overall program did significantly increase line workers' safety performance.

The following case history illustrates how to implement a multifaceted intervention with individual employees. The owner of a neighborhood grocery store was having problems with two clerks. Judi Komaki, William Waddell, and M. George Pearce helped the owner specify the problems in terms of desired behaviors to be increased.[16] Three behavior categories were identified: the location of the clerks in the store, the speed and nature of assistance given to customers, and the quantity of merchandise on the shelves. A functional analysis to determine what was preventing the desired behaviors from occurring revealed a general pattern of negative reinforcement. When the clerks did not perform as expected, the owner nagged them, so that nagging became an antecedent that prompted work. The consequence to clerks for working was that the owner stopped nagging; on the other hand, exactly what was expected of the clerks was never made explicit. To alter this counterproductive pattern, the Komaki team began by pinpointing the specific behaviors and outcomes expected: "When any customer requests assistance, the assistance should begin within five seconds of the request." To establish baseline on the frequency of pinpointed behaviors and outcomes, data were collected during four 15-minute observation periods scheduled at different times during the day (time sampling). Finally, *positive* consequences—feedback from the observer, self-recording to prompt self-reinforcement, and contingent time off with pay—were used as reinforcers instead of the negative consequence of the owner's stopping his nagging.

The change program did not focus on all behaviors immediately. Location of clerks was the target of the first phase. Increasing the quality of customer service was added a week later, followed in the third week by an increase in the quantity of merchandise available for sale. At the beginning of each of the phases, the pinpointed behaviors and outcomes were explained and demonstrated to the clerks. When necessary, clerks rehearsed the pinpointed behavior. Clerks were given a checklist for self-monitoring and were instructed to record results each time a school bell was sounded. The ringing of the bell eight times a day served as an antecedent to prompt self-recording. A graph depicting the baseline was posted. Clerks were told that whenever they engaged in the behaviors at a frequency of 90 percent or more (assigned goal), they would be rewarded by getting time off with pay.

The program evaluation substantiated three things. First, the program worked as was hoped—the level of performance for each behavior increased significantly: Appropriate location of clerks went from an average of 53 to 86 percent; speed of customer assistance, from an average of 35 to 87 percent; and quantity of groceries on the shelves, from an average of 57 to 86 percent. Second, the frequency of pinpointed behaviors increased only after the proper intervention was implemented. During the first phase, the amount of time the clerks spent in the store increased, but their speed of assisting customers and of keeping the shelves filled did not. (These other pinpointed behaviors increased only after they had become the focus of the change program.) Third, the evaluation demonstrated that the clerks accurately recorded their performance: A comparison revealed observers' and clerks' recordings to be almost identical. (See Figure 14.)

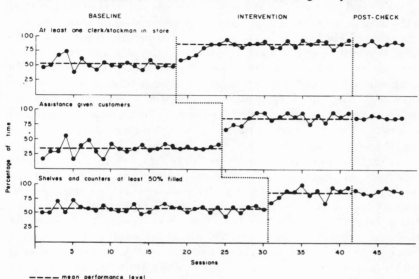

Figure 14. Increasing performance of clerks in a small grocery store.[17]

Maintenance is important. Behavioral change programs are designed to bring about change by manipulating the environment in a
structured way. Interventions are short term, and are not meant to be
ongoing programs. Ideally, one result is setting up an ecological system whereby factors in the environment continue to prompt and
reinforce a high frequency of the desired behavior. To accomplish
this in the grocery store, Komaki, Waddell, and Pearce focused on the
owner as the maintenance agent. During baseline and intervention
phases, the owner frequently served as the second observer. Through
this process, he learned how to observe and to give feedback. The
owner was also trained to praise or otherwise to reinforce clerks when
he saw them performing as desired. After 12 weeks, when the formal
program ended, the owner was able to maintain the clerks' behavior
at or close to the 90 percent criterion with a combination of feedback,
praise, and contingent paid time off. Presumably, the owner's behavior was maintained by increased profits and by an improvement in
customer relations.

Developing a Training Program

Too many sales personnel at Emery Air Freight were assuming
that promises—such as, "Sure, we'll call you next time we have an

urgent shipment"—were sales. A look at the actual sales statistics indicated a need for change. Ed Feeney knew the dangers of rushing into a training program before finding out exactly what behaviors needed changing.[18] He had to know what was happening during the sales calls. Proceeding in two ways, he identified the problem. With a questionnaire he asked all members of the sales staff precisely what they were doing. Second, Feeney went into the field and observed real sales calls. The questionnaires and observations revealed that too few calls were resulting in "observable actions." This is a specific act (such as writing a letter, calling a supplier, or signing a routing order) that would lead to a sale.

After this concrete outcome was identified, Feeney employed the principles of chaining (see Chapter 1) to identify the behaviors required to secure an observable act from the client. Using tape recordings of hundreds of sales presentations, Feeney worked backward from the desired terminal behavior in a step-by-step analysis of specific sales behaviors. The chain of essential behaviors that were identified included determining if the client was a viable customer, meeting with the decision maker, probing for needs, probing for objections, and asking for an observable action.[19]

Next Feeney developed a 40-hour programmed instructional package consisting of tape recordings and a workbook to shape each of the essential behaviors in the chain. Each of the modules was tested in the field. Those that worked were retained, and those that failed were revised. To make the training relevant and to make its application to the field as wide as possible, real-life examples taken from the observational tapes were used.

Most programmed instructional packages teach concepts about a skill, such as "A salesperson should probe for customer_____. (Answer: needs.)" At Emery, the program was designed to teach a skill: how to perform with a real customer. For example, after listening to a customer making an objection, the participant would be asked to identify the need expressed. Beginning with top management, personnel from all levels in all divisions of Emery went through the training. By the time the salespeople were trained, everyone at Emery knew how to sell the same way.

A post-call analysis procedure was introduced to maintain the new sales behavior. At the end of each call, regardless of the outcome, the salesperson was required to use the principles learned during training to systematically analyze and self-reinforce performance. Sales managers were trained to reinforce good sales performance and thorough and honest self-analysis. To evaluate effectiveness, the frequency of observable actions was monitored. The results indicated that in the first full year of operation the rate of observable actions tripled.

The Emery Air Freight program illustrates the step-by-step process of putting together a training program. Feeney specified the problem behavior by asking the salespeople about their calls and by going out into the field with them. He identified the behavior-in-situation: observable actions at the end of a sales call. Obviously, to elicit an observable action, the salesperson must engage in a complex series or chain of behaviors. If the salesperson failed to perform any one of the behaviors in the chain, he or she would fail to obtain an observable action. Therefore, the second step in problem specification was to conduct a functional analysis to identify each behavior in the chain. This, too, was accomplished by observing actual performance (listening to audio tapes of sales calls).

Notice that the problem was clearly defined in terms of an observable outcome. Collecting baseline data requires that the identification of an occurrence of the outcome be unambiguous. The frequency of observable actions was monitored. Evaluation consisted of comparing the frequency of observable actions after the end of the first year with the frequency before the training was instituted. During the training, each behavior in the chain was shaped through a series of programmed instructions. Programmed instructions allowed participants to work individually at their own rate. Built-in feedback provided immediate reinforcement for correct responses and information to improve incorrect ones.

Generalization from the classroom to real-life situations is always a serious problem. Newly acquired behavior not reinforced in the target setting will extinguish rapidly. This is often what happens after training: The behaviors acquired during the training are ignored or, worse yet, are punished in the setting in which they are intended to occur. Usually the problem is simply that the supervisor neglects to reinforce the new learning. More serious is the situation when supervisors and other members of the staff engage in (model) and respond to (reinforce) behaviors incompatible with the ones learned in their training.

For such a program to be effective, considerable attention should be devoted to developing a means of generalizing learning to the target setting and then maintaining it at a high frequency level. The Emery Air Freight program did this in four ways. First, examples in teaching and practice frames of the programmed instruction workbook were taken from actual sales calls. The closer the training approximates the target setting, the more likely it will be for generalization to occur. The second generalization technique was to alter the environment so that it became more like the training situation. To do this, Feeney had all levels—beginning at the top—go through the training; in this way, he eliminated conflicting contingencies. A companywide standard for sales calls had been established. The training and top-level support established exactly which sales behaviors were considered desirable. In this way the antecedents were introduced which elicited a particular kind of sales behavior. Third, reinforcement was built into the environment. Sales managers were instructed to use information from the post-call analysis to reinforce appropriate sales behavior. Finally, generalization and maintenance were further facilitated by arranging for self-reinforcement. The post-call analysis required that salespeople analyze their performance after the call. Not only does this promote self-reinforcement of those sales behaviors performed well, but it serves to pinpoint areas that need improvement.

Behavioral rehearsal (see Chapter 2) is a procedure in which trainees enact or practice the behavior being learned. A program conducted by Kenneth Wexley and Wayne Nemeroff with 27 first-level managers in an urban medical center illustrates how behavioral rehearsal can be used in training supervisory skills.[20] The managers (in groups of nine) attended two half-day training sessions. Training consisted of actively participating in a series of supervisory situations that simulated those the managers encountered on the job. For each situation, the trainer discussed effective and ineffective supervisory behaviors. During rehearsal, trainees took the role of supervisor and practiced the behaviors that had been pinpointed as effective in that situation. The roles of subordinates were enacted by assistants who were trained in eliciting the behaviors being focused on. At the end of each exercise the trainer made specific positive comments about those behaviors the manager had performed well (reinforcement) and assigned a specific behavioral objective or performance goal for the next exercise. For example, the trainer might have said, "Joe, you did a good job specifying standards. In the next exercise praise the subordinate for things he has done well." Or "Sally, the way you stated the purpose of the evaluation was excellent. Next time work on getting all the facts and considering them carefully before making a decision regarding the subordinate."

Telecoaching (a technique in which during the rehearsal trainees receive feedback through an ear device) was used with one of the three groups. During the telecoaching, the trainer elicited some of the pinpointed behaviors by suggesting specific ways in which to handle the subordinate. For example, through the tiny ear microphone the trainee might hear, "Good, now praise the subordinate for what he has done well." The immediacy of the feedback allowed the trainer to shape the trainee's behavior by reinforcing small steps toward the pinpointed behaviors. "You've got the right idea. Now be more specific and tell the subordinate exactly what behaviors she has performed well."

Following the formal training, self-monitoring and on-the-job coaching sessions with two of the three groups were used to generalize from the classroom to the job. Self-monitoring was accomplished with a 30-item behavioral checklist. Whenever the manager performed one of the pinpointed behaviors, he or she marked the appropriate item on the list. For example, after making positive comments to a subordinate for quality performance, the manager would check "praised a subordinate for a job well done." After a week of self-monitoring, the trainer met on the job with each manager. During this coaching session the trainer reviewed the checklists, discussed performance problems, and assigned a specific behavioral objective or performance goal for the next two weeks. During the second coaching session, the trainer reviewed the checklists, praised any progress that had been made toward the goal, and urged managers to practice those behaviors they had not yet attempted on the job. Managers were asked to continue self-monitoring for three more weeks, after which the study was terminated.

Program evaluation revealed a difference among managers who had received on-the-job coaching (the generalization phase) and those who had participated in the classroom training only. Subordinates gave managers who had been through the coaching sessions higher ratings on two leadership dimensions. In addition, subordinates of managers who had been coached were absent less often. Contrary to expectations, telecoaching did not boost performance. The data showed that those who had on-the-job coaching received somewhat higher leadership scores than those who had telecoaching.

The behavioral rehearsal provides trainees with an opportunity to practice pinpointed behaviors in all aspects. The trainee can perfect voice, movement, and timing. The ongoing dialogue provides an opportunity for the trainee to assess information gathered from the surrogate subordinate and to make a decision about an appropriate response. The addition of feedback and goal-setting between rehearsal exercises accelerates the learning process. The feedback differentiates what behavior is on target and what behavior needs improvement. The goal-setting provides a small step in a series of approximations of the eventual skill.

In theory, the telecoaching should maximize learning: The ear device allowed the trainer to provide guidance and immediate feed-back. Cueing correct performance and providing continuous immedi-ate reinforcement when it occurs should result in rapid learning. Comments from trainees indicated that the device was disruptive and made them nervous. A little tension is necessary for learning—it keeps one alert—but beyond an optimal level, tension is counterprod-uctive, and this is what apparently happened with the telecoaching. An alternative method of prompting and of giving immediate feed-back is for the trainer, sitting behind and somewhat to the side of the trainee, to coach that person during the rehearsal. In order to mini-mize anxiety, the rehearsal should proceed slowly and the trainer should explain that he or she will tap the trainee lightly on the shoul-der before speaking. This allows a moment to focus attention onto the coach and reduces the confusion of trying to act and listen simulta-neously. An additional benefit is that other trainees who observe the coaching have an opportunity to learn through modeling.

Wexley and Nemeroff's program emphasized the importance of building generalization into the training. The higher ratings of the managers who were coached on the job, as well as the reduced absen-teeism among their subordinates, indicates that the training must go beyond the experimental stage. Two important processes must occur if the behavior is to become part of the trainee's daily repertoire: The behavior must be generalized to the target setting, and once it occurs at the appropriate frequency it must be maintained. One generaliza-tion strategy is to take the training into the target setting. The on-the-job coaching sessions accomplished this: The manager received rein-forcement for performing on the job and was given a goal for further practice on the job. In this way the job setting was substituted for the classroom. The program at Emery Air Freight combined generaliza-tion and maintenance by making the on-the-job coaching sessions the responsibility of the sales manager. In this way, periodic coaching was established as a continuing on-the-job process.

Evaluating Your Behavior Change Program

Program evaluation is useful in many ways—most obviously in providing information about the effectiveness of your change pro-gram. This is vital in determining whether or not to continue the program. Positive results can help you persuade top management to provide funds and support for implementing your program on a broader basis. In addition, program evaluation provides concrete evi-dence of your managerial skills. Even when results are not as positive as you might have wanted them to be, merely having conducted a systematic evaluation demonstrates that you have essential managerial skills, such as planning and decision making. Publishing the results of your evaluations in in-house publications and trade journals will give others the opportunity to profit from your activities. Colleagues within your company can make use of tactics that you found effective. In the long run, this will help your company because others will not have to rediscover what you have discovered.

The final reason for careful evaluation has to do with recognizing the individuality of your employees. Management strategies presented in books such as this one or in seminars and workshops are general prescriptions and provide general guidelines. But each employee is an individual who has a unique learning history. Thus, change programs that were effective with loggers or bakery workers may not be effective with your employees. Likewise, an approach that works with employees in general may not be effective with a particular problem employee. At this time there are a limited number of controlled studies documenting the effectiveness of behavior change programs with individual employees. There is much work to be done in this area, and there are a number of popular organizational publications that are interested in such material. In this section I will briefly describe several common evaluation designs.

Intragroup Comparison

Evaluation involves comparing the outcome of your program with a standard. Without a standard or control, objective evaluation would not be possible. Evaluation designs are models for structuring programs, and each design has some kind of built-in comparison. Comparisons can be made within the target group (intragroup) or between the target and a control group. Intragroup comparison means that the behavior of a target person or group is compared with itself: The target's own behavior prior to the introduction of the change program provides the standard for comparison. Here are descriptions of three kinds of intragroup evaluation designs.

*The baseline design (AB).** This is the basic evaluation design. Data are collected on the frequency of the target behavior before any change is introduced. Pre-change data are called baseline, and collecting baseline data is continued until a pattern is revealed. The behavior change program is then introduced and data collection is continued. Evaluation consists of comparing the frequency of the target behavior during the baseline period with that same behavior during

---

*AB is commonly used to represent the evaluation design. A refers to the baseline phase and B to the intervention phase.

intervention. The problem with this design is that when a change is indicated it cannot be attributed unequivocally to the intervention or behavior change program; extraneous factors in the environment may have influenced the target behavior. Figure 15 illustrates results from a typical baseline design.

The reversal design (ABA). This design is similar to the baseline design, except that after the change program has been in effect for a designated period of time, it is withdrawn or reversed. During the reversal phase, if the frequency of the target behavior returns to baseline, then we can put more confidence in the effectiveness of the change program. The incentive program to reduce tardiness in the Mexican factory is an example of this design. The Hermann team reversed the intervention twice, and following each reversal the frequency of the tardiness increased, whereas when the incentive program was in effect it decreased. Figure 16 illustrates results from a typical reversal design.

The staggered design (AB₁B₂). The staggered design can be used when two or more behaviors are the target of the intervention. After baseline has been established, the change program is introduced on a staggered schedule. The program with the grocery store clerks illustrates a staggered design. There were three variables targeted: the location of clerks, the speed of customer assistance, and the quantity of merchandise on the shelves. Interventions to change each of these behaviors were introduced one at a time. The data revealed that each behavior changed only after the intervention targeting that behavior

Figure 15. Results from a typical baseline pattern.

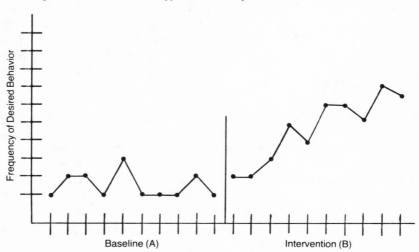

Figure 16. Results from a typical reversal design.

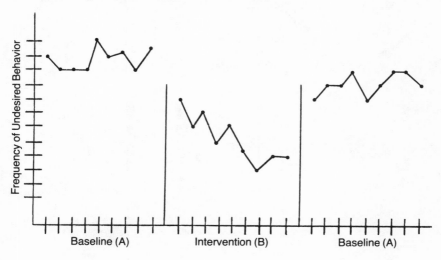

was introduced. Results from a typical staggered design are illustrated in Figure 17.

Intergroup Comparison

Intergroup comparison refers to an evaluation comparison between two different groups. Baseline data are collected on both groups (or individuals). The intervention is introduced with one group but not with the other, and the group that does not participate in the change program is called the control. This kind of design can— and, whenever possible, should—be combined with any of the intragroup designs. The purpose of the second group is to provide a control for factors in the environment which might affect the behavior of the target subject. The rule of thumb is that there should be only one difference between control and targets, and this difference should be the change program. Control employees should be from the same population—similar in age, sex, race, job title, and so forth. Controls should continue in the normal workaday routine, should not know they are serving as controls, and should be treated no differently from the way they would be were they not being evaluated.

An exception to this rule is a situation in which there is reason to believe that a noncritical aspect of the change program may affect behavior. An example is special attention. Research has demonstrated that special attention can influence productivity. Thus, productivity might increase in the target group as a result of attention—not of the

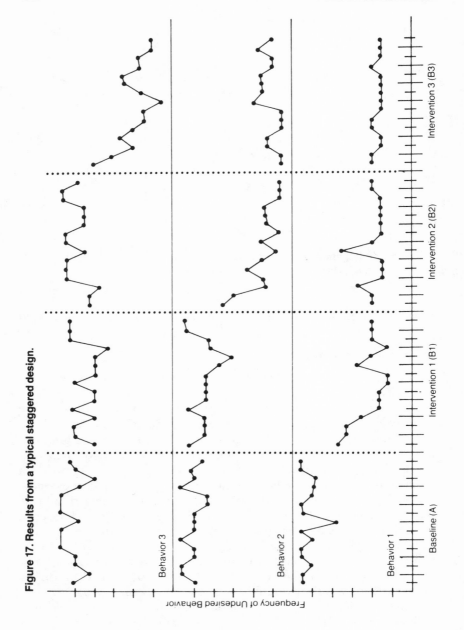

Figure 17. Results from a typical staggered design.

behavior change program. Without a control for attention, evaluators might wrongly conclude that the behavior change program caused the change.

One way to solve this problem is to expose the control group to special attention, but not to the conditions of the change program. Then, if the results indicate a difference between target and control, you can attach more weight to the conclusion that the change program was instrumental in causing the change. The program with the loggers conducted by Latham and Yukl illustrates this procedure: The controls were merely urged to do their best, whereas the target groups either participated in goal-setting or were assigned a goal. In this way, the control group was exposed to attention and promptings for increased performance, but not to the goal-setting.

When planning to introduce a change program in two departments or with two employees, you might consider using a staggered schedule in which a person is treated first as a control and later as a target of the intervention. The program to increase safety behavior conducted by Komaki, Barwick, and Scott illustrates this approach. After baseline data were collected on both departments, the program was introduced in the wrapping department eight and a half weeks before it was introduced into the makeup department. In this way, the makeup department served as a control for eight and a half weeks and then became a subject of the change program. The results showed that safety behavior increased in each department only after the intervention went into effect.

Conclusion

Behavior change programs can improve employee productivity. A key agent of change in all organizations at all levels is the immediate supervisor. With behavior management techniques, supervisors can increase employees' performance by teaching them how to work. Few schools teach people how to work; most people learn on the job. Goal-setting, self-reinforcement, self-monitoring, developing contingencies, and doing the least-liked work first are work behaviors. Learning by doing is a powerful and efficient educational process. Employees learn to come to work on time by coming to work on time and they learn to set goals by setting goals.

The challenge to the supervisor is to arrange the work environment so that employees are likely to do their work. With tardiness, the supervisor might add a contingent incentive; with goal-setting, the supervisor might guide the subordinate through the process many times. Learning to work is a continuous process: Accomplishing the objectives of one change program sets the stage for the next one. Once workers learn to be on time for an immediate continuous pay-off, for example, they need to learn to continue to arrive on time for a less frequent payoff. The first intervention might involve receiving an incentive every time the employee is on time; the second might use intermittent incentives and goal-setting. Supervisors are in a key posi-tion—they can facilitate or inhibit the performance of those they su-pervise. And by learning to use the skills and techniques outlined in this book, they can become agents of change—and teachers.

NOTES

1. Jaime A. Hermann, Ana I. DeMontes, Benjamin Dominquez, Francisco Montes, and B.L. Hopkins, "Effects of Bonuses for Punctuality on the Tardiness of Industrial Workers," *Journal of Applied Behavioral Analysis,* Vol. 6 (1973), pp. 563–570.
2. Reprinted with permission from Jaime A. Hermann, Ana I. DeMontes, Benjamin Dominquez, Francisco Montes, and B.L. Hopkins, ibid. (copyright 1973 by the Society for the Experimental Analysis of Behav-ior, Inc.), p. 567.
3. Christopher Orphen, "The Effect of a Behavior Modification Program on Workers' Absenteeism," *Journal of Behavioral Science,* Vol. 2, No. 4 (1977), pp. 249–252.
4. Walter Nord, "Improving Attendance Through Rewards," *Personnel Ad-ministration,* Vol. 33, No. 6 (November–December 1970), pp. 37–41.
5. Ed Pedalino and Victor V. Gamboa, "Behavior Modification and Absen-teeism: Intervention in One Industrial Setting," *Journal of Applied Psychol-ogy,* Vol. 59, No. 6 (1974), pp. 694–698.
6. Ted Gupton and Michael D. LeBow, "Behavior Management in a Large Industrial Firm," *Behavior Therapy,* Vol. 2 (1971), pp. 78–82.
7. Both figures are reprinted with permission from Ted Gupton and Mi-chael D. LeBow, ibid., pp. 80–81.
8. The conclusions in this paragraph are from a personal communication with Ted Gupton. Dr. Gupton was very helpful in assisting me in prepar-ing the material in this section.
9. Gary P. Latham and Sydney B. Kinne, "Improving Job Performance Through Training in Goal-Setting," *Journal of Applied Psychology,* Vol. 59, No. 2 (1974), pp. 187–191.
10. W.W. Ronan, Gary P. Latham, and S.B. Kinne, "Effects of Goal-Setting and Supervision on Worker Behavior in an Industrial Situation," *Journal of Applied Psychology,* Vol. 58 (1973), pp. 302–307.
11. Gary P. Latham and Gary A. Yukl, "Assigned Versus Participative Goal-Setting with Educated and Uneducated Wood Workers," *Journal of Ap-plied Psychology,* Vol. 60, No. 3 (1975), pp. 299–302.

12. Gary P. Latham, Terence R. Mitchell, and Dennis L. Dossett, "Importance of Participative Goal-Setting and Anticipated Rewards on Goal Difficulty and Job Performance," *Journal of Applied Psychology*, Vol. 63, No. 2 (1978), pp. 163–171.
13. John M. Ivancevich, J. Timothy McMahon, J. William Streidl, and Andrew D. Szilagyi, "Goal-Setting: The Tenneco Approach to Personal Development and Management Effectiveness," *Organizational Dynamics*, Vol. 6, No. 3 (1978), pp. 58–79.
14. Judi Komaki, Kenneth D. Barwick, and Lawrence R. Scott, "A Behavioral Approach to Occupational Safety: Pinpointing and Reinforcing Sales Performance in a Food Manufacturing Plant," *Journal of Applied Psychology*, Vol. 63, No. 4 (1978), pp. 434–445.
15. Reprinted by permission from Judi Komaki, Kenneth D. Barwick, and Lawrence R. Scott, ibid. (copyright 1978 by the American Psychological Association), p. 439.
16. Judi Komaki, William M. Waddell, and M. George Pearce, "The Applied Behavioral Analysis Approach and Individual Employees: Improving Performance in Two Small Businesses," *Organizational Behavior and Human Performance*, Vol. 19 (1977), pp. 337–352.
17. Reprinted by permission from Judi Komaki, William M. Waddell, and M. George Pearce, ibid., p. 342.
18. "Creating 'Instant' Salesmen," Marketing for Sales Executives, The Research Institute of America, Inc., 589 Fifth Avenue, New York, N.Y. 10017 (December 1970), pp. 4–7.
19. John C. Emery, "How to Double Your Sales and Profits Every 5 Years," speech presented to the Sales Executive Club of New York by the President of Emery Air Freight Corp. (1970).
20. Kenneth N. Wexley and Wayne F. Nemeroff, "Effectiveness of Positive Reinforcement and Goal-Setting as Methods of Management Development," *Journal of Applied Psychology*, Vol. 60, No. 4 (1975), pp. 446–450.

SUGGESTED READINGS

Connellan, Thomas K., *How to Improve Human Performance: Behaviorism in Business and Industry*. New York: Harper and Row, 1978.
Luthans, Fred, and Kreitner, Robert, *Organizational Behavior Modification*. Glenview, Ill.: Scott, Foresman and Company, 1975.
Miller, Lawrence M., *Behavior Management: The New Science of Managing People at Work*. New York: John Wiley, 1978.

Appendix A:

MANAGEMENT STRATEGIES

Dr. Beverly Potter

The Potter Principle: There Is No Peter Principle

Don't be too quick to assume that recently promoted managers who are not performing well have finally reached their level of incompetence. *What really happens:* Most companies fail to train managers after they promote them to a new job. As the managers flounder in their new positions, they damage themselves, those who report to them, and the whole company.

Classic case: The super salesperson who becomes an incompetent sales manager. *Why managers stumble as they move up:* Different skills are needed for lower-management, middle-management and top-management jobs. *The dilemma:*

• Lower managers function in one area of one department and generally have a *day-in, day-out* orientation to work.

• Middle managers have departmental responsibilities that require *delegation* and middle-range *planning.*

• Top managers generally shed day-to-day responsibilities but must be able to *integrate* departments to meet company goals.

Where the training problem is most common: In fast-growing companies that are forced to promote managers rapidly.

SIGNS OF AN UNTRAINED MANAGER

• *Avoids answering questions* from workers or requests for information from senior managers. *Reason:* Attempts to hide an inability to perform.

• *Has disgruntled subordinates.* Untrained managers ignite negative attitudes, complaints and excessive conflicts in their areas of responsibility. *Usual symptoms:* High worker turnover.

• *Shows increased personal stress,* indicated by heavy drinking or other behavioral changes. *Symptom:* Productivity loss.

TO SOLVE THE PROBLEM

Don't assume that the best *performer* is automatically the best person

The employee's responsibility to seek training

Many employees hesitate to seek training, *particularly* after they have been promoted. *Usual reasons:*

• They are afraid to reveal deficiencies.

• They really believe they *should* already possess all the skills and knowledge for the new job.

• They do not want to call attention to themselves by asking for money to pay for a course or by having to get approvals.

Best strategy when being promoted: Bring up the issue of training *before* stepping into the new job, as part of normal negotiations on job responsibilities, salary, etc. If train-

ing turns out to be insufficient, go back to the one who promised it and remind that person of the commitment.

To ask for training in a nondefensive, problem-solving way, say: Here's the difficulty I'm experiencing. And here's what I think I need. *Helpful:* Suggest courses or programs or on-the-job training.

Another approach: Don't wait for the company to provide training. Go out and *get* it. Employees who *really* want to move ahead by preparing for another, higher job should be willing to spend their own money, especially if the firm is not training-oriented.

for promotion. *Evaluate instead:* Potential to develop the *skills* needed in the *new* job.

Rather than suddenly promote a person into the new job, try to ease the manager in with some kind of apprenticeship process. *Ideal:* Managers-to-be accompany incumbent managers to meetings, watch them work and talk over various aspects of the job. Unfortunately, few companies do this.

Common problems:

• Incumbents who are leaving the company might not be interested in helping.

• Incumbents who are being promoted may be too busy themselves in

adjusting to a new position.

• Companies rarely encourage managers to communicate job skills to successors.

To make apprenticeship work, top management must set the example. Chief executives must groom their successors to let managers know they will be rewarded for training others. *Goal:* To get managers to overcome their self-protectiveness and become more committed to the *company*.

Good technique: Encourage managers to keep detailed accounts of situations they regularly encounter in their jobs. When new managers are promoted, the incumbent's collected notes will assist in the transition. □

Board Room Reports, June 1, 1981, Vol. 10, No. 11. Reprinted by permission, *Board Room Reports,* Management's Source of Useful Information, 500 Fifth Avenue, New York, N.Y., 10110.

Appendix B:

Job burnout: a management challenge

Absenteeism, on-the-job accidents, drug and alcohol use, conflict, sub-standard performance, and other signs of worker malaise are every-where—and the pulp and paper industry is no exception. The old methods of leading and motivating employees are no longer working. Job burnout is a motivational prob-lem. Skills lie dormant while interest in work wanes. Work becomes a chore. Any situation in which em-ployees feel they cannot win and feel helpless to change it is a poten-tial burnout situation.

The critical boss is the supervisor who consistently ignores good work and progress toward goals. The critical boss also zeroes in on errors and areas that need improvement. In a short time his or her employees feel that it's useless to attempt to please this boss; as a result they stop trying.

Feeling respected by others and having work acknowledged is a pri-mary source of self-respect for most working people. When good work goes unrecognized, self-esteem di-minishes and employees lose inter-est.

Not knowing how one fits into the organization can lead to a feeling that one's work is irrelevant. Recog-nition for work seen as meaningless has little motivational clout. Rather than feeling like a vital part of a team effort the employee feels like a cog in an unsympathetic system.

Incompatible demands create a no-win situation. Line workers, for example, are often expected to pro-duce both quality and quantity. Meeting such mutually exclusive demands is simply not possible be-cause succeeding at one means failing at the other. Similarly, opera-tions managers may see production goals as incompatible with comply-ing with EEOC requirements. Em-ployees whose jobs place them on the boundary between departments can also face double bind or damned-if-you-do-damned-if-you-don't situations; this situation exists because the priorities of different departments such as marketing and manufacturing rarely coincide.

Ambiguous goals make success difficult. Employees who misunder-stand what is expected of them can direct their efforts toward the wrong goal or in the wrong way, resulting in failure and discouragement. Clearly such a situation, if not cor-rected, impairs motivation and will be reflected in a drop in productivity.

When employees don't have enough information to set priorities and to make decisions they stand a small chance of accomplishing goals or of producing quality work.

No room for growth can create a feeling of being trapped. Monetary rewards and job security are neces-sary but rarely sufficient to sustain motivation. When employees feel there is no challenge in their work or that there is nothing to strive for and nowhere to go, they become bored and disgruntled.

Bureaucracy can place insurmountable barriers to accomplishing output goals with outdated rules and excessive paperwork. Absence of job impact eliminates a powerful motivator. When employees have little to say about the conditions or nature of their work they soon feel powerless. As a result the company loses their employees' commitment or enthusiasm.

In each burnout situation the worker doesn't get an expected payoff or reward. The worker feels powerless and ineffectual. Feeling like a helpless victim the worker becomes extremely stressful. If the double-bind situation continues unresolved, the employee experiences chronic stress. The resulting interpersonal irritations, alcohol or drug use, medical and homelife problems, and performance decline add to the feelings of powerlessness and futility. In my book, *BEATING JOB BURNOUT* (Harbor/Putnam, 1980) I discuss this vicious cycle and how, if left unchecked, it can damage ability to work. Also discussed are specific steps individuals can take to protect their motivation and renew their enthusiasm for working.

Most of us understand intuitively that there must be a reward or payoff for "doing;" if there is no reward workers will not continue to perform. This is common sense as well as a scientifically-verified fact.

Less understood is the importance of a feeling of control over work. To sustain performance workers must seek a cause and effect relationship between the "win" and their efforts. That is, the worker must feel that the win is a result of his or her actions and is not coincidental or something allotted to everyone. Employee benefits such as dental and health plans, for example, do not sustain motivation because all employees receive them regardless of their performance.

A substantial body of research indicates that a feeling of control acts as a buffer to the effects of stress. For example, a group of Harvard Graduate Business School researchers studied the job conditions of 2,000 high-status workers in three occupational groups: management, staff, and operations. They found that while all three groups experienced equally high levels of stress, stress-related disorders and worker malaise were not shared equally.

The operations group had a preponderance of health problems, emotional distress, and job dissatisfaction. Digging deeper the researchers found that operations people reported feeling frustrated by vague goals, mutually exclusive objectives, technically ignorant supervisors, and supervisors who couldn't be influenced.

While the management group also encountered high levels of conflict and ambiguity they reported fewer burnout symptoms. They reported less frustration, more satisfaction, and fewer illnesses.

The Harvard researchers concluded that the management group was less susceptible to stress and burnout because their decision-making power gave them a feeling that they could influence what happened to them.

A feeling of potency—being able to do something, to make a decision, and to act—enables us to tolerate more frustration and irritation at work. Organizations are structured in such a way that some people have a greater sense of control than others. And those who feel they

A burnout
prevention system

Most managers are aware that implementing basic management tactics will have a dramatic impact on staff satisfaction and motivation. The problem is how to do so.

Managing people's work requires sophisticated skills. Unfortunately, training in these skills, especially for lower level managers, is often scarce. I have developed some basic principles of managing people at work. I refer to the principles as TASC Plus. TASC Plus is an acronym that stands for a simple but effective managing process that incorporates all of these techniques. It is easy to remember and easy to use.

T stands for TELL. Tell the performer the output standard and how his or her performance compares. The standard is the performance goal or target and describes the specific output that the worker is responsible for producing. Effective standards are quantitatively stated in terms of cost, quality, quantity, or time. Effective standards incorporate more than one of these variables. If no standard has been set, then developing one is of primary importance. When feasible the employee should participate in the setting of the standard.

Feedback

Once the standard has been determined and agreed upon, tell the individual how his or her performance compares to that standard. This feedback should be given in a simple, straightforward manner, using objective terms and avoiding judgmental, emotional, and vague words. For example, to a floor supervisor you can say, "Joe, one of your important functions is to motivate those you supervise to peak performance. You can do this by making sure each of your people clearly understands his expected output and by checking each person's progress at least once a day. While checking the workers' charts you can let them know that you see what they're doing to meet output goals *(Standard)*. I've noticed that you check everyone each day and are readily available to answer questions and that you take time to make sure that they understand the answer. But I rarely hear you commenting on good work *(Comparison)*.

A stands for ASK. Ask the employees for information and suggestions. For example, "Joe, what are your ideas about using positive feedback as a 'motivator'?" When performance is above the standard, ask what will help to keep performance at that high level. "John, the accuracy of your cuts are exceptionally good. What can I do to help you stay at this high level?"

When performance is below the standard, ask what can be done to bring performance up to the standard. "Shirley, your average defect rate is 12% above the standard. What suggestions do you have for getting those defects down?" This communicates concern with Shirley's performance without being critical or blaming. Remember, the employee knows more about impediments to quality performance in his or her job than anyone else and probably has some good suggestions for solutions. Tap into this resource. By asking, you enlist participation. Make sure that you listen to what is suggested. If you ask and don't listen or dismiss without careful consideration, you risk increasing a sense of futility.

Start slowly

S stands for SET SMALL STEP OBJECTIVE. The suggestion is a natural springboard for setting a short-term objective aimed at achieving or surpassing the standard. Ideally the S step is a means of teaching the worker to self-manage or self-motivate. No step is too small as long as it represents movement forward. A series of successful, small steps is more effective than an objective that requires too much too soon, resulting in failure.

A good objective specifies *who* will do *what* under what conditions (*when* and *where*) for how *long*. For example, Joe replied that he had learned from his father that a "swift kick" was the best motivator. He agreed, however, that a positive approach might work better than threats; but he didn't know how to start. In such a situation the manager might negotiate a small step objective, "Okay, Joe, for the next week (how long), you're (who) going to pat each of your people on the back at least once a week (how much) by commenting on something he or she has done right (what). I'll come by this time next week to talk about how it worked out."

C stands for CHECK. Periodically check how the employee is doing. PLUS stands for acknowledging or reinforcing progress towards the objective. For example, upon hearing Joe giving Shirley feedback and acknowledging her "on-TASC" performance, the operations manager might give Joe an approving nod. On-TASC performance is any movement toward accomplishing the objective. Reinforcements don't have to be big things. Remember, your positive attention and comments have a lot of motivational power.

By following TASC Plus, supervisors can prompt participation as well as give feedback and reinforcement. Substandard performance need not be criticized. Rather, it can be used as an opportunity to use TASC Plus to motivate by eliciting participation in solving the problem and focusing on constructive solution. As a secondary gain, managers who use TASC Plus experience an increase in their own sense of controllability. Supervisors who use TASC Plus gain a feeling of "I CAN DO." *Beverly Potter.*

cannot grab their work and run with it are more susceptible to stress and worker malaise.

Management's decision-making powers provide a buffer but this does not mean that managers are immune to burnout. Within management some positions are more prone to burnout and distress than others. Middle management is one such position. Those below may feel the middle manager is betraying their concerns for company policy, while those above may look upon the middle manager as not quite seasoned and unable to step back to grasp the big picture.

Empowered employees—employees who have a sense of control over their job tasks—are resistant to burnout. By empowered I mean a feeling of "I can do and I can succeed by doing." Employees who feel they can impact on their work and can "win" by doing a good job retain their enthusiasm and are motivated. They are also an asset to the company. The challenge to managers is to orchestrate the work of employees, to draw upon and develop employee talents, to focus their energy and effort, and to coordinate the interaction of numerous employees and the flow of their output.

There are four ways in which an organization can increase the feeling of controllability among its personnel: goal setting, feedback, reinforcement, and participation. Each encourage a feeling of mastery at work. Used in unison, they are the most promising way to prevent burnout and they have a positive impact on productivity.

Goals are important because they provide a target. Without a goal the worker is like a ship without a sextant, going around and around, never making progress. A goal gives direction.

Encourage employees to participate in the goal-setting process. Industrial research indicates that when performers participate in setting their own goals, not only do they set higher goals, but they achieve them more often. Participation opens communication channels. The worker knows more about his or her job and impediments to performance than anyone else. Participation provides management with the access to this vital information.

For goals to be effective in increasing motivation a catalyst—feedback—must be present. The worker who receives no feedback on his or her performance is much like the blindfolded archery student. Without seeing where the arrow hits, the archery apprentice has little chance of becoming a master. Feedback is vital to learning. It tells us when to troubleshoot.

When and how you pay attention to employees is important. Often, managers forget about the power of personal attention, the most universally potent motivator. Notice and comment on good work. The effective manager is alert for and acknowledges small improvements. Acknowledgement that comes days or weeks after quality performance has little motivational clout. This is why Christmas bonuses, for example, fail to influence motivation. They arrive too late. The sooner the reinforcement is administered the greater its impact on future performance. □

© 1981 Beverly Potter

Originally printed in *PIMA*, The Magazine For Operating Managers, December 1981, Vol. 63, No. 12.

Index

cohesiveness, in groups, 161, 166–
175
commiseration, 6
committees, *see* meetings
company time reinforcers, 45
conditioned stimulus, 3
conditioning
classical, 2–6
extinction in, 15–16
higher-order, 4–5
operant, 2, 6–7, 15–16
Cone, John D., 254
conflicts, 187–190
control maintenance in, 191–195
215–216
failure of mediation in, 216–217
feelings expressed by disputants
in, 199–202
follow-up sessions and, 214–215
impartiality in, 196–199
information gathering for
resolution of, 190–208
manager as disputant in, 217–
219
mediation of, 209–214
sum-up technique used in, 202–
203
see also mediation in conflicts
conflict triggers, 216
consequences
of conflicts, 217
contingency, 46–47
defined, 2–3
desired, 16
in operant conditioning, 6
of target behavior, 31–34
contingencies, 8, 16, 21
addition of, as intervention
strategy, 43–46
consequences of, extinction and
punishment as, 46–47
rearrangement of, as intervention
strategy, 40–41
see also contracts, contingency

contingency relationships, *see*
contingencies
contingency shock, 53
contingency strategies, *see*
intervention strategies
continuous reinforcement, 17, 64
contracts, contingency, 54–55
in conflict mediation, 210–211
reinforcement menu in, 50–53
in relaxation training, 83–84
in self-management, 75
specificity in, 48–49
tokens in, 49–50
control
of conflict behavior, 216–217
in conflict management, 191–195,
215–216
in interviews, 117–118, 126–128
cooperation, in groups, 161
coping fantasy, 95, 109
coping practice, 90–91
crisis intervention, by management,
39–40

DAD process, for giving directives,
153–156
Darley, John M., 252
data behavioral
for baseline establishment, 36–38,
73–74
feedback as, 56–57
institutional sources of, 37
time samples and, 38
decision making
in conflict management, 208–209
stress and, 78, 95–98
DESC scripts, in conflict
management, 217–219
desensitization, 100–101
anxiety hierarchy and, 101–102
fears listing and, 101
reconditioning and, 103–104
relaxing and, 102–103
self-instruction and, 104–105

Author's Biography

Beverly A. Potter, Ph.D. specializes in the psychology of the workplace. Since the mid-70's she has been teaching managers at all levels how to help ordinary employees achieve extraordinary performance. She earned her doctorate from Stanford University and her masters from San Francisco State University.

Dr. Potter is a member of the Stanford University Staff Development Program.. She has provided consulting and management education to many corporations, government agencies and associations including Hewlett-Packard, TRW-CI, Tap Plastics, GTE, Department of Energy, Disability Evaluation, California State Bar, Design Management Institute, and International Association of Personnel Women. Her workshops have been sponsored by many universities including San Francisco State University, University of California at Berkeley and at Santa Cruz, De Anza College, and Hayward State University.

Her offices are located in Berkeley, California.

Workshops and Keynotes

Dr. Beverly Potter offers training management skills, self-management, career strategies, and working the organization. She can provide off-the-shelf training, tailor material to your team's needs or assist your staff in developing its own program. Popular topics include:

- Matching Personal Goals and Corporate Mission
- Managing Yourself for Excellence
- From Vision to Mission
- Beating Job Burnout
- Managing Authority: How to Give Directives
- Managing Conflict: Mediating an Action Plan
- Effective Interviewing: How to Pick a Winner

Consultation Intensives

Consultation Intensives are one-on-one problem solving sessions in which you develop strategies for accomplishing your objectives. Intensives are for business leaders who seek an advisor to assist them in working through specific "people" problems. Dr. Beverly Potter gets to the core issue so that you can step back and look at the situation objectively to develop a new perspective. She can provide tailor made tutorials when skill development is needed.

- *Mission Statement*: Create a vision of what can be accomplished and share it with your staff with a mission statement that articulates your purpose
- *Goal Setting*: Define priority goals to provide direction and sustain motivation
- *Managing Yourself Excellently*: Develop an action plan for accomplishing what you want to get done
- *Organizational Savvy*: Develop strategies for building allies and flowing with the company's culture
- *Managing Authority*: How to get accountability without being controlling
- *Supervisory Action Plan*: Analyze personnel problems and develop action plans for improvement
- *Career Strategies*: Start doing what you want to do

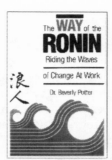

The Way of the Ronin
Riding the Waves
of Change
At Work
Dr. Beverly Potter
ISBN 0-914171-26-7
228 pages, Illustrated
$9.95

The Way of the Ronin is a different kind of business book. Drawing upon material from Aristotle to Bilbo Baggins and Don Juan to modern management experts like Tom Peters and Andrew Grove, *The Way of the Ronin* tells how to ride the waves of change at work.

Ronin translates "wave man" from Japanese and refers to masterless samurai. In feudal Japan only ronin were free. But such freedom in that rigid world was viewed as being tossed on the waves. Often the bushi master ordered a samurai to "do ronin" as a spiritual trial. Ronin became change masters. When feudalism collapsed in 1867 they lead Japan's remarkable industrialization. Mitsubishi, for example, was founded in 1870.

In *The Way of the Ronin*, Potter uses Ronin as a metaphor for an East/West approach to self direction and excellence in "corporate feudalism." She calls upon Corporate Ronin to lead the workplace into the Information Age with its promised renaissance. And she shows managers how to get accountability without controlling.

The Way of the Ronin outlines a career strategy for success in a changing workplace.

Introduction by Dennis Jaffe, Ph.D.

new insight on how to bolt past the competition to corporate success
R.G.H. Siu, The Craft of Power

extraordinary ... in culling out the best in contemporary thinking about the world and how people change within that world.
Job Wise

Recommended
Library Journal

stands out in its field
Midwest Book Review

Hardcover published by AMACOM, 135 W.50th St., NY., NY 10020, $17.95

Beating Job Burnout
How to Transform Work Pressure into Productivity
Dr. Beverly Potter
ISBN 0-914171-04-6
Illustrated, 212 pages
$9.95

Beating Job Burnout tells how to recognize the symptoms of burnout and explains how bureaucracy and poor management, including poor self-management, destroy motivation, diminish productivity and cause work malaise. More importantly, *Beating Job Burnout* tells how to overcome it. The key is to develop personal power -- an I-Can-Do feeling.

Beating Job Burnout describeseight paths to personal power including self-management, stress control, tailoring the job, changing jobs, mood management, and detached concern. *Beating Job Burnout* includes guidelines for how managers can help renewmotivation.

Beating Job Burnout is inspiring, provocative and useful. The many exercises, charts and examples translate easily into classes and workshops. The theoretical thread running through the book makes it a useful supplemental study to those interested in organizational dynamics.

Preventing Job Burnout: *A Workbook* $6.95
ISBN 0-931961-23-8, Illustrated, 80 pages, 9x11
A step-by-step workbook filled with self-tests and worksheets for developing a plan of action to prevent burnout.

Beating Job Burnout: *Audio Cassette* $7.95
Overview of causes and cures of job burnout.

To order books by Beverly Potter
Send your name, address with zip code, phone number and a check or money order (payable to Dr. Beverly Potter) or credit card number with expiration date. California residents add 7% sales tax. Add $2.50 for each book for UPS or 1st Class US Mail shipping and handling. Discounts available on quantity orders. Mail to Dr. Beverly Potter, PO Box 1035, Berkeley, Ca 94701, 415-540-6278